WITHDRAWN
UTSA LIBRARIES

I0454297

The Presidency and the Law

RENEWALS 458-4574

DATE DUE

MAY 13			
GAYLORD			PRINTED IN U.S.A.

The Presidency and the Law
The Clinton Legacy

Edited by David Gray Adler
and Michael A. Genovese

Foreword by Thomas E. Cronin

 University Press of Kansas

© 2002 by the University Press of Kansas
All rights reserved

Published by the University Press of Kansas (Lawrence, Kansas 66049), which was organized by the Kansas Board of Regents and is operated and funded by Emporia State University, Fort Hays State University, Kansas State University, Pittsburg State University, the
University of Kansas, and Wichita State University

Library of Congress Cataloging-in-Publication Data

The presidency and the law : the Clinton legacy / edited by David Gray
Adler and Michael A. Genovese.
     p. cm.
Includes bibliographical references and index.
   ISBN 0-7006-1193-2 (cloth : alk. paper) — ISBN 0-7006-1194-0 (paper : alk. paper)
    1. Presidents—Legal status, laws, etc.—United States—History—20th
century. 2. Executive power—United States—History—20th century. 3.
United States—Politics and government—1993–2001. I. Adler, David
Gray, 1954– II. Genovese, Michael A.
   KF5051 .P74 2002
   342.73'062—dc21

                       2002001897

British Library Cataloguing in Publication Data is available.

Printed in the United States of America

10 9 8 7 6 5 4 3 2 1

The paper used in this publication meets the minimum requirements of the American
National Standard for Permanence of Paper for Printed Library Materials Z39.48-1984.

Library
University of Texas
at San Antonio

Dedicated by David Gray Adler to
three Adler legacies:
Meggin, David, and Taylor,
and
by Michael A. Genovese to
Gabriela, the love of my life, air, and light:
you are my everything.

Contents

Tables

Foreword: The Presidency and the Law

Thomas E. Cronin

The constitutional Framers in 1787 created an American presidency of limited powers. They wanted a presidency strong enough to provide unifying political leadership and strong enough to match Congress, yet not so strong that presidents would be able to ignore the Constitution or overpower Congress.

The Framers of the Constitution were faced with a paradox that still challenges us today: give presidents too much power and they could become arbitrary and even tyrants, yet give presidents too little power and they will be enfeebled and ineffective.

Political scientists Michael A. Genovese and David Gray Adler bring together here several solidly researched, thorough, and perceptive essays that examine the American presidency and the law, with special attention to how recent presidents, including Bill Clinton, have exercised presidential power.

President Clinton is roundly criticized in many of these chapters. David Gray Adler argues that Clinton and his advisers repeatedly violated the Constitution's warmaking clause. Adler hints that this, not Clinton's lying about a sexual encounter, would have been plausible grounds for impeachment. Nancy Kassop concludes that Clinton used some of his powers, such as executive orders, in an aggressive and perhaps pathbreaking manner even as he suffered the setbacks of impeachment and especially strained relations with the Senate over numerous nomination issues. Mark J. Rozell claims that Clinton, like Nixon before him, gave the exercise of executive privilege a bad name. "The Clinton administration . . . made elaborate and mostly indefensible claims of executive privilege," he writes.[1] Clinton's prolonged legal difficulties, from Whitewater investigations to various suits involving Paula Jones and others, created major problems for the White House and resulted in a diminution of executive immunity and perhaps in lessened respect for the institution of the presidency. Robert J. Spitzer's analysis of the independent counsel operations is splendid on these points, as is the study of executive immunity by Evan Gerstmann and Christopher Shortell. Victoria Farrar-Myers provides an interesting analysis of Clinton's legacy in presidential fund-raising practices, and Louis Fisher's observations on the rise of presidential unilateralism are insightful and revealing. He points out that presidents often do what they think is "right," whether or not it is legally authorized.

The Clinton presidency will long be remembered for combative relations between the White House and Congress. Presidents and Congress regularly try to push each other's constitutional and legal boundaries. Tugs-of-war are nothing new in Washington, D.C. Yet Clinton and Congress, as you will read in these chapters, brought these clashes to a new level in several areas.

Readers should be reminded, however, that there is also a case to be made in favor of strong presidential leadership. Advocates of a strong presidency have long contended that Congress and the federal courts sometimes need to permit greater leeway to presidents than may be explicitly spelled out either in the Constitution or in the law. These chapters, then, should be read in the context of the ongoing debate on the scope of presidential legal authority.

The robust interpretation of presidential leadership is often associated with the constitutional Framer Alexander Hamilton and with Presidents Abraham Lincoln, Theodore Roosevelt, and Franklin Roosevelt. Hamilton, both at the Constitutional Convention of 1787 and during his distinguished service as secretary of the treasury under George Washington, had a well-defined and capacious conception of executive power. He was a gifted, aggressive person who clearly believed in a dominating executive. He had written persuasively in the *Federalist* of the need for energy in the executive and that this would be the leading characteristic in the definition of good government. Hamilton had lectured the delegates at the Constitutional Convention of 1787 about his view of the presidency: it would be an executive for life (or good behavior); it would virtually abolish the states; and it would have an absolute veto over the national legislature.

Hamilton, in effect, served as President Washington's floor leader in Congress, and he helped the Executive Department dominate the legislative process. Congress had yet to develop standing committees, and hence it was relatively weak in dealing with the executive. Hamilton quickly filled the vacuum, especially in fiscal policy and even in foreign policy and in matters such as Washington's response to the Whiskey Rebellion. In practice, Hamilton staked out wide claims for executive power, often acting as if he were President Washington's prime minister.

President Theodore Roosevelt espoused the Hamiltonian preference for broad executive powers when, reflecting on his own presidency, he wrote, "I declined to adopt this view that what was imperatively necessary for the Nation could not be done by the President, unless he could find some specific authorization to do it. My belief was that it was not only his right but his duty to do anything that the needs of the Nation demanded unless such action was forbidden by the Constitution or the laws. Under this interpretation of executive power I did and caused to be done many things not previously done by the President and heads of departments. I did not usurp power but I did greatly broaden the use of executive power."[2]

The Hamiltonian or Rooseveltian conception of presidential leadership has been embraced by many historians and political scientists. It is a view that sees the presidency as the primary institution or force in American life that can operate on a national scale, with the speed, focus, and direction needed to balance the complex social forces of today. "Only a President can move as swiftly as Truman did in the face of political deterioration in Western Europe," writes James Mac-Gregor Burns. "Only a President can mobilize public power along a lengthy line of action as did Kennedy and Johnson in the civil rights struggles of the 1960s. . . . Only the President, in short, can supply the powerful and sustained kind of collective leadership necessary to affect basic social forces."[3]

Modern-day Hamiltonians favor repeal of the Twenty-second Amendment's two-term limitations and repeal of the War Powers Resolution of 1973. They would also like to make the item veto available to presidents by constitutional amendment. They favor a strong presidency that will not be hemmed in by an assertive, intrusive Congress, especially a Congress that through its control over appropriations and confirmations limits the foreign policy leadership that presidents need to provide.

In contrast to the Hamiltonian viewpoint, the authors of the chapters in this book hold views that are more "Madisonian" in character. James Madison, who had more influence in drafting the U.S. Constitution than any other Framer, wanted a government of sharply limited powers, including a restrained presidency. Madison was sufficiently distrustful of governmental power that his central idea was to contain, constrain, and restrict political power wherever it arose—whether in majorities of the moment or in the presidency. Madison was more intent on constructing a safe government than in empowering national majorities or a president to enact needed laws.

Madison and his allies did not want to make it easy to bring about political change. Thus the Madisonian system of separated powers and interlocked gears requires substantial consensus among most groups and leadership institutions before the government can act. The Madisonian model is sometimes pejoratively called the "Buchanan" or "Taft" interpretation of presidential power, after Presidents James Buchanan and William Howard Taft. Buchanan largely became passive when faced with the issues leading up to the Civil War. Taft sided with Madison's preference for limited executive authority when he criticized Teddy Roosevelt's notions of the implied powers that come with the office of the president: "Ascribing an undefined residuum of power to the President is an unsafe doctrine and . . . it might lead under emergencies to results of an arbitrary character, doing irremediable injustice to private right." Taft continues: "The mainspring of such a view is that the Executive is charged with responsibility for the welfare of all the people in a general way, that he is to play the part of a Universal Providence and set all things right, and that anything that in his judgement will help the people he ought to do, unless he is expressly forbidden to do it. The wide field of action that this would give to the Executive one can hardly limit."[4]

Contemporary Madisonians and conservative constitutionalists rightly remind us that no one, including presidents, should be above the law. They know, too, that presidents make mistakes and sometimes become slaves to wrongheaded policies. Where Hamiltonians may see members of Congress as interfering with crucial UN, trade, or peacekeeping measures, Madisonians point to the constitutional virtues of checks and balances and of shared, collaborative policymaking. Senator Frank Church (D-Idaho) ably performed his Madisonian responsibilities in the 1960s and 1970s when he battled intellectually with Lyndon Johnson, Richard Nixon, Gerald Ford, and Secretary of State Henry Kissinger. Senator Church believed strongly that the United States had an important strategic role to play in international affairs, yet he agreed with John Quincy Adams's trenchant view that the nation should be cautious about going abroad in search of monsters to destroy. Church realized that although containment policies worked well in Europe for a lot of reasons, including shared values and institutions, it could be a mistake to believe a solution suitable for Europe would also be suitable for those regions of the world that had only recently cast off European colonial rule.

Church chaired congressional committees and investigations, wrote articles, gave provocative speeches, and provided countervailing arguments and opposition for both the White House and the conventional wisdom of the times. The historian David Schmitz writes, "In Frank Church, the nation found a penetrating and sometimes eloquent voice examining fundamental assumptions about policymaking. Weaving together the realist critique of a [Walter Lippmann] with the moral outrage of the Vietnam generation, Church asked Americans to consider many soul-searching questions about their own nation's conduct and to consider all the costs of containment."[5]

Church knew that nations often find it difficult to admit mistakes and policy errors. Yet he knew, too, that to leave questionable assumptions and policy unexamined might invite new tragedies. He was not entirely successful, and he was widely criticized; but his was an often clear, compelling, and courageous voice offering a needed balance to executive branch leadership.

Over the years considerable wisdom has been found in both our elected branches. Indeed, it is often out of the continuing clash between presidents and Congress that effective policies are forged.

In the context of this debate on presidential power, it is clear that President Clinton embraced a Hamiltonian conception of executive power; he wanted to be a Lincoln or a Roosevelt, not a Buchanan or a Taft. Clinton stretched the boundaries of the presidency, and his approach is examined in these chapters. He regularly contested with Congress and the courts. Doubtless he believed that in protecting the presidency he was doing what was "right" and advancing the national interests of the United States. But in some of his initiatives, as the authors attest here, Clinton caused his presidency, and indeed the institution of the presidency, some harm. To this extent he angered those individuals in Congress and the courts who believed he was violating laws or constitutional provisions.

In this book, the scholars often differ with the way Bill Clinton exercised many of his presidential powers. They criticize and question Clinton's interpretation of presidential legal authority. Clinton will certainly have occasion in his memoirs to defend his actions, and I trust he will read these arguments and let them frame his reflections on these matters.

The judicious chapters in this book once again remind us of what Clinton Rossiter wrote several decades ago: "A strong President is a bad President, a curse upon the land, unless his means are constitutional and his ends democratic, unless he acts in ways that are fair, dignified, and familiar, and pursues policies to which a 'persistent and undoubted' majority of the people has given support."[6]

NOTES

1. See Mark J. Rozell, "The Clinton Legacy," chapter 3 of this book.

2. Theodore Roosevelt, quoted in William Howard Taft, *The President and His Power* (New York: Columbia University Press, 1916), p. 143.

3. James MacGregor Burns, *Presidential Government* (Boston: Houghton Mifflin, 1966), p. 235. For a conservative defense of a strong presidency, see Terry Eastland, *Energy in the Executive: The Case for a Strong Presidency* (New York: Free Press, 1992).

4. William Howard Taft, *The President and His Powers*, pp. 144–145.

5. David Schmitz, "Senator Frank Church, the Ford Administration, and the Challenges of Post-Vietnam Foreign Policy," *Peace and Change* 21, no. 4 (October 1996): 458. See also LeRoy Ashby and Rod Gramer, *Fighting the Odds: The Life of Senator Frank Church* (Pullman: Washington State University Press, 1994).

6. Clinton Rossiter, *The American Presidency*, 2d ed. (New York: Harcourt, Brace, World, 1960), p. 257.

Acknowledgments

It is a pleasure to acknowledge the encouragement and support that we have received from friends and scholars. We thank Louis Fisher and Dean Alfange Jr. for their insights and advice on various chapters and for their counsel on scholarly matters. We are deeply indebted to Cheryl Hardy, secretary of the Department of Political Science of Idaho State University, for her superb typing, her administrative and organizational skills, and her abiding enthusiasm and good cheer. The librarians at Idaho State University, particularly those who labor in the reference, documents, and interlibrary loans departments, provided valuable assistance that is greatly appreciated. We thank Amy Montes and Kelli Lee of Loyola Marymount University for their research assistance. We gratefully acknowledge permission from the editor of *Presidential Studies Quarterly* to reprint material from Nancy Kassop, "The Clinton Impeachment: Untangling the Web of Conflicting Considerations," 30, no. 2 (June 2000): 363–368, and David Gray Adler, "The Clinton Theory of the War Power," 30, no. 1 (March 2000): 155–156. Finally, we are particularly grateful to Fred Woodward, director of the University Press of Kansas, for his commitment to this project, as demonstrated by his boundless patience, and for his stewardship, insights, and extremely helpful suggestions along the way.

Introduction

The historic American debate on the nature and scope of executive authority, punctuated and dramatized by the renowned eighteenth-century debate between James Madison and Alexander Hamilton and spiked in our time by sweeping assertions of unilateral presidential powers in foreign affairs and war making and by claims of privilege, secrecy, and immunity in domestic matters, took center stage once more in the clamor and conflict that marred and characterized the presidency of William Jefferson Clinton.[1] The legal controversies that enveloped the Clinton administration—the last-minute pardons, challenges posed by the independent counsel, unilateral war making, claims of immunity from civil lawsuits, and assertions of executive privilege for aides, agencies, and subordinates, among others—erupted in the intersection of law and politics. There, in the crossfire of toxic politics, hyperpartisanship, and personal rancor, entrenchment and obstinacy exacerbated policy differences, inhibited accommodation, and precluded resolution of issues by the familiar interbranch regimen of negotiation, barter, and compromise. The possibility of accommodation between the executive and the legislature became more remote with the hard-nosed, aggressive, and, for some, excessive investigatory pursuit of the president by the independent counsel, Kenneth Starr. The flames of personal acrimony between president and prosecutor, fanned by presidential arrogance and prosecutorial zeal, placed the two on a collision course that eventuated in the impeachment of President Clinton. The impeachment drama represented only the most conspicuous example of how the intersection of law and politics came to resemble Madison's "impetuous vortex," in which all three branches were ensnared and forced to confront issues and resolve disputes that, in more temperate times, most likely would have been resolved by informal means. But requests from both Congress and the independent counsel for information—for notes, memos, diaries, e-mail communications, and files—were met with executive refusal. Recalcitrance replaced accommodation, acrimony vanquished goodwill, and entrenchment dictated subpoenas, grand jury testimony, and courtroom trials. Thus it was that law and politics, public opinion and political wrangling, and personal posturing and constitutional maneuvering combined to propel the three branches into a cauldron of dispute over presidential power and independence. Here the executive, legislative, and judiciary came together to decide the fate of a president.

Lest we forget, these conflicts between the president and Congress were *legal* conflicts. At bottom, President Clinton invoked an expansive conception of executive power, one richly Hamiltonian in character, in foreign affairs and war making, in claims of executive power and privilege, and in the scope of both the pardon power and immunity from civil suits. His capacious view of the powers of the office boldly challenged the Madisonian view of the presidency and raised anew questions about constitutional purposes, powers, and limitations. These conflicts also spurred reconsideration of judicial interpretation of presidential power. The essential constitutional argument over the scope of presidential authority, now in its third century, pits those who extol the supposed virtues and values of broad executive power, including, most notably, Alexander Hamilton and Theodore Roosevelt, against advocates of a more limited and restrained presidential power, prominently represented in the views of James Madison and William Howard Taft. The conflict hinges in large measure on whether it is believed that the first sentence of Article 2, "The Executive power shall be vested in a President of the United States," is itself a grant of power or, as in the style of Articles 1 and 3, it is merely a designation of the office followed by an enumeration of the powers that are vested in the presidency. The debates in the Constitutional Convention are illuminating, but so are the actions that the Framers took, as reflected in the text of the Constitution.

The opening words of Article 2 state, "The executive power shall be vested in the President of the United States of America." Sections 2 and 3 enumerate presidential powers and responsibilities, including the duty that "he shall take care that the laws be faithfully executed." An understanding of the vesting clause, long the subject of academic debate, may be gathered from debates in the Constitutional Convention and in the several state ratifying conventions. It is instructive as well to recall the understanding of the term "executive power" on the eve of the Philadelphia Convention. The acclaimed legal historian, Julius Goebel, has observed that "executive," "as a noun, was not then a word of art in English law—above all it was not so in reference to the crown. It had become a word of art in American law through its employment in various state constitutions adopted from 1776 onward. . . . It reflected . . . the revolutionary response to the situation precipitated by the repudiation of the royal prerogative."[2] The use of the word "executive," as Robert Scigliano has demonstrated, was, among the founders, a term of derision, a political shaft intended to taint an opponent with the stench of monarchism.[3] The rejection of the use of the word "prerogative" in favor of the new and more republic-friendly noun of "executive" necessitated discussion and explanation of its scope and content.

The meager scope of authority granted to state executives is illustrated by the provisions of state constitutions. Despite intrinsic flaws and deficiencies in an omnipotent legislature under the Virginia Constitution of 1776, Thomas Jefferson noted in his 1783 "Draft of a Fundamental Constitution for Virginia," "By Executive powers, we mean no reference to the powers exercised under our former government by the Crown as of its prerogative. . . . We give to them these powers only which are necessary to execute the laws (and administer the government)."[4] This approach was reflected in the Virginia Plan, which Edmund Randolph introduced to the Constitutional Convention and which provided for a "national executive . . . with power to carry into execution the national laws . . . [and] to appoint to offices in cases not otherwise provided for."[5] For the Framers, the phrase "executive power" was limited, as James Wilson said, "to executing the laws, and appointing officers." Roger Sherman "considered the Executive magistracy as nothing more than an institution for carrying the will of the Legislature into effect." Madison agreed with Wilson's definition of executive power. He thought it necessary "to fix the extent of Executive authority . . . as certain powers were in their nature Executive, and must be given to that department" and added that "a definition of their extent would assist the judgment in determining how far they might be safely entrusted to a single officer." The definition of the executive's power should be precise, thought Madison; the executive power "should be confined and defined."[6] And so it was. In a draft reported by Wilson, the clause "the Executive Power of the United States shall be vested in a single person" first appeared. His draft included an enumeration of the president's powers to grant reprieves and pardons and to serve as commander in chief; it included as well the charge that "it shall be his duty to provide for the due and faithful execution of the Laws." The report of the Committee of Detail altered the "faithful execution" phrase to "he shall take care that the laws of the United States be duly and faithfully executed." This form was referred to the Committee on Style, which drafted the version that appears in the Constitution: "The executive power shall be vested in a president of the United States of America. . . . He shall take care that the laws be faithfully executed."[7]

The debate on executive power, to the extent that there was one, centered almost entirely on whether there should be a single or plural presidency. Edward Corwin has fairly remarked, "The Records of the Constitutional Convention make it clear that the purposes of this clause were simply to settle the question whether the executive branch should be plural or single and to give the executive a title."[8] There was no challenge to the definition of executive power held by Wilson and Madison, nor was there even an alternative understanding advanced. And there was no argument about the scope of executive power; indeed, any latent fears were quickly allayed. For example, in response to the Randolph Plan, which provided for a "national executive" that would have "authority to execute the national laws . . . and enjoy the executive rights vested in Congress by the Confederation," Charles Pinckney said he was "for a vigorous executive but was afraid the executive powers of the existing Congress might extend to peace and war which would render the executive a monarchy, of the worst kind, towit an elective one." John Rutledge shared his concern. He said "he was for vesting the Executive Power in a single person, tho' he was not for giving him the power of war and peace." Wilson sought to ease their fears; he "did not consider the Prerogatives of the British Monarch as a proper guide to defining the Executive Powers. Some of these prerogatives were of a legislative nature. Among others those of war and peace. The only powers he conceived strictly Executive were those of executing the laws, and appointing officers not (appertaining to and) appointed by the legislature."9 The absence of a challenge to the Madison-Wilson-Sherman understanding of executive power, the reassurance, moreover, that executive power did not constitute a source of warmaking authority or, more generally, a foreign affairs power, and the acknowledgment that the concept of prerogative was ill-suited to a Republic left little to fear about the office.10

If it is true, as Corwin has observed, that Wilson was the leader of the strong executive wing of the convention, a remark made comprehensible perhaps by the unwillingness of any other member to espouse a conception of executive power more expansive than Wilson's stated perimeters—to execute the laws and make appointments to office—what, we may ask, was the understanding of the phrase held by members of the various state ratifying conventions? In South Carolina, Charles Pinckney reported that "we have defined his powers, and bound him to such limits, as will effectually prevent his usurping authority." Similarly, Chief Justice Thomas McKean told the Pennsylvania Ratifying Convention that executive officers "have no . . . authority . . . beyond what is by positive grant . . . delegated to them." In Virginia, Governor Randolph asked, "What are his powers? To see the laws executed. Every executive in America has that power." That view was echoed by James Iredell in North Carolina and James Bowdoin in Massachusetts, who said the president's powers were "precisely those of the governors."11

And the powers of the governors strictly were limited. The Virginia Constitution of 1776, for example, stated that the governor shall "exercise the executive powers of government, according to the laws of the Commonwealth; and shall not, under any pretense, exercise any power or prerogative, by virtue of any law, statute or custom of England."12 As we have seen, moreover, Jefferson sought in 1783 in his "Draft of a Fundamental Constitution for Virginia" to place beyond doubt that "by Executive powers, we mean no reference to these powers exercised under our former government by the Crown as of its prerogatives."13 In short, as Madison concluded, state executives across the land were "little more than cyphers."14

It is not at all surprising that the founding generation would so sharply limit the power of its executives. In colonial America, the belief was prevalent, writes Corwin, that "the 'executive magistracy' was the natural enemy, the legislative assembly the natural friend of liberty."15 There was a deep fear of the potential for abuse of power in the hands of both hereditary and elected rulers. The colonial experience had laid bare the sources of despotism. "The executive power," wrote a Delaware Whig, "is ever restless, ambitious, and ever grasping at increase of power."[16] Thus Madison wrote in the *Federalist* no. 48: "The founders of our republics . . . seem never for a moment to have turned their eyes from the overgrown and all-grasping prerogative of an hereditary magistrate."[17]

It was in this context, then, that the Framers designed the office of the presidency. Far from establishing an executive resembling a monarch, the Framers, in fact, severed all roots to the royal prerogative. Their rejection of the British model, grounded in their fear of executive power and their embrace of republican principles, was repeatedly stressed by defenders of the Constitution. William Davie, a delegate in Philadelphia, explained to the North Carolina Convention that "that jealousy of executive power which has shown itself so strongly in all the American governments, would not admit" of vesting the treaty powers in the president alone, a principle reaffirmed by Hamilton in *Federalist* no. 75: "The history of human virtue does not warrant placing such awesome authority in one person."[18] Hamilton indeed was at the center of Federalist writings that attempted to allay any concerns about the creation of an embryonic monarchy. In *Federalist* no. 69, he conducted a detailed analysis of the enumerated powers granted to the president. In his capacity as commander in chief, for example, the president would be "first General and Admiral," a post that carried with it no authority to initiate war. The president's authority to receive ambassadors, moreover, "is more a matter of dignity than of authority," an administrative function "without consequence." Thus Hamilton concluded that nothing was "to be feared" from an executive "with the confined authorities of a President."[19]

The confined nature of the presidency, a conception reflected, for example, in Wilson's observation that the president is expected to execute the laws and make appointments to office or in Sherman's remark that "he considered the Executive Magistracy as nothing more than an institution for carrying the will of the legislature into effect," represented a characterization that was never challenged throughout the convention.[20] No delegate advanced a theory of inherent power. Madison justly remarked, "The natural province of the executive magistrate is to execute the laws, as that of the legislature is to make laws. All his acts, therefore, properly executive, must presuppose the existence of the laws to be executed."[21] The proposition that the president was subject to the law constitutes the essence of the rule of law, and at "the time of the Revolution and in the early days of the Republic, it was thought that republican government differed from the monarchies of Europe in precisely this respect."[22]

Despite the clarity of the convention's aims and the triumph there of Madison's conception of the presidency, as reflected in the meager textual allocation of power to the president, there is yet another tradition in America—the Hamiltonian model—that is represented in a large body of literature that extols the virtues of presidential power, a school that has its foundation in a broader, more expansive interpretation of executive power, a school that, if it cannot find its footing in the debates in Philadelphia—in the arguments, discussion, or train of thought of the convention—does purport to find its footing in the arguments, debates, and practices since the early days of the Republic. To borrow from Corwin, again, if the Framers did not intend by virtue of the term "executive power," to vest in the president a residual or inherent power, if they had no intent, by virtue of the vesting clause, to grant to the president a power to act beyond or in the absence of laws in what is commonly though incorrectly regarded as a Lockean prerogative, then perhaps the concept of inherent power was "grafted on the presidency" by presidents, jurists, and scholars, among others.[23] Indeed, given the absence at the convention of an understanding of executive power that challenged the Madison-Wilson-Sherman conception, it would seem fair to say that the broader, more expansive conception of executive power, as the embodiment of inherent, residual, prerogative or emergency authority, represents a gloss on the vesting clause.

In his famous defense of President George Washington's Proclamation of Neutrality in 1793, Hamilton, writing as Pacificus, applied the initial gloss on executive power in his claim of an "inherent" presidential power. In the course of his defense, Hamilton emphasized the differences between the Constitution's assignment to Congress in Article 1 of "all legislative powers hereinafter granted" and the more general grant in Article 2 of the executive power to the president. Hamilton contended that the Constitution embodies an independent, substantive grant of executive power. The subsequent enumeration of specific executive powers was, he argued, only "intended by way of greater caution, to specify and regulate the principal articles implied in the definition of Executive Power." He added, "The general doctrine then of our Constitution is, that the *Executive Power* of the nation is vested in the President; subject only to the *exceptions* and *qualifications* which are expressed in the instrument."[24] In *Myers v. United States* (1926), Chief Justice William Howard Taft seemed to embrace the Hamiltonian conception: "The executive power was given in general terms, strengthened by specific terms where emphasis was regarded as appropriate, and was limited by direct expressions where limitation was needed."[25]

Hamilton's interpretive effort to adduce a substantive conception of executive power, particularly from differences in terminology between Article 1 and Article 2, is fraught with difficulties. The convention debates provide no basis for ascribing any significance to the difference in phraseology between the legislative powers "herein granted" and "the Executive Power." Indeed, it was only in the last days of the convention, September 12, to be exact, that a change in the terms occurred through a report of the Committee on Style, which altered Congress's legislative powers to those "herein granted" but made no change in the phrase "the executive power." The change most likely represented an effort to reaffirm the limits of federalism and the regulatory authority of Congress and to allay concerns of the states, which feared for their legislative authority, rather than an effort to recognize a substantive conception of executive power. The change in language affected Congress and, on its face, had nothing to do with the executive, but if it did, the route to a substantive conception of executive power could not have been more circumlocutory by design.

Hamilton's claim of an independent, substantive conception of executive power is vulnerable on several counts. There is no evidence from the convention debates to support the claim. Given the Framers' aversion to executive authority and their consequent enumeration of presidential power one would expect to find at the convention some comment, some argument, or some shred of evidence to indicate that the convention intended to vest the president with a broad grant of executive authority. Indeed, it is difficult to imagine that such a full swing of the pendulum, from a deep-seated fear of the executive to an abiding confidence in it, strong enough to warrant a grant of broad discretionary authority, could be accomplished without comment; and yet the record reveals no such shift in thinking. Hamilton's explanation that the convention intended merely to specify and *regulate* what he termed the "principal" articles implied in the definition of executive power raises additional questions. His use of the word "regulate" implies limitations, a concept at the core of the Framers' effort, in Madison's words, to "confine and define" executive power, but one at odds with a broad grant of undefined residual authority. Moreover, why would the convention, from Hamilton's perspective, feel the need to enumerate a presidential power to require opinions in writing if the president possessed a broad residuum of executive authority? Pacificus's argument that only those executive articles that were "principal" articles seems at odds with the concept of inherent power, for is there anything more inherent in executive authority than the power to require a subordinate to place an opinion in writing? Justice James McReynolds's powerful dissent in *Myers* v. *United States* surely exposed this flaw in the Hamiltonian theory of inherent power, for it was, he wrote, "beyond the ordinary imagination to picture forty or fifty capable men, presided over by George Washington, vainly discussing, in the heat of a Philadelphia summer, whether express authority to require opinions in writing should be delegated to a president in whom they had already vested the illimitable executive power."[26]

However vulnerable Hamilton's conception of an inherent presidential power may be, it cannot be doubted that his view of the executive has prevailed; indeed, it has been dominant. Madison's view of the constitutional position of the president was superior to Hamilton's, as John Quincy Adams observed, but "history," writes Corwin, "has awarded the palm of victory" to Hamilton's conception of the office.[27] Presidents in the twentieth century, including Bill Clinton, routinely invoked a capacious understanding of presidential power—in foreign affairs and war making, in the use of executive orders and the grant of pardons, and in the claims of secrecy and privilege. It would seem beyond dispute that presidential power is circumscribed by the Constitution. But constitutional limitations often have been challenged and resisted by assertive presidents in pursuit of political goals and policy agendas. This certainly was true of the Clinton administration, which not only held an expansive view of the executive powers but which also undertook to exercise those powers in an extravagant manner that surpassed some previous claims of presidential power. In the chapters that follow, the authors have examined key legal and constitutional issues that in many ways define the Clinton presidency.

As Thomas E. Cronin reminds us in his foreword, the Framers sought to create a presidency strong enough to provide unifying political leadership and strong enough to match Congress, yet not so strong that presidents would be able to ignore the Constitution or overpower Congress. His point that the Framers faced a paradox resounds across a vista of 200 years: vest presidents with too much power and they can become arbitrary and tyrannical; give them too little, and they will be enfeebled and ineffective. These chapters reflect those twin concerns.

In chapter 1, "Expansion and Contraction: Clinton's Impact on the Scope of Presidential Power," Nancy Kassop observes that President Clinton exercised his powers in an aggressive manner. The interbranch conflicts that occurred during the Clinton years were particularly striking in their scope, intensity, and frequency, culminating in the impeachment crisis. Kassop reviews these skirmishes in the intersection of law and politics and concludes that the separation of powers law looks different from the way it did before Clinton arrived in Washington. Clinton's footprints cannot be ignored by his successors.

In chapter 2, "Clinton, the Constitution, and the War Power," David Gray Adler argues that Clinton frequently engaged in unilateral acts of war making in defiance of the war clause of the Constitution, which vests in Congress the exclusive authority to initiate hostilities on behalf of the American people. In spring 1999, Clinton ordered in concert with NATO allies a massive air and missile assault against the Federal Republic of Yugoslavia, an attack that ranks as the most intensive and sustained military campaign conducted by the United States since the Vietnam War. Adler analyzes the administration's legal and constitutional justifications and concludes that Clinton's actions violate the fundamental requirement of the war clause—authorization of hostilities by both houses of Congress. Clinton's "presidential war" against Yugoslavia marks the first time in our history that a president has waged war in the face of a direct congressional refusal to authorize the war. The war clause, it appears, has become a dead letter.

In chapter 3, "The Clinton Legacy: An Old (or New) Understanding of Executive Privilege?" Mark J. Rozell contends that President Clinton not only embraced an expansive conception of executive privilege but that he also exercised it in an indefensible manner. Indeed, Rozell argues that the elaborate use of executive privilege was a core issue that led to the impeachment of Bill Clinton. The Clinton administration scandals, he notes, revitalized the debate over executive privilege but did little to resolve the controversial nature of the power.

In chapter 4, "The Pardon Power Under Clinton: Tested but Intact," Michael A. Genovese and Kristine Almquist observe that the president's pardon power is all but unassailable and subject to few checks and balances. They argue that although Clinton's eleventh-hour pardons raised questions of propriety, provoked controversy, inspired suspicion about his motives, and invited cynical responses, they certainly were not the first to do so. While the firestorm surrounding the last-minute pardons triggered investigations by Congress and the Justice Department and provoked renewed discussion of impeachment and constitutional amendments of the pardon power, that authority, Genovese and Almquist conclude, was tested but remains intact.

Robert J. Spitzer, in chapter 5, "The Independent Counsel and the Post-Clinton Presidency," examines key political elements of the independent counsel law and their application to the Clinton presidency. Spitzer explains that the tendency to compartmentalize presidential scandals and venerate the presidency obscures the prevalence of the problem of scandal in the executive branch and heightens the perceived gap between allegedly great presidents of yore and the allegedly inadequate presidents of the present. He asserts that the attorney general's precarious political position and temptations for wrongdoing will generate the need for a revised version of the independent counsel law.

The issue of executive immunity, which has been brought before the Court on only a few occasions but which was central in the drama of the Clinton administration, is examined in chapter 6, "Executive Immunity for the Post-Clinton Presidency," by Evan Gerstmann and Christopher Shortell. They explore the underlying tension between the concepts of limited and absolute immunity and the concepts of permanent and temporary immunity in the context of *Clinton* v. *Jones,* the Supreme Court decision that permitted Paula Jones to proceed in her civil lawsuit against President Clinton and that arguably became the sine qua non of the impeachment effort.

In chapter 7, "In the Wake of 1996: Clinton's Legacy for Presidential Campaign Finance," Victoria A. Farrar-Myers examines the question of President Clinton's legacy in the area of presidential campaign finance. She observes that the 1996 presidential election set a precedent for campaign fund-raising and spending and that the money chase established new records, all of which serves to raise key concerns about current campaign finance laws and alternatives. Farrar-Myers follows the money trail with an eye on the proposed McCain-Feingold legislation.

In chapter 8, "The Impeachment of Bill Clinton," Adler and Kassop explore the complex, tumultuous, and unpredictable process of impeachment. They examine and critique the impeachment drive against President Clinton in the context of political, historical, and legal concerns and discuss the impact of the Clinton trial on standards of impeachment.

In chapter 9, "The Condition of the Presidency: Clinton in Context," Adler argues that the tremendous concentration of power in the modern presidency, some acquired through executive usurpation and some through legislative abdication, as represented in the rise of the imperial or personal presidency, has undermined the Framers' efforts to institutionalize and confine presidential power. The presidency was imperial when Clinton came to it, and it was imperial when he left it.

Louis Fisher brings the volume to a close in the epilogue, "Constitutional Violence," in which he offers sharp criticism of presidential conduct since 1950, which has been uninformed and undirected by statutory and constitutional constraints. Presidents do what they think is "right," whether or not it is authorized. Presidents seek to cut corners and circumvent legal and constitutional constraints; and as a result, laws are violated, cover-ups are successful, and political accountability disappears. Without adequate checks and balances, this constitutional violence will continue.

The contributors to this book have endeavored to provide a comprehensive assessment of the changes in the constitutional and legal understanding of the presidency that occurred during President Clinton's eight years in the White House. Scholarship, of course, requires normative criticism. In that spirit, these essays offer several criticisms of the Clinton administration's exercise of power and its interpretation of laws and constitutional provisions, not merely from a legal point of view but within a broader and, we believe, richer political and historical context. Finally, through their commentaries, analyses, and criticisms, our authors have offered their perspectives on the potential impact of the Clinton administration.

NOTES

1. The debate on the nature and scope of executive power has been canvassed by a vast and growing body of literature that defies illustration in a footnote, but see, for example, Thomas E. Cronin and Michael A. Genovese, *The Paradoxes of the American Presidency* (New York: Oxford University Press, 1998); Thomas E. Cronin, ed., *Inventing the American Presidency* (Lawrence: University Press of Kansas, 1989); Louis Fisher, *Constitutional Conflicts Between Congress and the President*, 4th ed., rev. (Lawrence: University Press of Kansas, 1997); Fisher, *Presidential War Power* (Lawrence: University Press of Kansas, 1995); Arthur Schlesinger Jr., *The Imperial Presidency* (Boston: Houghton Mifflin, 1973); Theodore Lowi, *The Personal President* (Ithaca, N.Y.: Cornell University Press, 1985); Forrest McDonald, *The American Presidency* (Lawrence: University Press of Kansas, 1994); Donald L. Robinson, *"To the Best of My Ability"* (New York: W. W. Norton, 1987); Richard Pious, *The American Presidency* (New York: Basic Books, 1979); Michael A. Genovese, *Presidential Powers* (New York: Oxford University Press, 2000); Mark J. Rozell, *Executive Privilege: The Dilemma of Secrecy and Accountability* (Baltimore: Johns Hopkins University Press, 1994); Robert J. Spitzer, *President and Congress: Executive Hegemony at the Crossroads of American Government* (New York: McGraw-Hill, 1993); David Gray Adler and Larry N. George, eds., *The Constitution and the Conduct of American Foreign Policy* (Lawrence: University Press of Kansas, 1996).

2. Julius Goebel Jr., "Ex Parte Clio," *Columbia Law Review* 54 (1954): 450, 474.

3. Robert Scigliano, "The President's 'Prerogative Power,'" in Cronin, ed., *Inventing the Presidency,* p. 24.

4. Quoted in Charles Warren, *The Making of the Constitution* (Cambridge: Harvard University Press, 1937), p. 177.

5. Max Farrand, ed., *The Records of the Federal Convention of 1787,* 4 vols. (New Haven: Yale University Press, 1911), 1: 62–63.

6. Ibid., pp. 65–70.

7. Ibid., 2: 171, 185, 572, 574, 597, 600.

8. Edward S. Corwin, "The Steel Seizure Case: A Judicial Brick Without Straw," *Columbia Law Review* 53 (1953): 53.

9. Farrand, ed., *Records,* 1: 62–70.

10. Although various presidents and commentators have sought to squeeze from the vesting clause a presidential authority to make war, the claim was considered and rejected at the convention; indeed, it caused much alarm. The Supreme Court, moreover, has never viewed the clause as a source of presidential power to initiate war or to conduct foreign policy. For discussion, see David Gray Adler, "The Constitution and Presidential Warmaking: The Enduring Debate," *Political Science Quarterly* 103 (1988): 14–17, and Louis Henkin, *Foreign Affairs and the Constitution* (Mineola, N.Y.: Foundation Press, 1972).

11. Farrand, ed., *Records,* 2: 540, 3: 201, 4: 107, 2: 128.

12. Ben P. Poore, *Federal and State Constitutions, Colonial Charters,* 2 vols. (Washington, D.C.: U.S. Government Printing Office, 1877), 2: 1910–1911.

13. Quoted in Warren, *Making of the Constitution,* p. 177.

14. Farrand, ed., *Records,* 2: 35.

15. Edward S. Corwin, *The President: Office and Powers, 1787–1957,* 4th ed., rev. (New York: New York University Press, 1957), pp. 5–6.

16. Quoted in Gordon Wood, *The Creation of the American Republic, 1776–1787* (Chapel Hill: University of North Carolina Press, 1969), p. 135. The colonists were virtually obsessed with power, "its endlessly propulsive tendency to expand itself beyond legitimate boundaries" (Bernard Bailyn, *The Ideological Origins of the American Revolution* [Cambridge: Harvard University Press, 1967], pp. 55–57).

17. *Federalist* no. 48, in Alexander Hamilton, James Madison, and John Jay, *The Federalist,* ed. Edward M. Earle (New York: Modern Library, 1937), p. 322.

18. Jonathan Elliot, ed., *The Debates in the Several State Conventions on the Adoption of the Federal Constitution,* 2d ed., 4 vols. (Washington, D.C.: Jonathan Elliot, 1836), 4: 120; *Federalist* no. 75, p. 487.

19. *Federalist* no. 69, pp. 448, 451.

20. Farrand, ed., *Records,* 1: 65.

21. James Madison, *The Writings of James Madison,* ed. Gaillard Hunt, 9 vols. (New York: Putnam, 1900–1910), 6: 145.

22. Francis D. Wormuth and Edwin B. Firmage, *To Chain the Dog of War* (Dallas: Southern Methodist University Press, 1986), p. 165.

23. See Scigliano's enlightening discussion of Locke's understanding of prerogative, which required a legislative act indemnifying the executive who violated the law, in contrast to a substantial body of literature that perceives the Lockean prerogative as justification for unilateral executive action in violation of the laws in the response to an emergency and that holds, as a consequence, that legislative indemnification is utterly

unnecessary (Scigliano, "President's Prerogative Power," pp. 236–256). See also Adler, "Presidential Warmaking," for the argument that the Framers did *not* incorporate a so-called Lockean Prerogative (pp. 32–33); Thomas S. Langston and Michael E. Lind, "John Locke and the Limits of Presidential Prerogative," *Polity* 24 (1991): 50–68; and Lucius Wilmerding, "The President and the Law," *Political Science Quarterly* 67 (1952): 321–338.

24. Hamilton, "Pacificus" no. 1 (June 29, 1793), reprinted in *The Papers of Alexander Hamilton,* ed. Harold C. Syrett et al., 27 vols. (New York: Columbia University Press, 1961–1987), 15: 33–34.

25. 272 U.S. 52 (1926), at 118.

26. Ibid. at 118.

27. J. W. Adams, *Eulogy on James Madison* (1836), cited in Edward S. Corwin, *The President: Office and Powers, 1787–1984,* 5th ed., rev. (New York: New York University Press, 1984), p. 473 n. 34; Corwin, *Total War and the Constitution* (New York: Knopf, 1947), p. 12.

1

Expansion and Contraction: Clinton's Impact on the Scope of Presidential Power

Nancy Kassop

Presidents and Congresses routinely try to push the boundaries of their constitutional power. Conflicting claims over such matters as war powers, budget authority, treaty power, executive privilege, executive orders, and appointment and removal powers form the backdrop for classic tugs-of-war that characterize the very way in which the principle of separation of powers operates. The Framers of the Constitution relied on this concept, along with its corollary of checks and balances, to distribute power among the three branches and to prevent the concentration of power in a single branch; of course, these checking devices have not stopped the branches from trying to frustrate the constitutional design in the name of self-protection from the encroachment of others. The interbranch contests that occurred during the Clinton administration were particularly striking in their intensity, their frequency, and their near-epic proportions. Separately, any one of the incidents—impeachment, a dramatic government shutdown provoked by budget conflicts, or testy confrontations over the confirmation process—would have been sufficient to establish difficult working relations between Congress and a president. The fact that these three episodes, and many others of similar magnitude, occurred during one president's administration only underscores just how contentious the relations were during the two-term Clinton presidency.

A discussion of the state of congressional-presidential relations over constitutional powers during the Clinton administration is, inevitably, one that rests on the convergence of politics and law. Shrill politics laid the groundwork for the intense legal and constitutional skirmishing that followed. The Republican takeover of Congress in the 1994 midterm elections, along with the smoothly orchestrated Contract with America, set the stage for a hardening of positions, as each political party retreated into its own branch for the next six years, and as an entrenched, institutional polarization widened over time.

1

How has this excessive combativeness affected the functioning of separation of powers, the governing principle that depends on some level of mutual respect, accountability, and accommodation among the branches? More specifically, what effect did this conflict have on the law of presidential power? Indeed, the effect has been both rich and decidedly mixed. Separation of powers conflicts abounded, and the result was an expansion of executive authority in some areas and contraction in others. Clinton was aggressive in his use of military force without congressional approval, his broad reliance on executive orders, and his use of the legislative process instead of treaties to advance trade agreements. Conversely, the effect of his unsuccessful assertions of assorted presidential privileges and immunities before the federal courts has been to contract the realm of confidentiality and to increase legal liability for his successors. His ability to achieve confirmation for his federal judicial nominees was adversely impacted by testy relations with Congress. And, not least, the residue left on the political system by his impeachment is subject to varying interpretations. The conclusion here is that on a variety of fronts and in various ways, the law of separation of powers as it applies to executive functions simply does not look the same as it did before Clinton's arrival in Washington. He has left fingerprints on a wide array of presidential powers that his successors will be unable to ignore.

The Clinton legacy for separation of powers might be described as "the constitutionalization of politics," the conversion of political differences into legal and constitutional battles. In other words, Clinton maximized his use of the tools in the president's constitutional "kit" to address partisan conflicts. All presidents, at times, have resorted to reliance on their constitutional powers to gain political advantage when accommodation with Congress seemed either unlikely or too costly. The Clinton years were distinctive because this strategy of reaching for the law in order to accomplish the standard business of politics—budgets, appointments, and treaties—became almost routinized, and it risked displacing the traditional methods of bargaining, negotiation, and compromise for the circular reason that reliance on those methods became strained and difficult in the poisoned environment between the Republican Congress and the Democratic president. Relationships between institutions in the governmental realm are no different from those in the personal realm: when two people find that they can no longer maintain constructive relations with each other, they turn to the law to sort out their mutual obligations and responsibilities. So, too, did Clinton in his interactions with Congress, which consequently spurred the reciprocal response in Congress to crank up the machinery of impeachment, the ultimate weapon for undermining the legal, constitutional, institutional, and political authority of a president.

What follows here is a kaleidoscopic view of how Clinton's actions served both to expand and contract the constitutional authority available to presidents. This is the state of presidential authority that his successor will inherit.

EXPANSIONS

War Powers

Clinton's use of military power illustrates that post-1973 Democratic presidents can misuse their commander-in-chief authority and can ignore the requirements of the War Powers Resolution every bit as well as, and perhaps even better than, their post-1973 Republican counterparts. Not only is one struck by the number of times Clinton used military force—cruise missile attacks in Iraq in 1993 and 1996, combat operations in Somalia in 1993, a threatened but rejected invasion of Haiti in 1993–1994, NATO air strikes in Bosnia in 1994, cruise missile strikes in Afghanistan and Sudan on August 17, 1998. and air strikes in Kosovo in spring 1999—but also by the fact that the legal justifications he offered are particularly dubious. He claimed, as previous presidents have, that he did not need authorization from Congress to use military force, but he was the first to use force in direct contravention of Congress's refusal to authorize such use in the air strikes against the Serbs in March 1999. He learned from George H. W. Bush how to argue that a United Nations Security Council Resolution can substitute for congressional action, and he expanded this formulation also to include NATO resolutions as another way to bypass Congress.[1]

Clinton's decision to wage air strikes against the Serbs in Kosovo in spring 1999 proceeded in utter disregard for congressional efforts to play a role in the determination of the use of force. Concededly, Congress sent mixed messages to the president on this matter, but it was clear that the administration gave little credence to congressional attempts to exert its war power. What was evident was an effort by Congress to assert itself, however fitfully and even incoherently, as the constitutionally authorized decision maker in matters of war and peace. The administration's arrogant unwillingness to include Congress as even an equal partner with collective responsibility for making decisions over the use of military force runs counter to both the intent of the Framers and the requirements of the War Powers Resolution.

The dizzying record of legislative actions began with Senate passage (58 to 41) of a concurrent resolution on March 23 authorizing the president "to conduct military air operations and missile strikes in cooperation with our NATO allies against the Federal Republic of Yugoslavia" (S. Con. Res. 21). The United States and its NATO allies began air strikes the next day. That same day, the House passed a resolution (424 to 1) that it "supports the members of the United States Armed Forces who are engaged in military operations against . . . Yugoslavia" (H.R. Res. 130). Then, on April 28, the House voted on four separate measures: "It defeated a joint resolution (2 to 427) that declared that a state of war existed between the United States and the Federated Republic of Yugoslavia; on a tie vote of 213 to 213, it rejected the concurrent resolution that the Senate had passed on March 23, authorizing the use of air strikes against Yugoslavia; it then defeated a concurrent resolution [139 to 290] that would have ordered the president, under the War Powers Act, to remove U.S. Armed Forces from their present operations against Yugoslavia [H.R. Con. Res. 82]; and it then passed a bill that prohibited the use of funds for ground troop deployment to Yugoslavia without specific congressional authorization [H.R. 1569]."

On May 4, the Senate voted, 78 to 22, to table a proposal to authorize the use of "all necessary force" in U.S. operations in Yugoslavia. On May 20, Congress passed a supplemental emergency appropriations bill, requiring the president to report on military operations in Yugoslavia; this act specifically omitted any statement that it constituted specific statutory authorization under the War Powers Resolution (P.L. 106-31, 113 Stat. 57.)[2]

The issues crystallized when Congressman Tom Campbell (R-Calif.) sued Clinton in federal district court, asking the court, first, to declare that the president had violated Article 1, section 8, clause 11 of the Constitution by "unconstitutionally continuing an offensive military attack . . . without obtaining a declaration of war or other explicit authority from Congress . . . , and despite Congress' decision not to authorize such action," and second, to declare that a report pursuant to the War Powers Resolution was required to be submitted and that such report would require the termination of the use of U.S. forces in hostilities after sixty days.[3] The district court concluded that the congressional plaintiffs did not have standing to sue, based on the conflicting and ambiguous messages that their legislative actions sent.[4]

It was not surprising that the court refused to permit this challenge to presidential war making to go forward. The "standing" analysis was similar to decisions in earlier congressional suits over presidential unilateralism in foreign affairs.[5] Until a case arrives in the courts in which Congress has acted in a coherent manner to reach a unified decision that is clearly and unambiguously at odds with the president, what the court has termed a "constitutional impasse," no president needs to fear the judiciary. But a sufficient number of federal court decisions now exist, positing that if those conditions are present, courts might give a decision on the merits. Clinton was saved in this instance because of the deficiencies of Congress. But every time a president ignores Congress in his foreign policymaking, it prompts members to file suit. The point is that now there are precedents on the record that could eventually find that the required conditions for standing are satisfied, and this growing body of precedents has hastened the day when the courts might actually decide these cases on the merits.

The language of justification used by a president is an indication of his true sense of the scope of his power, and this is the paper trail that remains behind, long after he leaves office. The president's constitutional positions emanate from the Office of Legal Counsel (OLC) in the Justice Department. In his tenure as assistant attorney general in charge of OLC for a good portion of the Clinton administration, Walter Dellinger articulated broad constructions of presidential power, and the area of war powers was no exception. During the consideration of the possible invasion of Haiti in 1994, he declared in a letter to four senators on the Foreign Relations Committee that the War Powers Resolution "recognizes and presupposes the existence of a unilateral presidential authority to deploy armed forces into hostilities or into situations where imminent involvement in hostilities is clearly indicated by the circumstances."[6] Utterly contrary to the explicit intent of the resolution's framers, Dellinger's letter maintained for the administration that the War Powers Resolution acknowledges unfettered executive authority to use force on its own without the participation of Congress.

Dellinger also used semantics to his advantage by asserting that the declaration of war clause in Article 1, section 8, clause 11 of the Constitution was not applicable to the deployment of troops in Haiti because "the operation was not a 'war' within the meaning of the Declaration of War Clause." The deployment was to have taken place, and did in fact take place, with the full consent of the legitimate government of the country involved. Taking that and other circumstances into account, the president, together with his military and intelligence advisers, determined that the nature, scope, and duration of the deployment were not consistent with the conclusion that the event was a "war."[7] That set of considerations was then formalized in that same OLC opinion into a standard for determining "war," a standard that suffered mightily from circularity and from abdication of all power to the president. This is not to suggest, however, that the United States cannot be said to engage in "war" whenever it deploys troops into a country at the invitation of that country's legitimate government. Rather, it is that "war" does not exist where U.S. troops are deployed at the invitation of a fully legitimate government in circumstances in which the nature, scope, and duration of the deployment are such that the use of force involved does not rise to the level of "war."[8]

Such a definition apparently had a sturdy shelf life, since an incarnation of it surfaced in a press briefing by Press Secretary Joe Lockhart on April 13, 1999. A reporter asked if "the president [is] ready to call this [air strikes against the Serbs] a low-grade war." Lockhart answered dismissively, "No, next question." The reporter pressed him, "Why not?" Lockhart replied, "Because we view it as a conflict." The reporter persisted: "How can you say that it's not war?" Lockhart responded, "Because it doesn't meet the definition as we define it." Finally, Lockhart conceded that there were "some constitutional implications" here that he was not prepared to handle and offered to get an answer for the reporter.[9]

The significance here is that Nixon, Reagan, and Bush had declared the War Powers Resolution unconstitutional and refused to abide strictly by its reporting requirements, choosing to report, instead, in a manner "consistent with," rather than "pursuant to" the resolution's section 4(a)(1) provision—a distinction with a difference that was certainly intended by these presidents. Clinton continued this same practice but went one step further and turned the resolution on its head and to his advantage, with his Justice Department's novel interpretation that it actually supports his exclusive use of the war power.[10]

Dellinger advanced another creative understanding of this statute when he sent to Congress separate reports on each distinct incident involving a military engagement, thus retriggering the sixty-to-ninety-day clock that begins with the reporting of hostilities. If he could justify that each of these incidents was a new outbreak, rather than part of "continuing hostilities," the sixty-day clock would never run its course, and the administration would not be faced with automatic termination of its use of force, as provided in section 5(b) of the resolution.

In all candor, virtually all presidents since Harry S. Truman have looked to the commander-in-chief clause as a fertile source of authority, and they have made claims to power that stretch well beyond what the Framers intended. Clinton is no different in that respect, but the paper trail he has left for his successors provides a formal, legal underpinning for what had previously been adopted primarily in practice. Moreover, it bespeaks an approach toward the separation of powers principle that does not simply protect the president from congressional encroachment in this area; rather, it is one that proactively claims executive primacy and exclusivity while marginalizing, dismissing, and preempting congressional power.

Executive Orders

As a president facing an opposition party in Congress, it is not surprising that President Clinton made bold use of executive orders as a means of circumventing the uncertainties of a legislature that was unlikely to be friendly to his initiatives. Here, too, as in war powers, Clinton followed in the paths of his Republican predecessors, who also operated under conditions of divided government. Thus, Clinton may not have blazed new trails for his successors by his use of executive orders to accomplish indirectly what he was unwilling to spend political capital on to accomplish directly. Rather, he solidified and made bipartisan the pattern of behavior that had already been established.

The role of executive orders in government cannot be determined by numbers alone. Numbers do not tell the full story, nor do they provide us with a context. "By the time Clinton left office he had signed 364 executive orders: 57 in 1993, 54 in 1994, 40 in 1995, 49 in 1996, 38 in 1997, 38 in 1998, 35 in 1999, 40 in 2000, 12 in 2001.[11] Bush had signed 166 (31 in 1989, 43 in 1990, 46 in 1991, 40 in 1992, 6 in 1993); Reagan had signed 381 (50 in 1981, 63 in 1982, 57 in 1983, 41 in 1984, 45 in 1985, 37 in 1986, 43 in 1987, 40 in 1988, 5 in 1989); Carter had signed 320 (66 in 1977, 78 in 1978, 77 in 1979, 73 in 1980, 26 in 1981); Ford had signed 169 (29 in 1974, 67 in 1975, 56 in 1976, 17 in 1977); Nixon had signed 346 (52 in 1969, 72 in 1970, 63 in 1971, 55 in 1972, 64 in 1973, 40 in 1974); and Johnson had signed 324 (7 in 1963, 56 in 1964, 74 in 1965, 57 in 1966, 65 in 1967, 56 in 1968)."[12] It is more useful to analyze some representative examples of executive lawmaking, both to understand the political forces at the time that would explain why this route was favored over the routine legislative process and to see if, in fact, these efforts withstood court and congressional challenges.

Clinton has made no secret of his willingness to use executive orders, especially after the 1994 elections. National Economic Council Director Gene Sperling noted, "In '93 and '94, we were very legislatively minded. After we lost Congress, we were just playing defense and fighting for our lives. But by the end of '95, we were learning how to explore the full range of presidential power."[13] Senior adviser Rahm Emanuel added to these comments: "Sometimes we use [administrative actions] in reaction to legislative delay or setbacks. Sometimes we do it to lead by example and force the legislative hand. . . . Obviously, you'd rather pass legislation that can do X, but you're willing to make whatever progress you can on an agenda item."[14]

Clinton signed a number of controversial executive orders. Not surprisingly, some sparked anger and frustration among Republicans in Congress who felt outmaneuvered by a president who could use his executive authority to achieve his policy goals and thereby exclude them from the process. Some orders were challenged in the courts and did not survive. Three policy areas, in particular, were focal points for executive lawmaking: the reversal of abortion restrictions from previous administrations, trade and employment matters, and the establishment of an environmental legacy.

From the start, Clinton wasted no time in using his executive authority, and within two days of taking office in January 1993 he issued no fewer than five separate orders or directives to departments, overturning restrictive abortion-related policies from the Reagan and first Bush administrations. These included reversing the gag rule on federally funded family planning clinics (58 Fed. Reg. 7455 [1993]), the ban on the importation of RU-486 (58 Fed. Reg. 1459 [1993]), the ban on abortions for U.S. servicewomen on military bases overseas (58 Fed. Reg. 6439 [1993]), the ban on fetal tissue research (58 Fed. Reg. 7457 [1993]), and the ban on U.S. aid to international organizations that promote abortion overseas.

Trade issues were an area in which Clinton relied on unilateral authority, and the most controversial example in this category was his 1995 executive order that authorized $20 billion in loan guarantees to Mexico from the Exchange Stabilization Fund to bail out the peso. Congress objected to this action, charging that Clinton was misusing the fund, which was never intended for rescuing a foreign country's currency. Hearings were held in 1995 to further investigate this matter, but Congress failed to take any official action.

Congress was critical of another plan by the president for exceeding his authority and using his power to accomplish an objective that was contrary to the purposes of the underlying legislation. In November 1999 Clinton proposed allowing states to use funds from the federal unemployment insurance trust fund to pay for temporary maternity and paternity leaves. Critics charged that such a policy would be contrary to six decades of history whereby this money had been used only to aid unemployed workers and only if they were actively seeking work.[15]

Executive Order 12954, which banned, through federal contracting policy, employers from replacing striking workers was one order that did not survive judicial scrutiny. Clinton issued it in 1995 after failing to get legislation on the matter in 1993 and 1994. In reaction, Congress countered with a legislative proposal that would overturn the order, but before that had a chance to be enacted, a federal appellate court declared the order invalid and preempted by a provision in the National Labor Relations Act.[16]

Clinton also used executive orders tactically to build an environmental legacy for his presidency. He set aside almost 2 million acres of southern Utah to create the Grand Staircase–Escalante National Monument under authority delegated to him from the Antiquities Act of 1906.[17] Similarly, he proposed a much larger initiative in October 1999 to protect almost 40 million acres of national forestland from commercial development. The massive scope of this effort would seal his environmental legacy.[18] Thus, as a lame-duck president late in his second term, facing a Congress that was in no mood to help to establish his place in history, Clinton turned one more time to his executive authority to accomplish this one massive policy. Predictably, Republican members and business groups protested both the policy and the president's method of achieving it. Senator Larry Craig of Idaho complained, "We have an attitude in this administration that not only does King William want to reign, he appears at this moment to be setting up a monarchy for Prince Albert. . . . These are not the King's lands, these are the people's lands, and we think he ought to come to the people's bodies to form and shape this kind of policy."[19] A spokesperson for the American Forest and Paper Association stated, "They are doing through a regulatory process what they can't do legislatively. . . . They don't have the votes, so they are doing an end-run around Congress to jam this elitist policy down the throats of the American people."[20]

Carl Cannon, in a June 2000 *National Journal* article, recounted vividly the three stages of Clinton's progression toward a "lands legacy," and he identified the day during the 1996 campaign when Clinton designated the Grand Staircase–Escalante National Monument as the turning point when the president realized the power of the stroke of his executive pen. "Something . . . happened that day at the Grand Canyon, according to well-placed sources in the environmental community: Clinton loved the feeling of setting aside that land, and relished the fact that he didn't need to talk to any Republicans or members of Congress to do it."[21] Of that day and that experience, Rindy O'Brien, vice president for policy at the Wilderness Society, said, "He was using his own tools of authority instead of working through the frustrating congressional process. It really geared him to use his legacy powers."[22]

Reliance on executive orders is sometimes a tactic that presidents use when the traditional avenues of politics are unpredictable or denied to them. It is a way of gaining a policy advantage, but only if congressional or judicial reversal seems unlikely. Clinton used this power generously, strategically, and across many different categories of policy. He set a standard that can be expected to be followed by his successors, especially if the institutions of government remain divided along partisan lines.

CONTRACTIONS

Appointments

All presidents look to their appointment power as a major prerogative of their office. Their executive branch appointments provide a way to solidify support for their policies, and their judicial appointments will have significance long after they leave office and may be part of their lasting legacies. Clinton's slow and troubled start with his cabinet appointments in 1993 is legendary for its misfires and mishandling, but the story of his judicial nominations is the one that captures the essence of presidential-congressional relations in times of partisan, polarized government and that had its origin in the judicial appointment battles of his predecessors.

Clinton approached his judicial appointments with the objective of de-emphasizing the importance of ideology, as had become so paramount and so poisoned in the Robert Bork and Clarence Thomas debacles of the Reagan and first Bush administrations. He endeavored, instead, to select for the federal bench those people whose outstanding judicial identity was moderate and centrist. For that matter, some Democrats were angered by his unwillingness to try to balance the conservatism of Reagan's and Bush's appointments with more distinctly liberal judges. But Eleanor Acheson, the assistant attorney general who headed the Office of Policy Development at the Justice Department, explained that, especially after the 1994 elections, "I think we were much more reactively cautious. . . . Right after the [1994] elections . . . I think the rule that . . . was only fair and responsible for the President to operate with was that until this thing settles out and we have a better sense of where we're going we just have to be very cautious."[23]

Indeed, some statistics tell the story that after Congress turned Republican in 1995, the confirmation rates of federal judges were lower than they had been with a Democratic Senate in the 103rd Congress. In 1993 and 1994 under a Democratic Senate, 90 percent of all judicial nominees were confirmed. In 1995 and 1996 under a Republican Senate, that confirmation number dropped to 70 percent of all nominees.[24] Significant slowdowns occurred in the rate of processing by the Senate in late 1996, exacerbated by the presidential candidacy of Bob Dole, who made the staffing of the federal courts a political issue in the 1996 campaign. Senate unwillingness to move judicial nominations late in an administration is not uncommon, although the sheer breakdown in the process was beyond the usual lethargy. Acheson described the delays of 1996 and 1997: "I wouldn't even call them delays. It was just a complete, almost destruction of the system."[25] Sheldon Goldman and Elliot Slotnick have termed this Republican strategy "court-blocking" and have analogized it as equal to and no less dramatic than Franklin Roosevelt's 1937 court-packing plan.[26] Consider the differences in the average number of days from the time a nomination was received by the Senate to the date of a hearing: for district judgeship nominees, it was 58 days in 1993–1994 and 76 days in 1995–1996. For circuit court judges, it was 75 to 80 days in 1993–1996 and 230 days in 1997–1998. For the average number of days between a committee vote and final floor action for district judgeships, it was 4 days in 1993–1994, 35 days in 1995–1996, and 38 days in 1997–1998. For circuit judgeships, the figures were 8 days in 1993–1994, 39 days in 1995–1996, and 42 days in 1997–1998.[27]

President Clinton addressed what he called the "mounting vacancy crisis in the courts" in a speech to the American Bar Association at the opening session of their 1999 annual meeting, noting that the progress that his administration had made in reducing the number of judicial vacancies in the federal courts came to a screeching halt in 1996, a presidential election year, when judges became grist for the mill of partisan politics. In that year, only seventeen judges were confirmed, and for the first time in forty years, not a single circuit court judge was confirmed by the Senate.[28] The most extreme example of hardball judicial nomination politics is found in the recent confirmation of Richard Paez to the Ninth Circuit Court of Appeals. Nominated by Clinton in January 1996, he waited four years in the confirmation twilight zone, and was finally confirmed in March 2000, setting the record of any judicial nominee in history to secure final confirmation.

The conclusion from these statistics and from the eight years of Clinton appointments to the federal judiciary is that the presidential power to appoint judges fell hostage to partisan politics, despite the intentions of the administration to try to avoid that very outcome. According to a Republican congressional staffer, Senate Majority Leader Trent Lott "uses the process of moving nominees as a price of moving legislation."[29]

The experiences of the Clinton administration may make it more difficult for future presidents to navigate this process with the Senate, if this recent scenario serves as any guide. As with war powers and executive orders, presidential-congressional relations on this matter were colored by the past history of previous administrations; but in this case, a difference emerged in that Clinton made a determined effort to ratchet down the roar of politics in judicial appointments. Yet the pull of historical memory proved too powerful to overcome, as Republicans viewed this as their chance to pay back a Democratic president and their Democratic counterparts in the Senate for the unsavory process and outcomes they had endured when they were in the minority. Efforts to break the cycle of mean-spiritedness proved unsuccessful (and it is anyone's guess whether that cycle will carry over to the next administration).

Presidential Privileges and Immunity

One unmistakable legacy that Clinton left to his successor is the string of court losses on matters of presidential privileges and immunity that arose during the impeachment proceedings. In both areas, Clinton chose to litigate matters that either had traditionally been resolved through negotiation and compromise or were so extraordinary as never to have arisen in such a context. And in both areas, the institution of the presidency lost legal and constitutional ground, now solidified in judicial precedents.

On the immunity issue, Clinton sued in federal district court in 1994 to claim that as president and as a defendant in a sexual harassment suit by Paula Jones, he had absolute immunity from civil liability. This claim was rejected by the district court, although it did find that he had temporary immunity from trial, a position that Clinton eventually maintained by the time the case reached the U.S. Supreme Court. But he fared no better in the high court, which, in May 1997, rejected his arguments for temporary immunity that were based on the uniqueness of the office, separation of powers, and the potential disruption that would be caused by a president's participation in a suit.[30] This case raised issues that went beyond the existing case law on presidential immunity from civil liability in presenting novel claims of presidential immunity for unofficial acts that occurred prior to his taking office as president.

The impact of the Court's opinion, denying such immunity, may be slight, given the unusual nature of the circumstances that gave rise to it. Perhaps significant, also, is the harsh criticism directed at the Court for its seeming naivete in failing to recognize the potentially immobilizing consequences of its decision to the institution of the presidency. In fairness, the Court could not possibly have imagined that its ruling would pave the way for a full-dress impeachment proceeding of a president down the road, with far more intrusion on the functioning of the presidential office than could ever have been expected from a civil trial. But this decision removed any legal impediment to the president's deposition in the trial court in the Paula Jones case, where he was asked pointed questions about his relationship with Monica Lewinsky, and where his answers would lay the predicate for the allegations of perjury that would form one part of Independent Counsel Kenneth Starr's investigation. In short, the Court's presumption of effective "case management" techniques at the district court level to ensure minimal intrusion into the president's official duties during a trial turned out to be utterly unrealistic and untrue.[31] Its resolution of the issue, in constitutional and legal terms, set the stage for an eventual outcome that would accomplish, in political and institutional terms, exactly the set of circumstances that the Court assumed it could avoid.

Of perhaps far greater practical significance to the routine functioning of the presidency than the immunity matter was the effect of the series of lower federal court decisions on three versions of presidential privilege: executive privilege, government attorney–client privilege, and Secret Service protective-function privilege. In the Secret Service case, the administration urged the court to create a protective function privilege that would provide an absolute shield to the president's protectors from having to testify in official proceedings. The lower courts rejected this invitation to fashion a wholly new privilege, suggesting, instead, that this was a matter that was more appropriate for Congress to determine, if it deemed such a privilege necessary.

The decisions on executive privilege and government attorney–client privilege have already affected the way business gets done in the White House: the judicial rejection of the assertion of these privileges in the Clinton matters has created an atmosphere where no one takes notes any longer, for fear of having them subpoenaed, now that the shields of executive privilege and government attorney–client privilege have been substantially eroded. Clinton White House Counsel Charles Ruff was explicit on this point: "We did not take notes. We were subject to subpoena. People were very careful not to put things down in writing."[32]

These two cases arose from subpoenas by Independent Counsel Starr to Sidney Blumenthal and Bruce Lindsey, ordering them to testify before the grand jury investigating perjury and obstruction of justice charges against Clinton that grew out of his trial deposition in the Paula Jones lawsuit. Blumenthal claimed executive privilege, as an assistant to the president, and Lindsey claimed a combination of executive and government attorney–client privilege, as both assistant to the president and as deputy White House counsel.

Judge Norma Holloway Johnson, in her district court decision, denied the application of the privileges asserted here but recognized the existence of both as qualified privileges and ruled that they were subject to a balancing test of need and availability. This meant that a president's claim of confidentiality was presumptively privileged but would be balanced against a prosecutor's showing that the covered communications were "directly relevant to the issues that are expected to be central to the trial" and that they were unavailable elsewhere. This was a slightly crisper test for privilege claims than the one that also presumptively privileged the president's claims of executive privilege to the extent that they "relate to the effective discharge of a president's powers" but that could be outweighed by the need for evidence in a pending criminal trial.[33]

Both parties to the Lindsey case argued absolutist positions: Starr argued that at least with government attorney-client matters, no such privilege should exist at all; Clinton's lawyers argued that his conversations with his government lawyers should be absolutely immune from judicial process. Given these diametrically opposed arguments, Judge Johnson found a middle ground between them. On appeal, the two-to-one decision in the District of Columbia Circuit Court of Appeals made further inroads into government attorney–client privilege by rejecting Judge Johnson's balancing test and ruling, instead, that government lawyers are different from private attorneys in that they have a legal duty to provide testimony to a grand jury.[34] The decision offered an escape hatch for the president, however, since Bruce Lindsey occupied both political and legal positions simultaneously. The court of appeals decision suggested that the specific communications claimed by the White House under government attorney–client privilege might actually fall more appropriately under a claim of executive privilege, so there was an alternative way to protect at least some of Lindsey's testimony. The overall conclusion from these two lower federal court decisions is that the courts recognized the existence of these claims and established tests for determining when they would apply but found that the specific facts in Clinton's case did not meet these tests.

Analysts have commented generally that the Clinton White House has narrowed considerably the protection of these privileges for future presidents by bringing them into the courts in the first place, contrary to previous incidents surrounding matters of privilege, which were resolved politically, not judicially, thus preserving the status of the privilege without specifically defining it in legal terms that could limit its future use. This is precisely the effect that these current decisions will have, much to the chagrin of former White House lawyers. Boyden Gray, the White House counsel to former President George H. W. Bush, lamented, "It's best not to litigate. No one's ever litigated it. Now there is no room to argue." But according to the Clinton White House lawyers, it was Starr who pushed them to the brink and who created a "frontal assault on something clearly privileged." Former Clinton White House counsel Charles Ruff explained, "There's always a choice. You can acquiesce. We ended up deciding that the principles involved were sufficiently important to the institution that they needed to be pursued."[35]

IMPEACHMENT—A DRAW

A common reaction to the impeachment of President Clinton was that the episode had lowered the bar for the future, that such attempts might now occur more frequently, and that they will be used as political weapons in the arsenal of confrontational politics.[36] Indeed, this worry may be overrated. The opposite argument can also be made, that there is just as much reason to predict a wariness toward the use of impeachment anytime soon, since it has proven itself to be so uncontrollable, unpredictable, and ultimately, unsuccessful for those who wish to employ it. In purely rational terms, then, is it worth the risk to undertake the process?

The answer to that question lies in the discretionary judgment and calculations of those who think a president's actions warrant the deadliest constitutional scrutiny. In the Clinton case, political opponents of the president underestimated the force of the legal, constitutional, and institutional factors and calculated that the potential benefit to them of removing a president was worth the political risk to their party and to the system. In fact, efforts to unseat a president that are motivated by extreme partisan polarization, as in the Clinton case, are unlikely to succeed and instead may diminish the fortunes of the party pursuing the president, as the 1998 midterm elections demonstrated. Only where enough members of a president's own party acknowledge the sufficiency of the evidence to make such an effort bipartisan will it make sense to pursue such a case.

Thus, any initial decision to undertake the impeachment process rests on the judgment by party leaders of the potential impact of the impeachment process on their party's short- and long-term interests. If this is so, then the decision of the House Republicans in 1998 can only be explained by either their belief that there was sufficient evidence to succeed in impeaching and removing Clinton or the fact that they were so motivated to move against him that they were willing to risk their party's reputation and interests, in the event that their efforts happened to fail.

Legally, the evidence for the charges against Clinton came either very close to or crossed the line of illegality. Yes, perjury and witness tampering by a president set an entirely unacceptable precedent for the orderly administration of justice by the nation's chief law enforcement officer. The flip side of that argument, however, is that it was the extraordinarily embarrassing nature of the subject matter (illicit sex) that the president was under obligation to disclose, an issue that is prone to provoking less than candid answers whenever it is under inquiry.[37] If one separates the fact of his sexual behavior from his misleading statements about it, then the veracity of his statements can be judged on its own. But the obstacle comes from the fact that the two cannot be separated. One grows out of the other. And as one journalist commented with reference to many of the independent counsel investigations, but the statement is equally relevant and aptly descriptive here, the sad lesson is that this is another case where "the cover-up became the crime even though there was no crime to cover up."[38]

Constitutionally, are we any closer to the certainty of defining what is an "impeachable offense"? The best we can say is that a majority of the House believed that lying to a grand jury and tampering with witnesses are such offenses, but the requisite two-thirds of the Senate did not. Guidance from the 1974 staff report of the House Judiciary Committee is instructive here and notes: "Not all presidential misconduct is sufficient to constitute grounds for impeachment. There is a further requirement—substantiality. In deciding whether this further requirement has been met, the facts must be considered as a whole in the context of the office, not in terms of separate or isolated events."[39] Did the charges here meet the test of substantiality? Reasonable people will disagree. But it may be worth noting the irony (and illogic) in the House votes that approved Article 1 perjury in the grand jury while defeating Article 2 in the Paula Jones deposition when the grand jury testimony (and thus perjury) of Article 1 would never have occurred if there had been no deposition (and thus no perjury) in the Paula Jones case of Article 2.

Indeed, the Clinton impeachment seems to be the embodiment of the "constitutionalization of politics" that I have already noted. The political choices by

House Republican leaders in 1998 to pursue impeachment to its very end reflected their conscious, single-minded determination to find any way to remove Clinton from office, and they were willing to sacrifice their party's standing, if necessary, to achieve their goal. Raw political strategy, converted into constitutional tactics, seemingly paved the way for their efforts, with little regard for the consequences to their party.

The selective analysis of topics covered here reveals some insights on the impact of the Clinton presidency on the scope of presidential power. I have examined the war power, executive orders, appointments, presidential privileges and immunity, and impeachment. Other topics that were excluded but that could be equally subjected to this same analysis are presidential use of signing statements to implement nonenforcement of laws and presidential use of legislation rather than treaties to conclude trade negotiations.

Some observers have suggested that the experience of the Clinton years has shrunk the presidency, has made it less relevant, and has diminished the office. As the title of this chapter suggests, the verdict may be more mixed and more complicated than that. Indeed, when it comes to an evaluation of the constitutional authority of the presidency, there may well exist a fundamental duality as a consequence of this eight years: an expansion of the war power and the use of executive lawmaking authority and a contraction of the appointment power, protection from presidential privileges, and immunity from civil liability.

The legacy for impeachment may fall into an ambiguous state—a draw, since the circumstances for invoking it are so fact-specific and context-dependent. In the long run, and with a bit of hindsight, history may judge the impeachment effort as partisan, predatory, and illegitimate, with less impact on the institution than assumed at the time, since the circumstances that gave rise to it were so idiosyncratic to the person of Bill Clinton and so perfectly timed with a polarized environment.

The damage to presidential privileges and immunity is clear and consequential, as it has already influenced White House behavior and has cast a pall over a president's ability to receive candid, confidential advice from his advisers. Charles Ruff has commented, "The practical result of the court's decision [the Court of Appeals ruling in the Lindsey case] is that the president and all other government officials will be less likely to receive full and frank advice about their official obligations and duties from government attorneys."[40] The lesson here, in hindsight, was that there was value after all in leaving some ambiguity over constitutional definitions and thus some maneuverability and flexibility in smoothing out the most sensitive of matters.

As for the war power and executive orders, what emerged from the evidence was the realization that the Clinton administration followed and perhaps solidified the same practices engaged in by its predecessors. Clinton gave no constitutional ground in either of these matters and probably strengthened them for his successor. Possibly, the explanation for this is that it was not so much a factor of the Clinton presidency as it was the coming of age and, consequently, the honing and refining of presidential tools with which to do business with an opposition-party Congress.

The loss of power in the judicial appointments process is a serious one, yet again one is struck by how much this current set of conditions was a product of the past. The paradox here is that if Clinton had chosen to make the process more overtly ideological and if he had nominated more liberal judges in order to balance the conservatism of the Reagan and Bush appointees, the reaction probably would not have been any more hostile than it already was here with moderate nominees. Instead of wearing the gloves, as the Clinton administration did, with only a chilly response to show for it, perhaps the next administration that faces an opposition Senate may just take them off completely and take their chances bare-handed. The cause of judicial independence would be ill-served by such conduct—and already we have seen that judicial appointments were visibly on the agenda in the 2000 presidential campaign. Clearly, this is an issue that may blossom over the next year and that may come center stage in the next administration. There may be no better (or, indeed, no worse) metaphor for the current state of presidential-congressional relations.

NOTES

1. For a detailed analysis of Clinton's use of the war power, see David Gray Adler, "The Clinton Theory of the War Power," *Presidential Studies Quarterly* 30 (March 2000): 155–168.

2. *Campbell v. Clinton*, 52 F. Supp. 2d. 34 (D.D.C. 1999); David Broder, "No Churchills," *Washington Post*, May 9, 1999, p. B9; Helen Dewar, "Senate Shelves McCain Proposal on Kosovo," *Washington Post*, May 5, 1999, p. A27.

3. Complaint for Declaratory Relief, *Campbell v. Clinton*, 52 F. Supp. 2d (D.D.C. 1999), at 99–1072.

4. *Campbell v. Clinton*, 52 F. Supp. 2d. 34 (D.D.C. 1999).

5. See, e.g., *Goldwater v. Carter*, 444 U.S. 996 (1979); *Dellums v. Bush*, 752 F. Supp. 1141 (D.D.C. 1990).

6. Walter Dellinger, "Deployment of United States Armed Forces into Haiti," 18 *Op. OLC* 34, September 27, 1994, pp. 572–573. For discussion, see Louis Fisher and David Gray Adler, "The War Powers Resolution," *Political Science Quarterly* 113 (spring 1998): 1, 11–12.

7. Dellinger, "Deployment," pp. 575–576.

8. Ibid., p. 576.

9. Joseph Lockhart, Office of the Press Secretary,White House Press Briefing, April 13, 1999, <*http://clinton6.nara.gov/1999/04/1999-04-13-press-briefing-by-joe-lockhart. html*>.

10. See Fisher and Adler, "War Powers," pp. 11–12, 19–20.

11. National Archives and Records Administration, Federal Register Home Page <http://www.nara.gov/fedreg/eo_clint.html>.

12. See online <http://www.nara.gov/fedreg/eo.html#top>. Individual sites for presidents here are <http://www.nara.gov/fedreg/eo_bush.html>; <http://www.nara.gov/fedreg/eo_reagn.html>; <http://www.nara.gov/fedreg/eo_cartr.html>; <http://www.nara.gov/fedreg/eo_ford.html>; <http://www.nara.gov/fedreg/eo_nixon.html>; <http://www.nara.gov/fedreg/eo_lgj.html>.

13. Alexis Simendinger, "The Paper Wars," National Journal, July 25, 1998, pp. 1732–1739.

14. Ibid., pp. 1736–1737.

15. Robert Pear, "Dispute over Plan to Use Jobless Aid for Parental Leave," Washington Post, November 8, 1999, p. A1.

16. Louis Fisher, "Legal Disputes in the Clinton Years," Presidential Studies Quarterly 29 (December 1999): 696.

17. Simendinger, "Paper Wars," p. 1736.

18. David Sanger and Sam Howe Verhovek. "Clinton Proposes Wider Protection for U.S. Forests," New York Times, October 14, 1999, p. A1; Tom Kenworthy, "Clinton Readies Forest Protection Initiative," Washington Post, October 8, 1999, p. A1.

19. Sanger and Verhovek, "Clinton Proposes," p. A20.

20. Kenworthy, "Clinton Readies," p. A1.

21. Carl Cannon, "Lands Legacy Gains Ground," National Journal, June 10, 2000, pp. 1837–1838.

22. Ibid.

23. Sheldon Goldman and Elliot Slotnick, "Clinton's First Term Judiciary: Many Bridges to Cross," Judicature 80 (May–June 1997): 257.

24. Ibid., p. 255.

25. Ibid., p. 270.

26. Ibid., p. 271.

27. Sheldon Goldman and Elliot Slotnick, "Picking Judges Under Fire," Judicature 82 (May–June 1999): 271.

28. "Remarks by the President at the Opening Assembly of the Annual Meeting of the American Bar Association," Atlanta, Georgia, August 9, 1999, Weekly Compilation of Presidential Documents 35 (1999): 1603.

29. Carrie Johnson, "Final Judgement: The President Has Been Criticized by Left and Right. Maybe He Got the Bench He Wanted," Legal Times, March 6, 2000, p. 10.

30. Clinton v. Jones, 520 U.S. 681 (1997).

31. Ibid.

32. Jim Oliphant, "Losing Privilege," Legal Times, March 10, 2000, p. 20.

33. In re Grand Jury Proceeding, 5 F. Supp. 2d. 21 (D.D.C. 1998); U.S. v. Nixon, 418 U.S. 683 (1974) .

34. In re Lindsey, 158 F. 3d. 1263 (D.C. Cir. 1998).

35. Oliphant, "Losing Privilege," p. 20.

36. This section is taken from Nancy Kassop, "The Clinton Impeachment: Untangling the Web of Conflicting Considerations," Presidential Studies Quarterly 30 (June 2000): 359.

37. As former senator Dale Bumpers remarked to the Senate during the trial, quoting H. L. Mencken, "When you hear somebody say 'this is not about sex,' it's about sex" (*Congressional Record,* 106th Cong., 2d sess., U.S. Senate, January 21, 1999, §845).

38. David Grann, "Starr Wars: The Finale. Background Noise," *New Republic,* June 28, 1999, p. 22.

39. Quoted in Michael J. Gerhardt, *The Federal Impeachment Process: A Constitutional and Historical Analysis* (Princeton: Princeton University Press, 1996), p. 27.

40. Ruth Marcus, "Court Rejects Privilege Claim," *Washington Post,* July 28, 1998, p. A1.

2

Clinton, the Constitution, and the War Power

David Gray Adler

President Bill Clinton frequently engaged in unilateral acts of executive war making in defiance of the war clause of the Constitution, which vests in Congress the sole and exclusive authority to initiate hostilities on behalf of the American people.[1] His use of U.S. military power ranged from the infliction of air and missile strikes against targets in Afghanistan and Sudan to global hot spots in Iraq and Bosnia. In spring 1999, in what amounted to one of the most flagrant acts of usurpation of the war power in the history of the Republic, President Clinton ordered in concert with NATO allies a massive air and missile assault against the Federal Republic of Yugoslavia in an effort to halt Slobodan Milosevic's slaughter of ethnic Albanians in Kosovo. That attack, which ranked as the most intensive and sustained military campaign conducted by the United States since the Vietnam War, may well have been justified on moral and policy grounds, but it nevertheless required authorization by Congress. The distinctive feature of Clinton's military action in Yugoslavia and what distinguished it from previous acts of usurpation lay in its raw violation of the fundamental requirement of the war clause—authorization of hostilities by both houses of Congress. It is regrettably true that for the past half century successive presidents have engaged in unilateral acts of war making without authorization from Congress, and it is true as well that on those occasions Congress took no action to preserve its powers from naked usurpation by the executive branch.[2] But Clinton's "presidential war" against Yugoslavia marked the first time in our history that a president waged war in the face of a direct congressional refusal to authorize the war.[3]

Clinton's action marked the further erosion of the war clause, the near "removal of a landmark power," by the introduction of arbitrary executive power, an act that the Framers sought to preclude by means of a written Constitution that limited governmental authority by assigning specific roles, responsibilities, and powers to each branch of government.[4] Viewed in historical perspective, Clinton's acts belong in a category with Harry Truman's war against Korea and his seizure of the steel mills and with Richard Nixon's assertion of an absolute executive privilege.[5] Claims of illimitable power ring hollow in a constitutional order that is at pains to cabin governmental authority at every turn. But parchment alone is no match for an executive who is determined to exert power that has not been granted. The war clause, it appears, is in jeopardy of becoming a "dead letter."[6]

The Clinton administration offered a variety of constitutional arguments, in different contexts, as justification for its unilateral actions, but they are unsubstantial and shatter upon analysis. On occasion—in Somalia, Afghanistan, and Sudan—Clinton, as we shall see, engaged in acts of war without bothering to adduce a constitutional rationale. When he troubled to supply justification, the strategy, if not the reasoning, was clear, and it was punctuated with obfuscation. Clinton's legal advisers contended that the Constitution is vague and ambiguous in its textual assignment of foreign affairs powers and that, incredibly, it is not even clear on the repository of the authority to "declare war."[7] On other occasions, the administration maintained, in terms and tones strikingly reminiscent of the imperial chords struck by Lyndon Johnson and Richard Nixon, that the president's voice is final on matters of war and peace.[8]

President Clinton's contention and actions have disfigured the war clause, and they have served to obscure the architectural blueprint of the Framers, for whom the concept of unilateral presidential power in foreign affairs was intolerable. The Constitution assigns to Congress senior status in a partnership with the president for the purpose of conducting foreign policy. Article 1 vests in Congress broad, explicit, and exclusive powers to regulate foreign commerce, raise and maintain military forces, grant letters of marque and reprisal, provide for the common defense, and initiate all hostilities on behalf of the United States, including full-blown war. As Article 2 indicates, the president shares with the Senate the treatymaking power and the authority to appoint ambassadors. The Constitution exclusively assigns only two foreign affairs powers to the president. He is designated commander in chief of the nation's armed forces, although, as we shall see, he acts in this capacity by and under the authority of Congress. The president also has the power to receive ambassadors, but the Framers viewed this as a routine, administrative function, devoid of discretionary authority. This list exhausts the textual grant of authority to the president with respect to foreign affairs jurisdiction. The president's constitutional powers pale in comparison to those of Congress.[9]

The Framers' studied decision to vest the bulk of foreign policy powers in Congress marked a deliberate and dramatic departure from the practice in England, which, like other nations, concentrated virtually unfettered authority in the hands of the executive. In his *Second Treatise of Government,* John Locke described three powers of government: the legislative, the executive, and the federative. Federative power was the power over foreign affairs—"the power of war and peace, leagues and alliances, and all the transactions with all persons and communities without the Commonwealth." The federative power was "almost always united" with the executive. Locke warned that the separation of executive and federative powers would invite "disorder and ruin."[10] Sir William Blackstone, the great eighteenth-century jurist, described in his distinguished four-volume work, *Commentaries on the Laws of England*, the vast foreign affairs powers that inhere in the Crown by virtue of the royal prerogative. Blackstone defined the king's prerogative as "those rights and capacities which the King enjoys alone." The monarch's *direct* prerogatives, those which are "rooted in and spring from the King's political person," included the authority to send and receive ambassadors and the power to make war or peace. The Crown, moreover, could negotiate "a treaty with a foreign state, which shall irrevocably bind the nation," and he could issue letters of marque and reprisal, which authorized private citizens to perform military actions on behalf of the nation. The king, according to Blackstone, was "the generalissimo, or the first in military command," and he possessed "the sole power of raising and regulating fleets and armies." In the exercise of his lawful prerogative the king "is, and ought to be absolute; that is, so far absolute, that there is no legal authority that can either delay or resist him."[11]

Placed in its historical context, then, the Constitutional Convention's decision to break from the prevailing foreign policymaking practices of other governments at the time was simply stunning. It is explicable, perhaps, only in terms of the Framers' intellectual orientation, their understanding of history, and their own practical experiences. The effective control and management of foreign policy and the use of armed force was, of course, a primary goal and an animating purpose of the convention. Indeed, given the widespread ramifications of foreign relations, "nothing," as Arthur Schlesinger Jr. has written, "was more crucial for the new nation than the successful conduct of its external relations."[12] The difficult search for an efficient foreign policy design was compounded by the Framers' heightened fear of the abuse of power. They were steeped in English history, and they well knew that "the management of foreign relations," as Madison stated, "appears to be the most susceptible of abuse of all trusts committed to a Government." War, alone, could plunder the nation's treasury, ravage its society, and destroy its very lifeblood. The Framers contemplated the possibility and consequences of treasonous acts, realized that fortunes were to be made in the dark and secretive world of espionage, and feared "the loss of liberty at home" that could result from "danger, real or pretended, from abroad."[13] They were also greatly influenced by the constitutional crises and political convulsions of the seventeenth-century English civil wars. The absolutist claims of the Stuart kings and the abuse of authority by manipulative ministers had hardened their view toward the executive. The pervasive fear of unbridled power and the specter of an embryonic monarch precluded presidential control of foreign policy. Even Alexander Hamilton, whose enthusiasm for executive supremacy was unsurpassed by members of the convention, shared these concerns as expressed in *Federalist* no. 75: "The history of human conduct does not warrant that exalted opinion of human virtue which would make it wise in a nation to commit interests of so delicate and momentous a kind, as those which concern its intercourse with the rest of the world, to the sole disposal of a magistrate created and circumstanced as would be a president of the United States."[14]

These deep-seated trepidations regarding the abuse of power, which resonated from the colonial period and reflected the Framers' reading of history, made the quest for an effective foreign affairs system an arduous task. The pervasive fear of a powerful executive, particularly a president who might wield unilateral authority in an area so sensitive and critical as that of foreign relations, was reinforced by the republican ideology that permeated the convention. The Framers' attachment to collective judgment and their decision to create a structure of shared power in foreign affairs provided, in the words of James Wilson, "a security to the people," for it was a cardinal principle of republicanism that the conjoined wisdom of the many is superior to that of one.[15] The emphasis on collective decision making came at the expense of unilateral presidential authority, but that consequence was of little moment, given the overriding aversion to unrestrained executive power. The structure of shared powers in the conduct of international affairs proved satisfactory to the Framers since it would deter the abuse of power and provide a means of airing the various political, social, and economic interests that were bound up in the nation's external relations.[16]

The Framers' belief in and commitment to collective decision making, reflected in their aspirations to effectuate a republican form of government, was perhaps no more dramatically affirmed than in their decision to vest in Congress the sole and exclusive authority to initiate military hostilities, short of and including full-blown war. Their historic decision to reconfigure the role of the executive in foreign affairs, to strip him of important prerogatives that at that juncture were universally admired and practiced, was immediately visible, palpable, and comprehensible. Thus the Framers replaced absolutist pretensions with congressional supremacy and erased the specter of a president swollen with power who might march the citizenry into war for less than meritorious reasons.[17] As James Madison explained it in a letter to Thomas Jefferson, "The constitution supposes, what the History of all Governments demonstrates, that the Executive is the branch of power most interested in war, and most prone to it. It has accordingly with studied care vested the question of war in the Legislature."[18]

Bald assertions of a unilateral presidential warmaking power, proceeding from assumptions that are at war with constitutional principles, have been frequently advanced. Efforts by presidents, publicists, and revisionists to supplant the congressional war power with executive supremacy, by means of obfuscation, contrived issues, casuistry, and juggled evidence, require fresh examination; otherwise, those efforts may be confused with convention.[19] Resort to historical sources and careful analysis of the relevant textual provisions will cast light on the Clinton theory of the war power and enable us to grasp the place of the war power in the constitutional design.

THE WAR CLAUSE

The fact that the power of war and peace was historically associated with the monarchy was addressed repeatedly at the Constitutional Convention. On June 1, 1787, Charles Pinckney said he was for a vigorous president but was afraid that some of the proposals "would render the Executive a Monarchy, of the worst kind, towit an elective one." John Rutledge wanted the executive power placed in a single person, "tho' he was not for giving him the power of war and peace." James Wilson sought to reassure the delegates. The prerogatives of the British monarchy were not "a proper guide in defining the executive powers. Some of these prerogatives were of a Legislative nature. Among others that of war & peace & c." Edmund Randolph worried about executive power, calling it "the foetus of monarch." The delegates at the convention, he said, had "no motive to be governed by the British Government, as our prototype." If the United States had no other choice he might adopt the British model, but the "fixt genius of the people of America required a different form of Government." Wilson agreed that the British model "was inapplicable to the situation in this Country; the extent of which was so great, and the manners so republican, that nothing but a great confederated Republic would do for it."[20]

Alexander Hamilton, a favorite among extollers of a strong presidency, also rejected the British model of executive prerogatives in the conduct of foreign affairs and the exercise of the war power. While he explained in a lengthy speech at the convention on June 18 that in "his private opinion he had no scruple in declaring . . . that the British Government was the best in the world," he nevertheless agreed that the English scheme would have no application in the United States. He proposed that the Senate would have the "sole power of declaring war" and, in language that would anticipate the role of the president as commander in chief, the president would be authorized to have "the direction of war when authorized or begun."[21]

The Framers' determination to preclude unilateral presidential authority to initiate military actions was demonstrated in the debates that surrounded the crafting of the war clause. On August 6, the Committee of Detail circulated a draft that provided that the legislature shall have the power "to make war."[22] This bore sharp resemblance to the Articles of Confederation, which vested the "sole and exclusive right and power of determining on peace and war" to the Continental Congress.

When the war clause was considered in debate on August 17, Charles Pinckney opposed placing the power in the full Congress. Its proceedings, he said, "were too slow. . . . The Senate would be the best depository, being more acquainted with foreign affairs, and most capable of proper resolutions."[23] Pierce Butler "was for vesting the power in the President, who will have all the requisite qualities, and will not make war but when the Nation will support it." Butler's opinion shocked Elbridge Gerry, who said that he "never expected to hear in a republic a motion to empower the Executive alone to declare war." Butler stood alone in the convention; there was no support for his opinion and no second to his motion.

The draft proposal to vest the legislature with the power to make war proved unsatisfactory to Madison and Gerry. As a consequence, they moved to substitute "declare" for "make," leaving the president "the power to repel sudden attacks." The meaning of the motion is unmistakable. Congress was granted the power to make, that is, initiate war; the president, for obvious reasons, could act immediately to repel sudden attacks without authorization from Congress. Roger Sherman spoke in support of the motion and thought it "stood very well. The Executive shd. be able to repel and not to commence war." George Mason "was agst giving the power of war to the Executive, because not <safely> to be trusted with it. . . . He was for clogging rather than facilitating war."[24]

The debates and votes on the war clause make it clear that Congress alone possesses the authority to initiate war. The warmaking power was specifically withheld from the president; he was given only authority to repel sudden attacks. Confirmation of that understanding was provided by remarks of ratifiers in various state conventions as well as by the early practice and contemporaneous statements of political actors.[25]

James Wilson, perhaps only slightly less important than James Madison in the Constitutional Convention, told the Pennsylvania Ratifying Convention, "This system will not hurry us into war; it is calculated to guard against it. It will not be in the power of a single man, or a single body of men, to involve us in such distress; for the important part of declaring war is vested in the legislature at large: this declaration must be made with the concurrence of the House of Representatives: from this circumstance we may draw a certain conclusion that nothing but our interest can draw us into war."[26] Similar assurance was provided in other state ratifying conventions. In North Carolina, James Iredell compared the limited powers of the president with those of the British monarch. The king of England was not only the commander in chief "but has the power, in time of war, to raise fleets and armies. He has also the authority to declare war." By contrast, the president "has not the power of declaring war by his own authority, nor that of raising fleets and armies. These powers are vested in other hands. The power of declaring war is expressly given to Congress." And Charles Pinckney, a delegate in Philadelphia, told the South Carolina Ratifying Convention that "the President's powers did not permit him to declare war."[27] Likewise, in New York, Chancellor R. R. Livingston responded to objections that the Continental Congress did not have "the same powers" as the proposed Congress. He explained that the two bodies shared "the very same" power, including the power "of making war and peace. . . . They may involve us in a war at their pleasure."[28]

The meaning of the war clause was thus settled at the dawn of the Republic. The word "declare" enjoyed a settled understanding and an established usage. As early as 1552, the verb "declare" had become synonymous with the verb "commence." They both meant the initiation of hostilities.[29] This was the established usage in international law as well as in England, where the terms "declare war" and "make war" were used interchangeably.[30] This practice was familiar to the Framers. As Chancellor James Kent of New York, one of the leading jurists of the founding period, stated, "As war cannot lawfully be commenced on the part of the United States, without an act of Congress, such an act is, of course, a formal official notice to all the world, and equivalent to the most solemn declaration." Though Kent interpreted "declare" to mean "commence," he did not assert that the Constitution requires a congressional declaration of war before hostilities could be lawfully commenced but merely that it must be initiated by Congress. What is "essential," according to Kent, is "that some formal public act, proceeding directly from the competent source, should announce to the people at home their new relations and duties growing out of a state of war, and which should equally apprize neutral nations of the fact."[31]

Given the equivalence of "commence" and "declare," it is clear that a congressional declaration of war would institute military hostilities. According to international law commentators, a declaration of war was desirable because it announced the institution of a state of war and the legal consequences that it entailed to the adversary, to neutral nations, and to citizens of the sovereign initiating the war. Indeed, this is the essence of a declaration of war: notice by the proper authority of an intent to convert a state of peace into a state of war. But all that is required under American law is a concurrent resolution or an explicit congressional authorization of the use of military force against a named adversary.[32] This may come in the form of a "declaration pure and simple" or in a "conditional declaration of war."[33] There are also two kinds of war, those which United States courts have termed "perfect," or general, and those labeled "imperfect," or limited wars. In 1782, the federal court of appeals, the prize court established by the Continental Congress, stated, "The writers upon the law of nations, speaking of different kinds of war, distinguish them into perfect and imperfect: A perfect war is that which destroys the national peace and tranquillity, and lays the foundation of every possible act of hostility. The imperfect war is that which does not entirely destroy the public tranquillity, but interrupts it only in some particulars, as in the case of reprisals."[34]

It was decided at the dawn of the Republic in three important Supreme Court cases that the power of determining perfect and imperfect war lay with Congress.[35] For example, in 1801, in *Talbot v. Seeman*, Chief Justice John Marshall held for the Court that the power of Congress comprises the power "to declare a general war" and also to "wage a limited war."[36] The power of Congress to authorize limited war is a necessary concomitant of its power to declare general war. If, as President Clinton and others have contended, the president might authorize relatively minor acts of war or perhaps covert military operations in circumstances not demanding full-blown war, that power could be wielded in a way that would easily eviscerate the Constitution's placement of the war power in Congress.[37] John Bassett Moore, the eminent American scholar of international law, justly rebuked that proposition: "There can hardly be room for doubt that the Framers of the Constitution, when they vested in Congress the power to declare war, never imagined that they were leaving it to the executive to use the military and naval forces of the United States all over the world for the purpose of actually coercing other nations, occupying their territory, and killing their soldiers and citizens, all according to his own notion of the fitness of things, as long as he refrained from calling his action war or persisted in calling it peace."[38]

Indeed, the Framers withheld from the president the power to work such mischief. As we have observed, he was granted only the authority to respond defensively to the initiation of war through sudden attack on the United States. In 1806, in *United States v. Smith,* Justice William Paterson of the Supreme Court, who had been a delegate to the convention, explained the rationale for a presidential response:

> If, indeed, a foreign nation should invade the territories of the United States, it would apprehend, be not only lawful for the president to resist such invasion, but also to carry hostilities into the enemy's own country; and for this plain reason, that a state of complete and absolute war exists between the two nations. In the case of invasive hostilities, there cannot be war on the one side and peace on the other. . . . There is a manifest distinction between our going to war with a nation at peace, and a war being made against us by an actual invasion, or a formal declaration. In the former case, it is the exclusive province of Congress to change a state of peace into a state of war.[39]

As described by Paterson, the rationale for vesting the president with the authority to repel sudden attacks rested on the fact that an invasion instituted a state of war, thus rendering a declaration of war by Congress superfluous. In such an event, the president was authorized to respond militarily against the attacking enemy. But contrary to Clinton's claims, the president's power of self-defense does not extend to foreign lands.[40] The Framers did not give the president the authority to intervene in foreign wars, or to choose between war and peace, or to identify and commence hostilities against an enemy of the American people. Nor did they empower him to initiate force abroad on the basis of his own assessments of U.S. security interests. These circumstances involve choices that belong to Congress under its exclusive province to change a state of peace into a state of war. The president's power is purely defensive and strictly limited to attacks against the United States.

The Constitution, then, grants to Congress the sum total of the nation's power to commence hostilities. Consistent with this constitutional theory, the convention gave the Congress the power to issue "letters of marque and reprisal."[41] Dating back to the Middle Ages, when sovereigns employed private forces in retaliation for an injury caused by the sovereign of another state or his subjects, the practice of issuing reprisals gradually evolved into the use of public armies. By the time of the convention, the Framers considered the power to issue letters of marque and reprisal sufficient to authorize a broad spectrum of armed hostilities short of declared war. In other words, it was regarded as a species of imperfect war. For example, Madison, Hamilton, and Jefferson, among others, agreed that the authorization of reprisals was an act of war and belonged to Congress.[42] As a direct riposte to the assertion of a presidential power to order acts of war, we may consider what Jefferson said in 1793 of the authority necessary to issue a reprisal: "Congress must be called upon to take it; the right of reprisal being expressly lodged with them by the Constitution, and not with the executive."[43]

By way of summary, when the Framers granted to Congress the power to declare war, they were vesting in that body the exclusive prerogative— a "single commitment" to Congress— to initiate military hostilities on behalf of the American people.[44] Congress might "declare" war, but a "declaration" was not required. Under the Constitution only congressional authorization of hostilities, great or small, was required. The congressional war power was regarded as omnicompetent. As a consequence, the president had no authority to engage in acts of war in the absence of congressional authorization.

THE COMMANDER-IN-CHIEF CLAUSE

Article 2, section 2, of the Constitution provides. "The President shall be Commander in Chief of the Army and Navy of the United States, and of the Militia of the several states, when called into the actual service of the United States." The commander in chief, in the words of Justice Robert H. Jackson, has been invoked for the "power to do anything, anywhere, that can be done with an army or navy."[45] While stated in the context of reviewing President Truman's invocation of the clause to support his seizure of the steel mills, Jackson's observations certainly anticipated the claims of recent executives, including Bill Clinton, who have seized the provision as a principal justification for their military adventures.[46] Clinton invoked the post to defend his unilateral decision to order missile strikes against Baghdad in 1993, air strikes in Bosnia in 1994, and his air war against Yugoslavia in 1999.[47] As we shall see, however, the title of commander in chief conferred no warmaking power whatever; it vested in the president only the authority to repel sudden attacks on the United States and to direct war, "when authorized or begun." In this capacity, he would direct these forces placed at his command by an act of Congress.

As Francis D. Wormuth has observed, "The office of commander in chief has never carried the power of war and peace, nor was it invented by the Framers of the Constitution."[48] What the Framers did do, however, was to adopt the title in light of the 150-year-old English tradition of entitling the office at the apex of the military hierarchy as commander in chief and of subordinating the office to a political superior, such as a king or parliament. The office carried no warmaking power whatever. This practice was thoroughly familiar to the Framers, and perhaps this settled understanding and the consequent absence of concerns about the nature of the post accounts for the fact that there was no debate on the commander-in-chief clause at the convention. Hamilton laid bare the dimensions of the office in *Federalist* no. 69: "The President is to be commander-in-chief of the army and navy of the United States. In this respect his authority would be nominally the same with that of the King of Great Britain, but in substance much inferior to it. It would amount to nothing more than the supreme command and direction of the military and naval forces, as first General and Admiral of the Confederacy; while that of the British King extends to the *declaring* of war and to the *raising* and *regulations* of fleets and armies,—all which, by the constitution under consideration, would appertain to the legislature."[49]

In sum, the president as commander in chief was to be "first General and Admiral" in "the direction of war when authorized or begun." But all political authority remained in Congress, as it had under the Articles of Confederation. As Louis Henkin has observed, "Generals and Admirals, even when they are 'first,' do not determine the political purposes for which troops are to be used; they command them in the execution of policy made by others."[50]

THE EXECUTIVE POWER CLAUSE

Article 2, Section 1, of the Constitution provides, "The executive power shall be vested in the President of the United States of America." In recent years various presidents and commentators have sought to squeeze from the executive power clause a presidential authority to make war. In 1966, for example, the State Department cited the president's role as chief executive to adduce constitutional support for Lyndon Johnson's entry into the Vietnam War.[51] Richard Nixon's legal advisers similarly invoked the clause to justify his adventures in southeast Asia.[52] In 1975, President Gerald Ford found constitutional warrant in the "President's Constitutional executive power" for the military activities he ordered in Cambodia.[53] On April 26, 1980, President Jimmy Carter authorized an attempted rescue of American citizens held hostage by Iran. He justified the attempt as being "pursuant to the President's powers under the Constitution as chief executive and as commander-in-chief."[54] Like his predecessors, Bill Clinton has advanced his position as chief executive as a source of unilateral presidential warmaking power. When he deployed troops against Yugoslavia, he justified the order "pursuant to my constitutional authority to conduct U.S. foreign relations and as commander-in-chief and chief executive."[55]

The claim asserted by Johnson, Nixon, Ford, Carter, and now Clinton—that the grant of executive power includes authority to initiate hostilities—was considered and rejected by delegates to the Constitutional Convention; indeed, it caused them much alarm. The Randolph Plan provided for a "national executive," which would have "authority to execute the national laws . . . and enjoy the executive rights vested in Congress by the Confederation." Charles Pinckney said he was "for a vigorous executive but was afraid the executive powers of the existing Congress might extend to peace and war which would render the executive a monarchy, of the worst kind, towit an elective one." John Rutledge shared his concern: "He was for vesting the Executive Power in a single person, tho' he was not for giving him the power of war and peace." James Wilson sought to ease their fears; they "did not consider the Prerogatives of the British Monarch as a proper guide to defining the executive powers. Some of these prerogatives were of a legislative nature. Among others that of war and peace. The only powers he conceived strictly executive were those of executing the laws, and appointing officers not (appertaining to and) appointed by the legislature." He added, "Making peace and war are generally determined by the writers on the Law of Nations to be legislative powers—executive powers ex vi termini, do not include the rights of war and peace."[56]

No delegate to the convention ever suggested or even intimated that the executive power is a fountainhead of power to make war. For the Framers, the phrase "executive power" was limited, as Wilson said, to "executing the laws, and appointing officers." Roger Sherman "considered the Executive magistracy as nothing more than an institution for carrying the will of the Legislature into effect." Madison agreed with Wilson's definition of executive power. He thought it necessary "to fix the extent of executive authority . . . as certain powers were in their nature executive, and must be given to that department" and added that "a definition of their extent would assist the judgment in determining how far they might be safely entrusted to a single officer." The definition of the executive's power should be precise, thought Madison; the executive power "shd. be confined and defined," and so it was.[57] The president's powers were enumerated. There was no challenge to the definition of executive power held by Wilson and Madison, nor was there even an alternative understanding advanced. And there was no argument about the scope of executive power; indeed, any latent fears were quickly arrested by assurances from Madison and Wilson that the power of peace and war was not an executive but a legislative function. Given the Framers' conception of the chief executive as little more than an institution to effectuate the "will of the legislature," that is, to execute the laws and to appoint officers, there was little about the office to fear.

Clearly, the widespread "aversion of the people to monarchy," the "unhappy memories of the royal prerogative; fear of tyranny, and distrust of any one man, kept the framers from giving the President too much head."[58] That the Framers did not vest the president with too much authority is evidenced by the relative calm with which the state ratifying conventions discussed the presidency. No doubt this is attributable to the careful and specific enumeration of the president's full powers. In South Carolina, Charles Pinckney reported that "we have defined his powers and bound him to such limits, as will effectually prevent his usurping authority."[59] Similarly, Chief Justice Thomas McKean told the Pennsylvania Ratifying Convention that executive officers "have no . . . authority . . . beyond what is by positive grant . . . delegated to them." In Virginia, Governor Randolph asked, "What are his powers? To see the laws executed. Every executive in America has that power." That view was echoed by James Iredell in North Carolina and by James Bowdoin in Massachusetts, who said the president's powers were "precisely those of the governors, which were strictly limited."[60]

It is not at all surprising that the founding generation would so sharply limit the power of its executives. In colonial America, the belief was prevalent, writes Edward Corwin, that "the 'executive magistracy' was the natural enemy, the legislative assembly the natural friend of liberty."[61] There was a deep fear of the potential for abuse of power in the hands of both hereditary and elected rulers. The colonial experience had laid bare the source of despotism. "The executive power," wrote a Delaware Whig, "is ever restless, ambitious, and ever grasping at increase of power."[62] Thus James Madison wrote in the *Federalist* no. 48: "The founders of our republics . . . seem never for a moment to have turned their eyes from the overgrown and all-grasping prerogative of an hereditary magistrate."[63]

It was in this context that the Framers designed the office of the presidency. Far from establishing an executive resembling a monarchy, the Framers, in fact, severed all ties to the royal prerogative. Executive powers amounted to little more than the execution of laws and appointment of various officers. There is no intimation whatever in the records of the Constitutional Convention or in any state ratifying conventions that executive power includes the power to make war or even to initiate hostilities.

SOLE ORGAN OF FOREIGN AFFAIRS

When President Clinton ordered U.S. forces to wage war against Yugoslavia, he adduced as justification his "constitutional authority to conduct foreign relations," for it is "beyond peradventure, and a long-established bedrock principle of constitutional law" that the president acts "as the sole organ of the federal government in the field of international relations."[64] Invocation of the sole organ doctrine, the unhappy judicial creation of Justice George Sutherland in his bizarre opinion for the Court in the 1936 case of *United States v. Curtiss-Wright Export Corp.,* has become a commonplace for presidents and commentators who seek executive supremacy in matters of war and foreign affairs.[65]

The *Curtiss-Wright* opinion represents the Court's primary contribution to the growth of executive power over foreign affairs. Its declaration that the president is the "sole organ" of American foreign policy is a powerful, albeit unfortunate, legacy of the case. Even when the sole organ doctrine has not been invoked by name, its spirit, indeed its talismanic aura, has provided a common thread in a pattern of cases that has exalted presidential power above constitutional norms.[66]

The dominance of *Curtiss-Wright* is reflected in the fact that is quite likely the most frequently cited case involving the allocation of foreign affairs powers.[67] It possesses uncommon significance even though it raised merely the narrow question of the constitutionality of a joint resolution that authorized the president to halt the sale of arms to Bolivia and Paraguay, then involved in armed conflict in the Chaco, in order to help stop the fighting. In his opinion for the Court, Justice Sutherland upheld the delegation, but he strayed from the issue and, in some ill-considered dicta, imparted a disturbing legacy—the chimerical idea that authority in foreign affairs was essentially an executive power, which he explained "as the very delicate, plenary, and exclusive power of the President as the sole organ of the federal government in the field of international relations—a power which does not require as a basis for its exercise an act of Congress."[68]

Let us consider the historical context from which Sutherland ripped the sole organ doctrine. In short, the justice greatly expanded on Congressman John Marshall's speech in 1800 in which he noted that "the President is the sole organ of the nation in its external relations . . . of consequence, the demand of a foreign nation can only be made on him."[69] Marshall was defending the decision of President John Adams to surrender to British officials a British deserter, Jonathan Robbins, in accordance with the Jay Treaty. The Robbins affair involved a demand upon the United States, according to Marshall, and it required a response from the president on behalf of the American people. At no point in his speech did Marshall argue that the president's exclusive authority to communicate with foreign nations included a power to formulate or develop policy. Edward S. Corwin has properly concluded, "Clearly, what Marshall had foremost in mind was simply the President's role as an instrument of communication with other governments."[70] By way of affirming that Congressman Marshall had only a communicative role in mind, we may note his consistency on the point, as reflected in his view as Chief Justice Marshall. While on circuit, he held in 1812, in *United States v. Brig Diana,* that although it was for Congress to formulate policy, "the president was the only constitutional channel of diplomatic intercourse with foreign nations; and the only organ of communication to the people of the United States upon this subject."[71] This point of procedure had been acknowledged as uncontroversial in 1793 by then secretary of state Thomas Jefferson, who remarked that since the president is the only channel of communication between this country and foreign nations, it is from him alone that foreign nations or their agents are to learn what is or had been the will of the nation; and whatever he communicates as such, they have a right and are bound to consider it as the expression of the nation, and no foreign agent can be allowed to question it.[72]

This view has not been challenged. Thus it was Sutherland who infused a purely communicative role with a substantive policymaking function and thereby manufactured a great power out of the Marshallian sole organ doctrine. To have done this, as Myres McDougal and Asher Lans have observed, was to confuse the "organ" with the "organ grinder" and effectively to undermine the constitutional design for cooperation and collective decision making in the conduct of foreign relations.[73]

The sole organ doctrine—Clinton's "bedrock principle of constitutional law"—is merely so much fanciful rhetoric. It lacks paternity, and it has no roots in either the Constitutional Convention or the Constitution. In point of fact, the enumeration of foreign affairs powers in the text of the Constitution represents a fundamental repudiation of the doctrine on definitional grounds alone. Finally, let us consider Sutherland's own view on the issue of whether the sole organ doctrine embraces a unilateral presidential warmaking power. In 1919, Senator George Sutherland wrote, "Generally speaking, the war powers of the President under the Constitution are simply those that belong to any commander-in-chief of the military forces of a nation at war. The Constitution confers no war powers upon the President as such."[74]

JUDICIAL DECISIONS

The meaning of the war clause was put beyond doubt by several early judicial decisions. No court since has departed from the view that Congress enjoys the sole and exclusive authority to initiate hostilities on behalf of the United States. In 1800, in *Bas v. Tingy,* the Supreme Court held that it is for Congress alone to authorize an "imperfect" (limited) war or a "perfect" (general) war.[75] In 1801, in *Talbot v. Seeman,* Chief Justice John Marshall, a member of the Virginia Ratifying Convention, stated that the "whole powers of war [are] by the Constitution of the United States, vested in Congress."[76] In *Little v. Barreme,* decided in 1804, Marshall held that President John Adams's instructions to seize ships were in conflict with an act of Congress and were therefore illegal.[77] In 1806, in *United States v. Smith,* the question of whether the president may initiate hostilities was decided by Justice William Paterson, riding circuit, who wrote for himself and district judge Tallmadge: "Does [the president] possess the power of making war? That power is exclusively vested in Congress. . . . It is the exclusive province of Congress to change a state of peace into a state of war."[78] In the *Prize Cases* in 1863, the Court considered for the first time the power of the president to respond to sudden attacks: Justice Robert C. Grier delivered the opinion of the Court: "By the Constitution, Congress alone has the power to declare a natural or foreign war. . . . If a war be made by an invasion of a foreign nation, the president is not only authorized but bound to resist force, by force. He does not initiate the war, but is bound to accept the challenge without waiting for any special legislative authority. And whether the hostile party be a foreign invader, or states organized in rebellion, it is none the less a war, although the declaration of it be 'unilateral.'"[79]

These decisions, some of which are older than *Marbury v. Madison* (1803), the graybeard of all judicial precedents, established at the dawn of the Republic that it is for Congress alone to initiate hostilities, whether in the form of general or limited war; the president, in his capacity as commander in chief, is granted only the power to repel sudden attacks against the United States.[80] This constitutional fact was reaffirmed in 1990, in the closely watched case of *Dellums v. Bush*. In *Dellums,* Federal District Judge Harold H. Greene dismissed as not ripe for review a congressional challenge to President George Bush's claim of unilateral authority to wage war in Kuwait, but in his decision he forcefully rejected many of the sweeping claims made by the executive branch.[81] In words that echo those of John Bassett Moore, Judge Greene stated that if the president "had the sole power to determine that any particular offensive military operation, no matter how vast, does not constitute war-making but only an offensive military attack, the congressional power to make war will be at the mercy of a semantic decision by the Executive. Such an interpretation would evade the plain language of the Constitution, and it cannot stand."[82]

It is thus against the intentions of the Framers, against the debate and vote on the war clause, and against a wealth of judicial precedents that President Clinton and other recent executives have invoked a presidential power to initiate hostilities. The evidence against their case is overwhelming. Their claims ignore the text of the Constitution, and they find no authority in our legal history.

President Clinton's conception of a capacious presidential warmaking power was manifested on several occasions. Among other contentions, he consistently asserted a unilateral power to deploy troops as he wished—even into combat—without authority from Congress. From his perspective, moreover, Congress may not interfere with the president's power and responsibility to act as the "ultimate decision making authority" in matters of war and peace.[83] A brief review of his military actions and legal rationales will enable us to examine his record in light of constitutional principles.

CLINTON'S MISSILE ATTACK ON BAGHDAD

On June 26, 1993, President Clinton ordered the launching of twenty-three Tomahawk cruise missiles against Iraq's intelligence command and control center in Baghdad in retaliation for an assassination attempt against former president George Bush during his trip to Kuwait. While the trial of sixteen suspects, including two Iraqi Nationals, was under way, the CIA determined that there had in fact been a plot to assassinate Bush that was "directed and pursued by the Iraqi intelligence service" and that involved the "use of a powerful bomb" produced in Iraq. Clinton characterized the assassination effort as "an attack against our country and against all Americans."[84] In a message to Congress, Clinton defended the air strike on grounds that it was "in the exercise of our inherent right of self defense as recognized in Article 51 of the UN Charter and pursuant to my constitutional authority with respect to the conduct of foreign relations and as commander-in-chief."[85]

President Clinton did not consult Congress before ordering the attack, which killed eight people and injured a dozen others. He adduced several policy justifications for the attack: it "was essential to protect our sovereignty, to send a message to those who engage in state-sponsored terrorism, to deter further violence against our people, and to affirm the expectation of civilized behavior among nations."[86] The president's power of self-defense, which pivots on an invasion of the United States, does not extend to foreign lands. The Framers did not grant the president the power to intervene in foreign wars, or to choose between war and peace, or to identify and commence hostilities against an enemy of the American people. Nor did they empower him to initiate force abroad on the basis of his own assessments of U.S. security interests. These circumstances involve policy choices and value judgments that belong to Congress under what Hamilton, echoing the view of the convention, characterized as its "exclusive province" to authorize military force. The president's power is purely defensive and strictly limited to attacks against the United States. If, as John Bassett Moore and Judge Harold Green have warned, the president might authorize relatively minor acts of war or perhaps covert military operations in circumstances not demanding full-blown war, that power could be wielded in a way that would eviscerate the congressional war power.

Clinton's legal defense crumbles under the weight of analysis. As we have observed, the commander-in-chief clause affords the president no offensive authority. Hamilton explained in *Federalist* no. 69 that the president is to direct military hostilities *after* they have been "authorized or begun" by Congress. Congress never authorized the air strikes against Iraq; indeed, as we have seen, Congress was not even consulted. Nor can Clinton derive authority for the attack with the invocation of a vague reference to his "constitutional authority" to conduct foreign affairs. As we have observed, the president is not the "sole organ" of American foreign policy, and the limited role assigned to him by the constitutional text grants him no authority to commence hostilities. Nor can he invoke Article 51 of the UN Charter as justification for his military attack against Baghdad. Clinton's actions exceeded the limitations of self-defense under Article 51 of the charter. For purposes of international law, the charter prohibits the use of force unless it is authorized by the Security Council or undertaken by nations in self-defense and in response to "armed attack."[87] As a matter of principle Article 51 permits measures of self-defense that are genuinely defensive. Under international law, the key criterion is a factual finding of the status of the attack. In the event of an attack a nation may defend itself. If, however, the attack has been completed and there is no immediate threat of a renewed attack, the offended nation must seek intervention by the United Nations. In the absence of a threat of a renewed attack, a nation may no longer characterize its military response as defensive. In that case, its response becomes a reprisal.[88] In truth, Clinton's military assault on Baghdad clearly was an act of reprisal—a retaliatory use of military force to inflict injury. The asserted motive, retaliation for an assassination attempt against President Bush, did not satisfy the Article 51 criterion for self-defense. The armed attack had ceased, and there was no immediate threat of a renewed attack. In short, Clinton usurped the power of Congress to order reprisals. If he believed a military response was in order, he should have made the case to Congress because, as Jefferson said in 1793 of the authority necessary to issue a reprisal, "Congress must be called upon to take it; the right of reprisal being expressly lodged with them by the Constitution, and not with the executive."[89]

MILITARY FORCE IN SOMALIA

President Clinton continued the humanitarian relief effort in Somalia, which involved U.S. troops deployed by President Bush after the 1992 election as part of a UN mission to rescue millions from famine. Bush explained that the United States would play a limited role in the mission: "To open the supply routes, to get the food moving, and to prepare the way for a U.N. peacekeeping force to keep it moving. This operation is not open-ended. We will not stay one day longer than is absolutely necessary."[90] Congress had not authorized the intervention of U.S. troops, but Bush assured congressional leaders that he had no intention of allowing U.S. forces to become "involved in hostilities."[91]

The landscape and the nature and scope of the mission changed suddenly in June 1993 when twenty-three Pakistani peacekeepers were killed. UN officials believed that the warlord, Mohamed Farad Aideed, was behind the deaths. Clinton ordered a retaliatory air strike against a radio station and four weapons-storage sites. Clinton defended the use of force on policy grounds, including the need to undermine Aideed's capacity to inflict "military havoc in Mogadishu" and to punish him for "the deaths of countless Somalis from starvation, from disease, and from killing."[92] But Clinton offered no legal justification for his retaliatory attack. His usurpation of the war power could not have been defended on any grounds. His action, strictly speaking, did not constitute a reprisal for the technical reason that Aideed had not attacked any American soldiers or interests. Clinton, quite simply, committed an act of war against a foreign nation, for which he had no legal or constitutional authority.

CLINTON AND HAITI

In October 1993, President Clinton dispatched some 600 troops to Haiti as part of a plan to restore to power the democratically elected president, Jean-Bertrand Aristide. The soldiers, principally military engineers, were part of a UN effort to force Haiti's military regime to resign by October 15. When the troops arrived, however, an armed group of Haitians prevented them from landing. At that juncture, President Clinton implied that he might resort to the use of military force. On October 15 he set the stage for American intervention: "First, there are about 1,000 American citizens living in Haiti or working there. Second, there are Americans there who are helping to operate our Embassy. Third, we have an interest in promoting democracy in this hemisphere."[93]

On July 31, the UN Security Council adopted a resolution "inviting" all states to use "all necessary means" to oust the military regime of Haiti.[94] Within a few days, the Senate, perhaps mindful of George Bush's reliance on a Security Council resolution as authority for Desert Storm in 1991, at the expense of Congress,[95] adopted by a vote of one hundred to zero an amendment that the Security Council resolution "does not constitute authorization for the deployment of United States Armed Forces in Haiti under the Constitution of the United States or pursuant to the Powers Resolution."[96] At a news conference on August 3, Clinton declared that he did not need support or authority from Congress to invade Haiti: "Like my predecessors of both parties, I have not agreed that I was constitutionally mandated to get it."[97] On September 15, during a televised address, he stated that he was prepared to use military force "to carry out the will of the United Nations." He emphasized, moreover, the importance of honoring our commitments: "I'd like to mention just one other thing that is equally important, and that is the reliability of the United States and the United Nations once we say we're going to do something."[98]

President Clinton never ordered an invasion of Haiti, although about 20,000 troops were sent to occupy the island. Instead, he appointed former president Jimmy Carter to negotiate with the Haitian military, and leaders agreed to abandon their reign in favor of Aristide. Both houses of Congress were critical of Clinton's indifference toward the legislative body and its jurisdiction over the war power. Both chambers passed legislation that provided that "the President should have sought and welcomed congressional approval before deploying United States forces to Haiti."[99] Even legislators who voted against the legislation, including Senator Bill Bradley (D-N.J.), agreed that Clinton should have first obtained approval from Congress.[100]

Let us assess Clinton's legal justification for his threat to invade Haiti. His claim that as president, he is not "constitutionally mandated" to seek prior authorization from Congress is untenable. The entire legislative history of the Constitutional Convention makes it pellucidly clear that the Framers were opposed to a unilateral executive warmaking power and placed the war power solely and exclusively in Congress. The Supreme Court reaffirmed that history in several important decisions nearly 200 years ago, and these decisions have not been overturned. Until 1950, no president ever asserted a unilateral constitutional power to take the nation to war. It is irrelevant, from a constitutional perspective, that Harry Truman laid claim to that power and that several of his successors or, in other words, Clinton's "predecessors," have adduced either the claimed constitutional authority or the recent practice of executive war making as precedent. These arguments are irrelevant, as Chief Justice Earl Warren held for the Supreme Court: "That an unconstitutional action has been taken before surely does not render that action any less unconstitutional at a later date."[101] Or, as Justice Felix Frankfurter explained it, in more pungent terms, "Illegality cannot attain legitimacy through practice."[102] In sum, it cannot be maintained that constitutional power, in this case, the war power, can be acquired through practice. The Court has rightly and repeatedly denied claims that the president can acquire power through a series of usurpations. If it were otherwise, the president might aggrandize all governmental power. Neither Congress nor the judiciary could lawfully restrain the exercise of the president's accumulated constitutional powers.[103] Clearly, this practice would scuttle our entire constitutional jurisprudence. Thus, the most recent act of usurpation stands no better than the first.

The policy arguments that Clinton cited as a rationale for invasion may have bolstered his political efforts, and they may have been relatively wise, but they would not have furnished a legal foundation for his intervention. Congress may initiate war for any reason, including the promotion of democracy in Haiti, but the president has no such constitutional authority. The protection of Americans abroad, moreover, is retained by Congress as well, so far as it pertains to the use of military force. In the Hostage Act of 1868, which is still good law, Congress provided that the president, in his efforts to protect citizens in foreign lands, may use all measures, short of hostilities.[104] The question of whether military force ought to be used to protect or rescue Americans abroad falls within the constitutional province of Congress.

We shall defer for a moment Clinton's invocation of a Security Council resolution as authorization for an invasion of Haiti, but let us consider his very peculiar argument about the War Powers Resolution.[105] Ever since President Richard Nixon vetoed the resolution in 1973, executive officials have objected that it was too restrictive and that it encroached on the president's authority as commander in chief.[106] But the Clinton theory of the resolution, developed by Assistant Attorney General (and now Professor) Walter Dellinger, claimed that the statute "recognizes and presupposes the existence of unilateral presidential authority to deploy armed forces [quoting from the statute] 'into hostilities or into situations where imminent involvement in hostilities is clearly indicated by the circumstances.'"[107] Dellinger carefully refers to the resolution as an *acknowledgment,* not a *source,* of executive power, because what Congress grants it may take away.

For Dellinger, the structure of the resolution "makes sense only if the President may introduce troops into hostilities or potential hostilities without prior authorization by the Congress."[108] By declining to prohibit the president from deploying troops into situations like that in Haiti, Dellinger stated that Congress "has left the President both the authority and the means to take such initiatives."

Later, at a law school conference, he elaborated on that point: "By establishing and funding a military force capable of being sent around the globe, and declining in the War Powers Resolution or elsewhere to forbid the President's use of his statutory and constitutional powers to deploy troops into situations of risk such as Haiti, Congress left the President both the authority and the means to take such initiatives."[109]

Read in that light, the War Powers Resolution grants to the president an unlimited, discretionary authority to choose war and peace. As such, it does great violence to the law of delegation. The statute does not attempt, for example, to delegate the war power for specified contingencies, nor does it provide a governing policy or standard. The president is vested with the authority to choose an enemy and to decide when to make war. The law of delegation stands for the proposition that Congress is the principal and the president is the agent. The War Powers Resolution makes the president the principal.[110]

CLINTON IN BOSNIA

In the context of U.S. participation in a "no-fly zone" over Bosnia-Herzegovina, under the auspices of United Nations and NATO leadership, President Clinton threatened to order air strikes, but he vacillated on the question of whether he required "support" or "authorization" from Congress. At a press conference on May 7, 1993, Clinton explained, "If I decide to ask the American people and the United States Congress to *support* an approach that would include the use of airpower, I would have a very specific, clearly defined strategy."[111] Minutes later, he stood on different ground: "I assure you today that if I decide to ask for the *authority* to use airpower from the Congress and the American people. . . ."[112] On September 8, he said he would endorse U.S. participation in a NATO–led effort in Bosnia, but said, "Of course in the United States, as all of you know, anything we do has to have the support of the Congress. I would seek the support of the Congress to do that. . . . If we can get the Congress to support it, then I think we should participate. . . . [Military action in Bosnia] has to be able to be enforced or, if you will, be guaranteed by a peacekeeping force from NATO, not the United Nations but NATO and of course, for me to do it, the Congress would have to agree."[113] On October 20, he sent a letter to congressional leadership in which he noted that he "would welcome and encourage congressional authorization of any military involvement in Bosnia."[114]

At the same time, Clinton objected to congressional efforts to limit his military options. He opposed any amendment "that affects the way our military people do their business, working with NATO and other military allies," or any measure that "unduly restricted the ability of the President to make foreign policy."[115] Further, he opposed any effort to "tie the President's hands" and render "us unable to fulfill our NATO commitments."[116] Thus the president, not Congress, has the authority to make military commitments to NATO. Further, Clinton indicated that he might veto legislation that required him to seek authorization from Congress before using troops in Haiti and Bosnia. Apparently, Congress could advise, but the president must decide whether or not to use military force: "All I can tell you is I think I have a big responsibility to try to appropriately consult with members of Congress in both parties . . . whenever we are in the process of making a decision that might lead to the use of force. I believe that. But I think that, clearly, the Constitution leaves the President, for good and sufficient reasons, the ultimate decisionmaking authority. . . . The President must make the ultimate decision, and I think it's a mistake to cut those decisions off in advance."[117]

At bottom, Clinton remained "fundamentally opposed" to legislative efforts that "improperly limit my ability to perform my constitutional duties as Commander-in-Chief." Such efforts would "insert Congress into the detailed execution of military contingency planning in an unprecedented manner. The amendment would make it unreasonably difficult for me or any President to operate militarily with other nations when it is in our interest to do so—and as we have done effectively for half a century through NATO."[118] But as Louis Fisher has observed, "for that half-century, NATO had never used military force."[119]

NATO air strikes were commenced in February 1994, and they were followed by further attacks in April and November and by additional strikes in August and September 1995. Throughout this long period of heavy, although periodic, bombings, President Clinton never sought authorization from Congress. Rather, he invoked the commander-in-chief clause and sought to bolster it with "authorization" from "U.N. Security Council resolutions and NATO decisions."[120] Those resolutions and decisions by international organizations, coupled with his claims of broad constitutional foreign affairs authority, were adduced as justification for his decision to deploy 20,000 American grounds troops in Bosnia, without authorization or support from Congress.

The consequences of Clinton's theory for American constitutionalism are profound. NATO allies such as England and France replace Congress, as do Security Council "allies" such as Russia and China, in matters of war and peace. On this reasoning, the president may draw authorization from Russia for the purpose of sending U.S. military forces to Haiti while ignoring Congress. There is no logic to the theory that extraconstitutional bodies may direct or replace creatures of the Constitution,[121] but for the sake of completeness, let us consider the procedures that govern the U.S. decision to supply troops to the UN and NATO. As we shall see, there is nothing in the history of those organizations to indicate that Congress transferred the war power to the president.

Article 43 of the UN Charter invites members to make available to the Security Council "on its call and in accordance with a special agreement or agreements" military forces and other assistance for the purpose of maintaining international security and peace. The agreements, concluded between the Security

Council and member states, "shall be subject to ratification by the signatory states in accordance with their respective constitutional processes."[122] With the procedures and mechanisms for deploying troops among the many and varied governmental systems represented in the UN, member states were left to determine for themselves the meaning of "constitutional processes." The U.S. Congress resolved that issue with the passage of the UN Participation Act of 1945. Under Section 6 of that act, the U.S. agreements with the Security Council to supply military forces "shall be subject to the approval of the Congress by appropriate Act or joint resolution."[123] As a consequence, the agreements would not be produced by unilateral presidential action but by action by both the House and Senate, a procedure in accord with our "constitutional processes" for going to war. The legislative history of the UN Participation Act clearly reflects congressional understanding that the executive could not contribute troops without legislative authorization.[124] Thus Clinton's claim of a presidential power to carry out Security Council resolutions without authorization from Congress are hollow and derive no support from the Constitution, the UN Charter, or the UN Participation Act of 1945.[125]

President Clinton's invocation of the NATO treaty as authorization of military action in Bosnia fares no better. The question of defining "constitutional processes" for the use of force reappears in the 1949 NATO treaty, which provides that an armed attack against a member state in Europe or North America "shall be considered an attack against them all."[126] Moreover, in the event of an attack, member states, in accordance with Article 51 of the UN Charter, may assist the nation under siege by resort to "such action as it deems necessary, including the use of armed force."[127] Article 2 of the treaty provides that it shall be ratified "and its provisions carried out by the Parties in accordance with their respective constitutional processes."[128] Since our constitutional process vests in Congress the decision to commence hostilities, it follows that the president may not choose to send troops to aid a fellow NATO member. Congress must make that choice, after it has reviewed all of the circumstances surrounding the attack and weighed all of its options. Our nation has recognized, moreover, for more than two centuries, that mutual defense and mutual security treaties do not automatically require a response. In 1793, Alexander Hamilton denied that the 1778 Mutual Defense Treaty with France could commit us to war on behalf of France as the new republic rampaged throughout Europe.[129] Further, the legislative history of congressional debates on NATO make it clear that the United States would not automatically be drawn into war if a NATO state were attacked. During hearings in 1949, Secretary of State Dean Acheson told the Senate Foreign Relations Committee that membership in NATO "does not mean that the United States would automatically be at war if one of the other signatory nations were the victim of an armed attack. Under our Constitution, the Congress alone has the power to declare war."[130]

AFGHANISTAN AND SUDAN

On August 20, 1998, President Clinton ordered missile strikes at sites in Afghanistan and Sudan. The missile strikes destroyed a pharmaceutical plant located in Sudan's capital of Khartoum. The United States also fired missiles at training facilities in Afghanistan that were thought to be under the control of Osama bin Laden, whom the Clinton administration characterized as the "terrorist mastermind" behind the recent bombings of the American embassies in Nairobi, Kenya, and Dar es Salaam, Tanzania. Clinton explained that he had selected these targets "because of the imminent threat they presented to our national security."[131] Clinton tried, but never adequately explained, why the pharmaceutical plant in Sudan constituted an "imminent threat." He contended that the factory was "involved in the production of materials for chemical weapons," but questions remained as to whether the plant was producing a precursor chemical for a nerve gas or an agricultural insecticide.[132] Insufficient information forced the Pentagon to concede that it was unaware of the fact that the factory produced "a large share of the medicine used in the Sudan."[133] The United States informed the UN Security Council that the missile strikes were legally justified as a measure exacted in self-defense, under Article 51 of the UN Charter. President Clinton explained that the United States had obtained "convincing evidence" that bin Laden was behind the embassy bombings and that he planned to attack other American targets in the immediate future. Further, the Clinton administration claimed that the Sudanese factory "was producing chemical warfare-related weapons" and that it, too, was part of bin Laden's terrorist network.

Clinton offered no constitutional justification for his unilateral acts of war making. Though he advanced the rationale of self-defense under Article 51 of the UN Charter, a claim that has been met with scholarly criticism, the most promising rationale available to the United States was that of an act of reprisal.[134] That justification would hinge on fact-finding, but in any case, it would have to be ordered by Congress, which, under the Constitution, is vested with the executive authority to issue reprisals. Clinton did not seek such authorization; indeed, he did not even consult with Congress on the matter. His action was arbitrary and preemptive.

BOMBING IRAQ—AGAIN

In February 1998, President Clinton was prepared to order heavy air strikes against Iraq to force Saddam Hussein to permit UN inspectors to search sites for weapons of mass destruction. The bombing was postponed when UN Security General Kofi Annan visited Baghdad and negotiated a settlement with Iraq. The

Clinton administration accepted the settlement, with reservations, but made clear that military force remained an option if Iraq failed to comply with the new agreement.[135]

The administration never saw fit to offer a legal defense of its contemplated action. Perhaps it came close to supplying a rationale on February 19, 1998, when Secretary of State Madeleine Albright, while on a visit to Tennessee State University, was asked how Clinton could order military action against Iraq after opposing American policy in Vietnam. Albright responded, "We are talking about using military force, but we are not talking about a war. This is an important distinction."[136] As a matter of constitutional law, this is a distinction without a difference. The Constitution vests in Congress the sole and exclusive authority to initiate all military hostilities, regardless of their scope or magnitude. Semantic efforts like Albright's would eviscerate the war clause.

Predictably, perhaps, President Clinton's February 1998 agreement with Saddam Hussein collapsed. As a consequence, nine months later, in December, Clinton ordered four days of bombing in Iraq. He defended the assault as an effort to "attack Iraq's nuclear, chemical and biological weapons programs"; moreover, Iraq had failed to cooperate with UN weapons inspectors.[137] Clinton also observed that the credibility of the United States was on the line. He explained the necessity of carrying out threats to use military force if Hussein did not cooperate with UN inspectors: "If Saddam can cripple the weapons inspection system and get away with it, he would conclude that the international community—led by the United States—has simply lost its will. . . . If we turn our backs on his defiance, the credibility of U.S. power as a check against Saddam will be destroyed."[138] As a foreign policy, these may be laudable goals. But because they involve the use of force, they must be authorized by Congress.

WAR IN YUGOSLAVIA

On March 24, 1999, President Clinton announced that U.S. armed forces in concert with eighteen NATO allies had begun air strikes against Serbian military targets in the Federal Republic of Yugoslavia.[139] Clinton stated that he had ordered U.S. military forces into action "pursuant to my constitutional authority to conduct U.S. foreign relations and as Commander-in-Chief and Chief Executive."[140] The avowed purpose of the intervention was to allay the repression and dislocation of hundreds of thousands of ethnic Albanians and to deter a wider war.

The U.S. role in the massive deployment of airpower constituted the most intensive and sustained military campaign since the Vietnam War. General Joseph Ralston, vice chairman of the Joint Chiefs of Staff, characterized the military operation as "a major war theatre, as far as the air war is concerned."[141] Indeed, as of May 6, 1999, 800 U.S. airplanes had been committed to the war. As of May 14, there had been a total of 20,772 air sorties, of which 7,135 were strike sorties, and over 9,000 munitions had been launched at over 1,900 targets. U.S. forces bombed bridges, power lines, industrial facilities, oil refineries, and other targets throughout Yugoslavia.[142]

The destructive capacity of the war effort was overwhelming, but Congress provided no authorization. It is true that Congress considered several pieces of legislation relevant to the war. On April 28, 1999, the House of Representatives by a vote of 2 to 427 defeated a joint resolution declaring a state of war between the United States and the Federal Republic of Yugoslavia.[143] The House also defeated by a vote of 139 to 290 a concurrent resolution that would have directed the president to remove U.S. forces from Yugoslavia under section 5(c) of the War Powers Act.[144] The House passed a bill that prohibited the use of Department of Defense funds for deployment of U.S. ground troops in Yugoslavia without specific congressional authorization.[145] But the single most important measure from a constitutional law standpoint considered by the House was legislation that would have authorized the president to conduct military air operations and missile strikes against Yugoslavia. The Senate had passed the measure on March 23, but on April 28, the House, by a tie vote of 213 to 213, rejected the concurrent resolution.[146] That was the vital issue before Congress, since the war clause requires authorization by both chambers. By its refusal to pass the measure, the House, as a consequence, denied President Clinton the constitutional authority he needed to wage war. But he defied the House and waged war anyway. It is true that the various votes by the House cast mixed signals and left its observers unclear as to its ultimate disposition on the war in Yugoslavia. But it is also true that the constitutional mechanism for authorizing military hostilities—an affirmative vote by both houses—was not forthcoming. Clinton's defiance of the House vote raised arbitrary executive power to a new and dangerous pitch. It is one thing, and quite a contemptible thing at that, for either chamber to indulge presidential usurpation of the war power while doing nothing to preserve its constitutional powers. But it is, indeed, dismaying for a president to make war in the face of a congressional refusal to authorize the war. When that occurs, usurpation gives way to evisceration.

Clinton's legal justifications were unavailing. Neither the commander-in-chief clause nor the executive power clause, as we have seen, affords him any authority to engage the nation in hostilities. Equally unpersuasive is Clinton's reference to his constitutional authority to conduct foreign policy. His role, which pales in comparison to that assigned to Congress, includes no warmaking power whatever.

Clinton's military actions triggered a lawsuit, *Campbell v. Clinton*, in which twenty-six plaintiffs, members of the House, sought a judicial determination that the war was unconstitutional. The federal district court dismissed the case on grounds that the legislators lacked standing to bring the suit. The district court's ruling was affirmed by the D.C. Circuit, and the U.S. Supreme Court refused to grant a writ of certiorari.[147] But the lawsuit forced Clinton's legal advisers to supply the administration's most detailed explanation to date of its view of the war clause of the Constitution. The argument was frivolous. Clinton's counsel told the Court, "Certainly there is no single commitment of the war-making power to Congress. The Constitution in three words grants Congress the power to 'declare war.' The Constitution does not elaborate on when such declarations are required, on the branch or branches of government which makes those determinations, or on appropriate actions which may be taken in absence of a declaration of war. Indeed, there have been only five such declarations of war in U.S. history, and none since World War II."[148]

This riot of language and the conclusions to which it gives flight find no foundations in the architecture of the Constitution. Clinton's attempt to obscure the meaning of the war clause is sheer casuistry. The Madison-Gerry motion at the convention gave Congress the power to declare, that is, commence, military hostilities, "leaving to the Executive the power to repel sudden attacks." This meaning, the quintessence of the war clause, was immediately captured by Roger Sherman, who agreed that the executive "should be able to repel and not to commence war," an uncontested principle echoed by James Wilson and others in the state ratifying conventions.[149] As a logical matter, the exception for a presidential power "to repel sudden attacks" would not have been necessary if the president had been given the authority to make war. Indeed, after the Madison-Gerry motion had been introduced, there was no other motion presented to give the president the power to make war. Such a motion would have been an irreducible prerequisite. Madison and Gerry envisioned an attack on the United States. When they attributed to the president the authority to repel such a sudden attack, they did not impute to him a discretionary power to choose between war and peace or the power to make a judgment concerning the security of the United States. Their motion was not intended to recognize any powers in the president to institute hostilities, let alone a state of war; it recognized that foreign countries are able to institute a state of war. The Constitution makes an exclusive commitment of the nation's war power to the Congress. The war power of Congress, drawn from the war clause and the marque and reprisal clause, is omnicompetent; it covers every species of international military hostilities except for sudden attacks on the United States. The Constitution recognizes that the power to initiate war is lodged in two places: in Congress and in a foreign enemy. It recognizes no such power in the president. Thus there is no parallel clause in the Constitution that says of the president, "He shall have the power to make war."

If the Framers had desired to construct such a clause, they certainly had the tools and equipment to do it. If they had, however, one would expect to find some discussion of it in the convention, or at least some passing reference to such a power. There was none. There is not a scintilla of evidence to suggest or even to intimate that the Framers embraced the concept of a unilateral presidential war making power.

Clinton's attempt to extract a presidential war power from historical practice is equally unpersuasive. His attorneys represented to the court that there have been only "five" declarations of war in our history, and none since World War II. The assertion is demonstrably false. Congress issued six declarations of war alone in World War II.[150] And it has passed perhaps dozens of resolutions declaring general war, conditional war, contingent war, and limited war, in addition to all of the acts "authorizing" but not "declaring" war, including the 1991 Gulf War.[151] The false numerical assertion obscures the fundamental point that military hostilities must be authorized but not necessarily declared by Congress.

In a footnote to the administration's brief, it was asserted, "U.S. Armed Forces have acted without a declaration of war in scores of instances from the presidency of George Washington to the present."[152] The assertion was more strategy than history, more tactical than historical. The aim, quite clearly, was to demean the need for congressional authorization of hostilities. This shopworn argument, another effort at obfuscation, rests on the premise that the president has frequently exercised the war power without congressional authorization. The actual number of these episodes varies among the several compilations, but defenders usually list between 100 and 200 unilateral acts, each of which is supposed to constitute a legitimizing precedent for future executive wars. As we have seen, however, the Court has repeatedly denied claims that the president can acquire power through a series of usurpations.[153]

In detail and in conception the argument is flawed. Francis D. Wormuth has thoroughly deflated their claims with a "painstaking analysis."[154] Though space does not permit a critical analysis of each alleged assertion of executive precedents, there is no evidence whatever that Washington engaged in unilateral war making, and the Clinton administration has not supplied any. Consider, moreover, an error common to the lists: the claim that unilateral war making was initiated by the "undeclared" war with France in 1798. The claim, as Professor Wormuth justly observes, "is altogether false. Congress passed a series of acts that amounted, so the Supreme Court said, to a declaration of imperfect war; and Adams complied with those statutes."[155] As Dean Alfange Jr. has observed in a detailed study of the Quasi-War, Adams's action "certainly provides no precedent for a claim of presidential prerogative to commit the United States to war without congressional authorization. Adams made absolutely no claim of a general presidential power to initiate hostilities."[156] Moreover, many of the episodes involved initiation of hostilities by a military commander, not by authorization from the president. If practice establishes law, then the inescapable conclusion is that every commander of every military unit has the power to initiate war. What is perhaps most revealing about presidential understanding of the constitutional locus of the war power is that in the one or two dozen instances in which presidents have personally made the decision unconstitutionally to initiate acts of war, they have not purported to rely on their authority as commander in chief or chief executive. In "all of these cases the Presidents have made false claims of authorization, either by statute or by treaty or by international law."[157]

CONCLUSION

For the first century and a half of our history, the practice of war making largely adhered to the scheme of the Constitution, which placed in Congress the sole and exclusive authority to initiate all military hostilities on behalf of the American people. On those few occasions where presidents initiated the use of force, they invoked statutes or treaties to color their actions and assertions, ever mindful of the need in a republic to steer clear of pretensions to arbitrary power. But with the immense accretion of presidential power in the post–cold war era, congressional fires have been damped and the congressional control of the war power has been eclipsed. Suddenly, rapacious, aggressive, and impatient presidents have turned to unilateral war making, leaving constitutional norms in their wake. The tides of power, which once flowed steadily from congressional control, now run toward the executive.

The absolutist pretensions of Bill Clinton, which harken to the swollen claims of the Stuart kings, virtually eviscerated the war clause. He asserted the executive power to commence war at his pleasure and to determine its course and direction, its intensity and duration. The Framers produced a Constitution that granted these prerogatives to Congress. "Those who are to conduct a war," said Madison, "cannot in the nature of things, be proper or safe judges, whether a war ought to be commenced, continued or concluded."[158]

As things stand today, however, power has replaced law, usurpation has replaced amendment, and executive fiat has replaced constitutionalism. The English knew something about this chain of events, and they plunged their nation into a civil war, at least partly in pursuit of a vision that would rescue law from power. The leaders of the American Revolution knew something of these circumstances as well, and they vigilantly pursued the idea of subordinating the executive to the rule of law. And the Framers, standing on the shoulders of tall thinkers, effectuated the idea and implemented it in a written constitution. It surely was one of their great, if not lasting, achievements, for the very marrow of constitutionalism consists of the subordination of the executive to the rule of law.

Since the object of the war clause had been to break the back of the absolutist aspirations of the executive and thus to ensure that the collective judgment of Congress would be brought to bear in the use of military force, surely a life-sized remedy was available for presidential usurpation of the war power. Of course. In a presidency engulfed by impeachment, it is well to recall that few violations of the Constitution more richly deserved the punishment of impeachment than executive usurpation of the war power. The Framers' fear of unilateral presidential war making, the deep-seated concern that one person might plunge the nation into a rush of chaos, misery, and disaster, drove them to vest the war-making authority in Congress, and they did so in clear and unmistakable terms. Presidential aggrandizement of that power—an act subverting the Constitution—is precisely the sort of abuse of power, trust, and office that epitomized what

George Mason characterized as the "great and dangerous offenses" that would invite impeachment.[159]

But a Congress unwilling to exercise its constitutional authority in making decisions on war and peace could hardly be expected to impeach a president for exercising the authority that it has abdicated. It is supremely ironic that Congress, ignoring what could constitute genuine grounds for impeachment, instead chose to impeach Bill Clinton for lying about a sexual encounter. But there is yet hope that a future election might produce a president who admires and values the fibers of the war clause, for we have had others. Even Abraham Lincoln, caught in the clutches of America's gravest crisis, never claimed a unilateral warmaking power. Representing the Lincoln administration before the Supreme Court in the *Prize Cases* (1863), Richard Henry Dana Jr. told the Court that what Lincoln had done in response to the Civil War had nothing to do with "the right to initiate a war, as a voluntary act of sovereignty. That is vested only in Congress."[160]

NOTES

1. The war clause, Article 1, section 8, paragraph 2, provides, "The Congress shall have power . . . to declare war [and] grant Letters of Marque and Reprisal." A considerable body of literature has addressed the intense and acerbic debate on the question of whether Congress or the president is constitutionally empowered to commence war. See the landmark article by Francis D. Wormuth, "The Nixon Theory of the War Power: A Critique," *California Law Review* 60 (May 1972): 623. See also his earlier monograph, *The Vietnam War: The President versus the Constitution* (Santa Barbara, Calif: Center for Study of Democratic Institutions, 1968), reprinted in *The Vietnam War and International Law,* ed. Richard Falk, 4 vols. (Princeton: Princeton University Press, 1969), 2:711, and his collaborative effort with Edwin Firmage, *To Chain the Dog of War: The War Power of Congress in History and Law* (Dallas: Southern Methodist University Press, 1986). See also Raoul Berger, "War-Making by the President," *Pennsylvania Law Review* 121 (November 1972): 29; Charles Lofgren, "War-Making Under the Constitution: The Original Understanding," *Yale Law Journal* 81 (March 1972): 672; and Arthur Bestor, "Separation of Powers in the Domain of Foreign Affairs: The Intent of the Constitution Historically Examined," *Seton Hall Law Review* 5 (spring 1974): 527.

Several new and excellent works have recently appeared. See Louis Fisher, *Presidential War Power* (Lawrence: University Press of Kansas, 1995); John Hart Ely, *War and Responsibility* (Princeton: Princeton University Press, 1993); Michael Glennon, *Constitutional Diplomacy* (Princeton: Princeton University Press, 1990); Harold Hongju Koh, *The National Security Constitution: Sharing Power After the Iran-Contra Affair* (New Haven: Yale University Press, 1990); Edward Keynes, *Undeclared War: Twilight Zone of Constitutional Power* (University Park: Pennsylvania State University Press, 1982). See also David Gray Adler, "The Constitution and Presidential Warmaking: The Enduring Debate," *Political Science Quarterly* 103 (spring 1988): 1; Adler and Larry N. George, eds., *The Constitution and the Conduct of American Foreign Policy* (Lawrence: University Press of Kansas, 1996); Louis Fisher and David Gray Adler, "The War Powers Resolution: Time to Say Goodbye," *Political Science Quarterly* 113 (spring 1998): 1. This represents a longer and more detailed version of my article, "The Clinton Theory of the War Power," *Presidential Studies Quarterly* 30 (March 2000): 155, and it reflects further thoughts and considerations found in my essay, "Virtues of the War Clause," *Presidential Studies Quarterly* 30 (December 2000): 777, written in response to a critique of my views by David Mervin, "Demise of the War Clause," *Presidential Studies Quarterly* 30 (December 2000): 770.

2. Unilateral acts of presidential war making, from Truman in Korea, to Reagan in Grenada, to Bush in Panama, to Clinton in Iraq and Bosnia, among others, have faced little or no formal opposition from Congress. See, generally, Fisher, *Presidential War Power,* pp. 92–161; Adler and George, eds., *The Constitution,* pp. 57–132, 158–182; Fisher and Adler, "War Powers," pp. 1–6, 10–18.

3. The phrase, often used in the literature, is borrowed from Wormuth, "Presidential Wars: The Convenience of 'Precedent,'" *Nation,* October 9, 1972, p. 301.

4. Writing in 1793 in opposition to a novel construction of presidential power that, to him, seemed foreign to the Framers' conception of the office, James Madison warned that a "people [who enjoy] the blessing of a free and defined constitution, cannot be too watchful against the introduction, nor too critical in tracing the consequences, of new principles and new constructions, that may remove the landmarks of power" (quoted in Richard Loss, ed., *The Letters of Pacificus and Helvidius* [Delmar, N.Y.: Scholars' Facsimiles and Reprints, 1976], p. 87).

5. Fortunately, the Supreme Court rejected the unfettered claims of Truman and Nixon in *Youngstown Sheet and Tube Co. v. Sawyer,* 343 v.s. 579 (1952), and in *United States v. Nixon,* 418 U.S. 683 (1974).

6. Attorneys representing Congressman Tom Campbell and twenty-six other plaintiffs in *Campbell v. Clinton* justly argued that if "congressional consent for the current offensive military action against Yugoslavia is not required, the War Powers Clause is a dead letter, so soon after the *Dellums* Court refused to 'read [it] out of the Constitution'" (*Campbell v. Clinton,* 52 F. Supp. 2d. 34 [D.D.C. 1999], plaintiffs' Memorandum in Opposition to Defendant's Motion to Dismiss, p. 19). In *Dellums v. Bush,* Judge Harold H. Greene warned that if the president "had the sole power to determine that any particular offensive military operation, no matter how vast, does not constitute war-making but only an offensive military attack, the congressional power to declare war will be at the mercy of a semantic decision by the Executive. Such an 'interpretation' would evade the plain language of the Constitution, and it cannot stand" (752 F. Supp. 1141, 1145 [D.D.C. 1990]). He added that he was "not prepared to read out of the Constitution the clause granting to the Congress, and to it alone, the authority 'to declare war'" (ibid.). The suit was dismissed by the district court for lack of standing, a ruling that was affirmed on appeal (203 F. 3d 19 [D.C. Cir. 2000]).

7. Clinton's attorneys made this argument in their Memorandum of Points and Authorities in Support of Defendant's Motion to Dismiss (p. 34 in *Campbell v. Clinton,* 52 F. Supp. 2d. 34 [D.D.C. 1999]).

8. In a speech in Omaha on June 30, 1966, President Johnson stated, "The American people have chosen only one man to decide." Walter Lippmann objected that this was "a claim to arbitrary power," which violates "the prevailing principle in the whole constitutional system" (*Newsweek,* July 18, 1966, p. 17, quoted in Wormuth, "Vietnam," p. 1).

Arthur Schlesinger Jr. cut to the quick in his analysis of Nixon's theory of a presidential war power. Nixon, he wrote, "had effectively liquidated the constitutional command that the power to authorize war belonged to Congress" (*The Imperial Presidency* [Boston: Houghton Mifflin, 1973], p. 198). Clinton's arguments have been no less strident, but his actions in Kosovo brought to a new pitch the executive claim to a unilateral warmaking power.

9. See, generally, Adler, "Court, Constitution, and Foreign Affairs," in Adler and George, eds., *The Constitution*, pp. 19–56.

10. John Locke, *Two Treatises of Government*, ed. Peter Laslett (Cambridge: Cambridge University Press, 1960), *Second Treatise*, sec. 146–148.

11. Sir William Blackstone, *Commentaries on the Laws of England*, 4 vols. (Oxford: Oxford University Press, 1765–1769) 2: 238–250.

12. Arthur Schlesinger Jr., *The Imperial Presidency*, p. 2.

13. Madison to Jefferson, May 13, 1798, quoted in Leonard D. White, *The Federalists* (New York: Macmillan, 1948), p. 65.

14. Hamilton, *Federalist* no. 75, in Alexander Hamilton, James Madison, and John Jay, *The Federalist*, ed. Edward M. Earle (New York: Modern Library, 1937), p. 487. In the First Congress, Roger Sherman, who had been a delegate in Philadelphia, argued in defense of the shared-powers arrangement in foreign affairs and stated, "The more wisdom there is employed, the greater security there is that the public business will be well done" (*Annals of Congress* 1 [1789] 1085).

15. Jonathan Elliot, ed., *The Debates in the Several State Conventions on the Adoption of the Federal Constitution*, 2d ed., 5 vols. [1861; reprint, New York: Burt Franklin, 1974), 2: 507.

16. Collective decision making would ensure consideration of the various interests and values of the different regions of the nation, interests and values that could be in conflict, not only in matters of war, as reflected in the War of 1812, but also in such other areas as treaty making. Sectional interests and regional rivalries boiled over in the context of the proposed Jay-Gardoqui Treaty of 1786, which was advantageous to northern merchants at the expense of southern exporters. See Adler, "The Framers and Treaty Termination: A Matter of Symmetry," *Arizona State Law Journal* (1981): 891–893. The Framers, in fact, were preoccupied with the effect that war and treaties might have on economic and sectional interests; see Bestor, "Separation of Power," pp. 613–619.

17. In 1848, the House adopted a resolution that the Mexican-American War had been "unconstitutionally begun by the President [Polk]." As a member of the House of Representatives, Abraham Lincoln voted for the resolution and explained his reasoning in a famous letter to his law partner, William Herndon: "The provision of the Constitution giving the war-making power to Congress was dictated, as I understand it by the following reasons: Kings had always been involving and impoverishing their people in wars, pretending generally, if not always, that the good of the people was the object. This our convention understood to be the most oppressive of all kingly oppressions, and they resolved to so frame the Constitution that no one man should hold the power to bring oppression upon us." See Arthur B. Lapsley, ed., *The Writings of Abraham Lincoln* (New York: Putnam's, 1905), 2: 51–52.

18. Letter of Madison to Jefferson, April 2, 1798, in *The Writings of James Madison*, ed. Gaillard Hunt, 9 vols. (New York: Putnam, 1900–1910), 6: 312.

19. For recent efforts to establish executive supremacy in war and foreign affairs, see John C. Yoo, "Clio at War: The Misuse of History in the War Powers Debate," *University of Colorado Law Review* 70 (1999): 1169; H. Jefferson Powell, "The Founders and the President's Authority over Foreign Affairs," *William and Mary Law Review* 40 (May 1999): 1471; Powell, "The President's Authority over Foreign Affairs: An Executive Branch Perspective, " *George Washington Law Review* 67 (1999): 527. See also Mervin, "The Demise of the War Clause," pp. 770–776.

20. Max Farrand, ed., *The Records of the Federal Convention of 1787,* 4 vols. (New Haven: Yale University Press, 1966), 1: 65–74.

21. Ibid., 1: 288, 292.

22. Ibid., 2: 182.

23. Ibid., 2: 318.

24. Ibid., 2: 318–319.

25. For an accurate historical discussion, see Wormuth and Firmage, *To Chain the Dog of War,* pp. 17–167. For a concise discussion of the early practice, see Fisher, *Presidential War Power,* pp. 13–44, and Adler, "The Constitution and Presidential Warmaking," pp. 17–26. For examination and discussion of specific military actions and issues in the early years, see Casper, "The Washington Administration, Congress, and Algiers," pp. 259–273, Dean Alfange, "The Quasi-War and Presidential Warmaking," pp. 274–290, Daniel Hoffman, "Secrecy and Constitutional Controls in the Federalist Period," pp. 291–312, and Louis Fisher, "The Barbary Wars: Legal Precedent for Invading Haiti," pp. 313–319, all in Adler and George, eds., *The Constitution.*

26. Elliot, ed., *Debates,* 2: 528.

27. Ibid., 4: 107, 287.

28. Ibid., 2: 278.

29. Huloet's dictionary provided this definition: "Declare warres. Arma canere, Bellum indicere." We have here two meanings: to summon to arms; to announce war (quoted in Wormuth and Firmage, *To Chain the Dog of War,* p. 20).

30. In 1744 *Comyn's Digest,* an authoritative treatise on English law, stated, "To the King alone it belongs to make peace and war," and "The King has the sole authority to declare war and peace" (in Wormuth and Firmage, *To Chain the Dog of War,* p. 20). For a discussion of the understanding of international law, see Lofgren, "War Making," pp. 685–695.

31. James Kent, *Commentaries on American Law,* 2d. ed., 4 vols. (Boston: Little, Brown, 1896), 1: 55.

32. For an excellent historical discussion of various declarations and authorizations of war, see Wormuth and Firmage, *To Chain the Dog of War,* pp. 53–74.

33. According to Emerich de Vattel, the leading international law publicist, a conditional declaration of war, an ultimatum demanding satisfaction of grievances, ought properly to precede a declaration of general war (Vattel, *The Law of Nations,* trans. C. Fenwick (Washington, D.C.: Carnegie Institution, 1916), 254–257.

34. *Miller v. The Ship Resolution,* 2 U.S. (2 Dall.) 12, 21 (1782).

35. Manifestly, these opinions reflected the understanding of the war clause held by delegates to the Constitutional Convention and the various state ratifying conventions.

36. 5 U.S. (1 Cranch) 1, 28 (1801).

37. John Norton Moore and others have contended that acts of military force short

of war might be committed by the president; see Moore, "The National Executive and the Use of Armed Forces Abroad," in Falk, ed., *Vietnam*, 2: 814. Senator Paul Douglas defended President Truman's unauthorized venture in Korea on this ground (*Cong. Rec.* 96 [1950]: 9648). Senator Barry Goldwater argued that when the convention deleted from the working draft of the Constitution the authorization of Congress to make war, "the Framers intended to leave the 'making of war' with the President" (*Cong. Rec.* 119 [daily ed., July 19, 1983]: S14141). For a more recent effort supporting a presidential warmaking power, see John C. Yoo, "The Constitution of Politics by Other Means: The Original Understanding of War Powers," *California Law Review* 84 (March 1996): 167.

38. J. B. Moore, *The Collected Papers of John Bassett Moore,* 7 vols. (New Haven: Yale University Press, 1944), 5: 195–196.

39. 27 F. Cas. 1192, 1230 (C.C.D. N.Y. 1806).

40. Early presidents, beginning with Washington, exhibited remarkable sensitivity to the congressional power to initiate hostilities, principally by refusing requests to intervene militarily. This modesty is striking in an era in which presidents, including Clinton, believe they may intervene militarily, anytime, anywhere. For a superb discussion of presidential refusals to act, see Wormuth and Firmage, *To Chain the Dog of War,* pp. 75–86; see also Fisher, *Presidential War Power,* pp. 13–44.

41. For an excellent discussion of the origins and development of the use of letters of marque and reprisal, with an application to contemporary covert war, see Jules Lobel, "Covert War and Congressional Authority: Hidden War and Forgotten Power," *Pennsylvania Law Review* 134 (June 1986): 1035.

42. Ibid., pp. 1045–1047. See Wormuth and Firmage, *To Chain the Dog of War,* pp. 36–39.

43. Quoted in John Bassett Moore, *A Digest of International Law,* 8 vols. (Washington, D.C.: U.S. Government Printing Office, 1906), 7: 123. A reprisal is an act of war and therefore requires congressional authorization.

44. In an effort to obscure the meaning of the war clause, the administration told the *Campbell* court that the allocation of foreign affairs and warmaking powers is not clear, but "certainly there is no single commitment of the war-making power to Congress" (quoted in Memorandum of Points and Authorities in Support of Defendant's Motion to Dismiss, p. 34). But Clinton's bald assertion flies in the face of early judicial decisions that confirmed the exclusive warmaking authority as belonging to Congress (see following discussion). His claim finds no support in the architecture of the Constitution.

45. *Youngstown Sheet and Tube Co. v. Sawyer,* 343 U.S. 579, 643 (1952). But Jackson said that nothing would be "more sinister and alarming than that a President whose conduct of foreign affairs is so largely uncontrolled, and often even is unknown, can vastly enlarge his mastery over the internal affairs of the country by his own commitment of the nation's armed forces to some foreign venture' (ibid., p. 642).

46. Presidents Lyndon Johnson, Richard Nixon, Gerald Ford, Jimmy Carter, Ronald Reagan, and George H. W. Bush have asserted the clause as a source of warmaking authority. For example, the State Department justified Johnson's involvement in Vietnam on the basis of the commander-in-chief clause (*Department of State Bulletin* 54 [1966]: 474, 484). For the same justification by Reagan with respect to his actions in Lebanon and Grenada, see *Weekly Compilation of Presidential Documents* 18 (September 29, 1982): 1232, and 19 (October 25, 1983): 1494. Bush defended his invasion of Panama on the

same rationale (*Congressional Quarterly Weekly Report* 44 [April 19, 1986]: 882). For discussion, see Wormuth and Firmage, *To Chain the Dog of War,* pp. 105–125, and Fisher, *Presidential War,* pp. 139–148.

47. Arthur Schlesinger Jr. had said of the Framers' understanding of the clause: "There is no evidence that anyone supposed that his office as commander in chief endowed the President with an independent source of authority. Even with Washington in prospect, the Founders emphasized their narrow and military definition of this presidential role" (*The Imperial Presidency,* p. 6).

48. Wormuth, "Nixon Theory," p. 630.

49. Hamilton, *Federalist* no. 69, p. 448. Similar assurance was provided by James Iredell, later a U.S. Supreme Court justice, in the North Carolina State Ratifying Convention (Elliot, ed., *Debates,* 4: 107–108).

50. Louis Henkin, *Foreign Affairs and the Constitution* (Mineola, N.Y.: Foundation Press, 1972), pp. 50–51. Moreover, no court ever has held that the clause is a source of warmaking power. Even George Sutherland denied that the office vested the war power in the president. He said that the "Constitution confers no war powers upon the President as such [commander in chief]." See George S. Sutherland, *Constitutional Powers and World Affairs* (New York: Columbia University Press, 1919), p. 73.

51. Leonard Meeker, "The Legality of the United States Participation in the Defense of Vietnam," *Department of State Bulletin* 54 (1966): 474.

52. William Rogers, "Congress, the President, and War Powers," *California Law Review* 59 (September 1971): 1194, 1207–1212.

53. *Public Papers of the Presidents, 1975,* (Washington, D.C.: U.S. Government Printing Office, 1975), 670.

54. *Cong. Rec.* 126 (daily ed., April 28, 1980): H2991.

55. *Weekly Compilation of Presidential Documents* 35 (March 26, 1999): 528.

56. Farrand, ed., *Records,* 1: 62–70.

57. Ibid., 1: 65–70.

58. Hamilton, *Federalist* no. 67, p. 436. Henkin has observed that the "powers vested in [the president] are few and seem modest, far fewer and more modest than those bestowed upon Congress" (*Foreign Affairs,* p. 37).

59. Elliot, ed., *Debates,* 4: 329.

60. Ibid., 2: 540, 3: 201, 4: 107, 2: 128. Madison said that state executives across the land were "little more than cyphers" (Farrand, ed., *Records,* 2: 35).

61. Edward S. Corwin, *The President: Office and Powers, 1787–1984: A History and Analysis of Practice and Opinion,* 5th ed., rev. (New York: New York University Press, 1984), pp. 5–6.

62. Quoted in Gordon Wood, *The Creation of the American Republic, 1776–1787* (Chapel Hill: University of North Carolina Press, 1969), p. 135.

63. Madison, *Federalist* no. 48, p. 322.

64. Memorandum of Points and Authorities in Support of Defendant's Motion to Dismiss, p. 37, in *Campbell v. Clinton.*

65. 229 U.S. 304 (1936). For discussion, see Lofgren, "United States v. Curtiss-Wright Export Corporation: An Historical Reassessment," *Yale Law Journal* 83 (November 1973): 1; David M. Levitan, "The Foreign Relations Power: An Analysis of Mr. Justice Sutherland's Theory," *Yale Law Journal* 55 (April 1946): 467.

66. For discussion of its impact, see Adler, "Court, Constitution and Foreign Affairs," in Adler and George, eds., *The Constitution*, pp. 19–56.

67. Gerhard Casper, "Constitutional Constraints on the Conduct of Foreign and Defense Policy: A Nonjudicial Model." *University of Chicago Law Review* 43 (spring 1976): 463.

68. 299 U.S., at 320.

69. *Annals of Congress* 10 (1800): 613–614.

70. Corwin, *President*, p. 216.

71. Quoted in Jean Edward Smith, *John Marshall: Definer of a Nation* (New York: Henry Holt, 1996), p. 408; I owe this reference to Clayton Olgilvie.

72. Thomas Jefferson, *The Writings of Thomas Jefferson*, ed. P. L. Ford, 10 vols. (New York: Putnam, 1892–1899), 6: 451.

73. Quoted in Raoul Berger, "The President's Unilateral Termination of the Taiwan Treaty," *Northwestern Law Review* 75 (1980): 530, 591.

74. Sutherland, *Constitutional Power and World Affairs*, p. 73.

75. 4 Dall. 37 (1800).

76. 5 U.S. (1 Cranch) 1, 28 (1801).

77. 6 U.S. (2 Cranch) 170, 177–178.

78. 27 F. Cas. 1192, 1230 (No. 16342) (C.C.D. N.Y. 1806).

79. 67 U.S. (2 Black) 635, 668 (1863).

80. The Supreme Court never has held that the commander-in-chief clause confers power to initiate war. The Court has noted a crucial limitation on presidential power: "As commander in chief, he is authorized to direct the movements of the naval and military forces placed by law at his command, and to employ them in the manner he may deem most effectual to harass and conquer and subdue the enemy" (*Fleming v. Page*, 50 U.S. [9 How.] 603, 615 [1850]). Thus Congress may establish the policy to which the president must adhere.

81. 752 F. Supp. 1141 (D.D.C. 1990).

82. Ibid., at 1145.

83. That pillar of presidential power. George Sutherland, denied in 1919 that the president has such powers: "The Constitution confers no war powers upon the President" (*The Constitutional Power and World Affairs*, p. 731. And Hamilton, another favorite among extollers of presidential power, described in *Federalist* no. 69 how the Framers had denied to the president *any* authority to initiate hostilities. He consistently maintained that position. In 1801, for example, he addressed the war clause and stated: "The plain meaning of which is, that it is the peculiar and exclusive province of Congress, *when the nation is at peace* to change that state into a state of war; whether from calculations of policy, or from provocations or injuries received; in other words, it belongs to Congress only *to go to war*" (Letters of Lucius Crassus, No. 1," quoted in *The Works of Alexander Hamilton*, ed. H. C. Lodge, 12 vols. [New York: Putnam, 1904], 8: 249–250 [emphasis in original]. See also, the opinion of Chief Justice Harlan Stone in *Ex parte Quirin:* "The Constitution thus invests the President with power to wage war which Congress has declared" (317 U.S. 1, 26 [1942]).

84. *Weekly Compilation of Presidential Documents* 29 (June 26, 1993): 1181.

85. Ibid., p. 1183.

86. Ibid., p. 1181.

87. See Oscar Schachter, "The Right of States to Use Armed Force," *University of*

Michigan Law Review 82 (1984): 1620; Louis Henkin et al., *International Law*, 3d ed. (St. Paul, Minn.: West, 1993), pp. 911–944.

88. For a discussion of the international law governing reprisals, see, generally, Henkin et al., *International Law*, pp. 870–873, and M. N. Shaw, *International Law*, 3d ed. (Cambridge: Cambridge University Press, 1995), pp. 690–699.

89. Quoted in Moore, *Digest of International Law*, 7: 123.

90. *Public Papers of the Presidents, 1992–1993*, 2: 2175.

91. Ibid., p. 2180.

92. *Weekly Compilation of Presidential Documents* 29 (June 17, 1993): 1101.

93. Ibid., 2082.

94. "UN Authorizes Invasion of Haiti," *Washington Post*, August 1, 1994, p. A1.

95. For discussion see, generally, Fisher, *Presidential War Power*, pp. 148–151.

96. Senate, *Cong. Rec.* 140 (daily ed., August 3, 1994): S10415–10433, and Public Law 93-148.

97. *Public Papers of the Presidents, 1994*, 2: 1419.

98. Ibid., p. 1780.

99. United States Policy Towards Haiti, Public Law 103-423, 108 Stat. 4358, sec. 1 (b) (1994).

100. Senate, *Cong. Rec.* 140 (daily ed., October 6, 1994): S14340.

101. *Powell* v. *McCormack*, 395 U.S. 486, 546 (1969).

102. *Inland Waterways Corp. v. Young*, 309 U.S. 518, 524 (1940).

103. Edward Corwin has observed that "none of the departments may abdicate its powers to either of the others" (*The President*, p. 9). See also *Panama Refining Co. v. Ryan*, 293 U.S. 388, 421 (1935).

104. For discussion, see Berger, "The Protection of Americans Abroad,"*Cincinnati Law Review* 44 (1975): 741.

105. For discussion, see, generally, Fisher and Adler, "The War Powers Resolution: Time to Say Goodbye," *Political Science Quarterly* 113 (1998): 1.

106. See Fisher, *Presidential War Power*, pp. 128–134, 191–194.

107. See Fisher and Adler, "War Powers Resolution," pp. 11–12.

108. Ibid.

109. See Walter Dellinger, "After the Cold War: Presidential Powers and the Use of Military Force," *University of Miami Law Review* 50 (1995): 107.

110. See, generally, the excellent discussions in Wormuth, "Nixon Theory," pp. 640–644, and Edward Keynes, "War Powers Resolution," in Adler and George, eds., *The Constitution*, pp. 246–249.

111. *Public Papers of the Presidents, 1993*, 1: 594.

112. Ibid.

113. Ibid., 2: 1455.

114. Ibid., p. 1781.

115. Ibid., p. 1763.

116. Ibid., p. 1764.

117. Ibid., p. 1768.

118. Ibid., p. 1770.

119. Louis Fisher, "Sidestepping Congress: Presidents Acting Under the UN and NATO," *Case Western Reserve Law Review* 47 (1997): 1237.

120. *Weekly Compilation of Presidential Documents* 31 (September 1, 1995): 1474.

121. In *Reid v. Covert,* Justice Hugo Black stated for the Court: "The United States is entirely a creature of the Constitution. Its powers and authority have no other source. It can only act in accordance with all the limitations imposed by the Constitution" (354 U.S. 1, 16–17 [1957]). In the *Steel Seizure* case, Justice Robert H. Jackson delivered a weighty rebuke to the claim of extraconstitutional "executive power" (*Youngstown Sheet and Tube Co. v. Sawyer,* 353 U.S. 587 [1952]).

122. UN Charter, Article 43.

123. United Nations Participation Act of 1945, Public Law 264, 59 Stat. 621, sec. 6 (1995).

124. See Fisher, "Truman in Korea," in Adler and George, eds., *The Constitution,* pp. 320–335.

125. See Fisher, *Presidential War Power,* pp. 70–91.

126. 63 Stat. 2244, Art. 5 (1949).

127. See, generally, Michael Glennon, *Constitutional Diplomacy* (Princeton: Princeton University Press, 1990), pp. 205–222.

128. 63 Stat. 2246.

129. See David Gray Adler, *The Constitution and the Termination of Treaties* (New York: Garland, 1986), pp. 151–160; Adler, "The President's Recognition Power," in Adler and George, eds. *The Constitution,* pp. 140–148.

130. North Atlantic Treaty (part 1). Hearing Before the Senate Committee on Foreign Relations, 81st Cong. 1949. S. Doc. 48, 11.

131. *Weekly Compilation of Presidential Documents* 34 (August 20, 1998): 1643.

132. Ibid., 1644. See "Possible Benign Use Is Seen for Chemical at Factory in Sudan," *New York Times*, August 27, 1998, A1.

133. Ibid., "Flaws in U.S. Account Raise Questions of Strike in Sudan," August 29, 1998, A1, A4; see also, "U.S. Notes Gaps in Data About Drug Plant," September 3, 1998, A6. The decision to launch the strikes hinged on the quality of evidence; and a year after the attack, it was disclosed that numerous officials were suspicious of the quality of the evidence. See "To Bomb Sudan Plant, or Not: A Year Later, Debates Rankle," October 27, 1999, A1.

134. For a critical review of this suggestion, see Jules Lobel, "The Use of Force to Respond to Terrorist Attacks: The Bombing of Sudan and Afghanistan," *Yale Journal of International Law* 24 (1995): 537.

135. The administration failed to offer a legal rationale to defend its contemplated use of force. See Fisher and Adler, "The War Powers Resolution," pp. 18–20. For an analysis of Clinton's use of force against Iraq, see Louis Fisher, "Military Action Against Iraq," *Presidential Studies Quarterly* 28 (1998): 793.

136. Albright's attempt at obfuscation calls to mind President Harry Truman's response on June 29, 1951, to a question posed at a news conference, on whether the United States was at war. "We are not at war," he said. When he was asked if it would be more accurate to call the conflict "a police action under the United Nations," he agreed: "That is exactly what it amounts to" (quoted in Fisher, "Truman in Korea," p. 327). These semantical plays are futile; Congress has the exclusive authority to initiate hostilities, great or small.

137. *Weekly Compilation of Presidential Documents* 34 (December 16, 1998): 2494.

138. Ibid., p. 2496.

139. Ibid., 35 (March 24, 1999): 513.

140. Ibid., p. 528.

141. *Meet the Press* transcript, May 2, 1999, quoted in Plaintiffs' Memorandum in Opposition to Defendant's Motion to Dismiss, in *Campbell v. Clinton*, 52 F. Supp. 2d. 34 (D.D.C. 1999).

142. Within a week of the initiation of the air strikes against Yugoslavian targets, Serbian troops accelerated their violence against residents of Kosovo, which triggered the forced exodus of over 1 million Kosovans from their homes and villages into the neighboring states of Albania, Macedonia, and Montenegro (*Weekly Compilation of Presidential Documents* 35 (April 7, 1998): 602. Clinton indicated that he would "intensify our actions" and reiterated the open-ended nature of his commitment: "It is not possible to predict" the length "of these operations" and "the durations of the deployments" (ibid., 603). The Framers vested all of these decision-making responsibilities in Congress, but they have been usurped by Clinton.

143. H. R. J. Res. 44, 106th Cong., 2d sess., 1999.

144. H. R. Con. Res. 82, 106th Cong., 2d sess., 1999.

145. H. R. 1569, 106th Cong., 2d sess., 1999.

146. S. Con. Res. 21, 106th Cong., 2d sess., 1999.

147. 52 F. Supp. 2d. 34 (D.D.C., 1999); affirmed, 203 F. 3d 19 (D.C. Cir. 2000); Cert. Denied, 531 U.S. 815 (2000).

148. Memorandum of Points and Authorities in Support of Defendant's Motion to Dismiss, p. 34, *Campbell v. Clinton*.

149. For discussion, see Adler, "Constitution and Presidential Warmaking," pp. 3–5.

150. The assertion of "five" declared wars is a pervasive error in the literature. A recent and, given the finger-pointing nature of the title of his article, an ironic example of this mistake may be found in John C. Yoo, "Clio at War: The Misuse of History in the War Powers Debate," *University of Colorado Law Review* 70 (1999): 1170. Yoo had committed the same error in a longer, more detailed article, "The Continuation of Politics by Other Means: The Original Understanding of War Powers," *California Law Review* 84 (March 1996): 167. He stated, "Congress has issued a declaration of war only five times in its history" (p. 172). Let us substitute fact for fiction and borrow from the compendious research of Wormuth and Firmage. On December 8, 1941, Congress by joint resolution declared that a state of war existed with Japan; "on December 11, 1941, with Germany; on the same day, with Italy; on June 5, 1942, with Bulgaria; on the same day, with Hungary and with Rumania. All these resolutions authorized the president to use the army, the navy, and the militia for the prosecution of war" (*To Chain the Dog of War,* pp. 53–54).

151. On January 12, 1991, Congress voted to authorize President George Bush to use military force against Iraq. Following passage of the resolution by votes of 52 to 47 in the Senate and 250 to 183 in the House, Speaker Thomas Foley asserted that Congress had adopted "'the practical equivalent' of a declaration of war" *New York Times,* January 13, 1991, p. 1. For a critique of the debate preceding the authorization vote, see Keynes, "War Powers Resolution," pp. 241, 249–253; Donald Robinson, "Presidential Prerogative and the Spirit of American Constitutionalism," in Adler and George, eds., *The Constitution,* pp. 114, 126–129.

152. Memorandum of Points and Authorities in Support of Defendant's Motion to Dismiss, p. 27 n. 9, *Campbell v. Clinton.*

153. As Justice Frankfurter wrote for the Court, "Illegality cannot attain legitimacy through practice." (*Inland Waterways Corp. v. Young,* 309 U.S. 513, 524 [1940]).

154. Raoul Berger, *Executive Privilege: A Constitutional Myth* (Cambridge: Harvard University Press, 1974), p. 76. See Wormuth, "Nixon Theory," pp. 652–664, and Wormuth and Firmage, *To Chain the Dog of War,* pp. 133–149.

155. Wormuth, "Vietnam War," p. 718.

156. Alfange, "The Quasi-War and Presidential Warmaking," p. 281.

157. See Wormuth and Firmage, *To Chain the Dog of War,* pp. 53–86.

158. "Letters of Helvidius" in Hunt, ed., *Writings of James Madison,* 6: 148.

159. Farrand, ed., *Records,* 2: 550.

160. *The Prize Cases,* 67 U.S. 635 (1863).

3

The Clinton Legacy: An Old (or New) Understanding of Executive Privilege?

Mark J. Rozell

A core issue in the scandal that led to the impeachment of Bill Clinton was the president's elaborate use of executive privilege. Although nowhere mentioned in the Constitution, executive privilege has a long history in presidential politics. Presidents since George Washington have claimed the power to withhold information from the legislature, the judiciary, and ultimately the public. Despite this long history and the many precedents for its exercise, executive privilege remains a controversial power. The Clinton administration scandals revitalized the national debate over executive privilege but did little to resolve its controversial nature.

On the fringes of the debate are those scholars such as the late Raoul Berger, who have argued that executive privilege simply does not exist in our constitutional system, and those such as former president Richard Nixon, who maintained that this power is absolute and not open to challenge by the coordinate branches of government.[1] In between these two extremes, presidents and Congresses oftentimes have tried to strike a balance through the accommodation process. The relevant debate today is over the proper scope and limits of executive privilege. Few people any longer argue that executive privilege is a "myth." Fewer still cling to the belief that the privilege is an absolute presidential power not subject to the compulsory powers of the other branches.

One of the original proposed articles of impeachment against President Clinton concerned abuse of powers, in particular executive privilege. Many of the advocates of Clinton's impeachment argued reasonably that the use of executive privilege to conceal wrongdoing and to frustrate and thwart the legitimate inquiries of the Office of Independent Counsel (OIC) constituted an abuse of presidential powers. Yet the executive privilege language did not stay in the article eventually voted out by the House Judiciary Committee (and later rejected by the full House). The authors of this article of impeachment either lacked sufficient confidence in their own constitutional argument, or they simply believed that the chances of House approval were too slim.

The confusion over whether to proceed with the charge of abuse of executive privilege evidenced the fact that for many observers the proper parameters of this constitutional doctrine remain unclear. During much of 1998, Clinton's lawyers argued that the president has a broad-based authority to assert executive privilege and that to deny that claim was nothing less than to strip away the legal protections for confidential White House deliberations. The OIC countered that the Clinton scandal involved personal, rather than official, governmental matters, and therefore the White House's various claims of executive privilege could not stand. Each side cited substantial constitutional law, scholarly opinion, and historic precedents in defense of its case.

Federal District Judge Norma Holloway Johnson ultimately sided with the OIC—not because she believed that Clinton's arguments in defense of executive privilege were weak but because Independent Counsel Kenneth Starr had made a compelling showing of need for access to the information shielded by executive privilege. Judge Johnson applied the classic constitutional balancing test, similar to that of the unanimous decision in *U.S. v. Nixon:* in a criminal investigation the need for evidence outweighs the presidential claim to secrecy.[2]

Judge Johnson's decision resolved the immediate controversy, but it did little to clarify the parameters of executive privilege. As a consequence, the OIC declared victory because it achieved access to testimony crucial to the investigation. The White House declared victory because the judge had upheld the principle of executive privilege. After declaring that the president was dropping any claim of executive privilege, the White House later asserted additional claims as the investigation moved forward.[3]

In light of these events, there are competing interpretations of remedies to clarify the meaning and application of executive privilege. One interpretation is that these events evidence the need for legal certainty with regard to executive privilege. That is, either through further clarification in the courts or preferably legislation, there needs to be a clear definition of executive privilege followed by explicit guidelines for its application. Presumably, statutory guidelines would eliminate the lack of certitude over the future exercise of executive privilege and perhaps even eliminate much of the kind of legal wrangling that characterized the Clinton scandal. The appeal of such an outcome is obvious.

A second interpretation—and the one presented here—is that general guidelines on the exercise of executive privilege are necessary, but legalistic precision over the application of this presidential power is neither feasible nor desirable. Executive privilege is a presidential power, but one that is open to challenge by the coordinate branches. It is a power that requires the exercise of presidential discretion on behalf of the public interest. It is impossible to determine today all of the possible circumstances under which presidents in the future may need to use executive privilege. Precise standards of application would unduly constrain presidents from being able to exercise this sometimes-necessary power. Rather than looking toward precise legalistic boundaries, those individuals concerned with the proper application of executive privilege would do better to reexamine the constitutional Framers' understanding of the separation of powers.

THE HISTORICAL DEVELOPMENT OF EXECUTIVE PRIVILEGE

Critics are quick to point out that the phrase "executive privilege" does not appear in the Constitution. To be precise, that phrase was not a part of our constitutional vocabulary until the Eisenhower administration, leading some to suggest that executive privilege therefore could not be constitutional.[4] This argument ultimately fails because every president since Washington has exercised some form of what we today call executive privilege, regardless of the words used to describe their actions. As Louis Fisher has pointed out, "One could play similar word games with 'impoundment,' also of recent vintage, but only by ignoring the fact that, under different names, Presidents have from an early date declined to spend funds appropriated by Congress."[5]

Executive privilege is an implied power derived from Article 2. It is most easily defined as the power of the president and high-level executive branch officers to withhold information from those who have compulsory power—Congress and the courts (and therefore, ultimately, the public). This power is not absolute. The modern understanding of executive privilege has evolved over a long period, the result of presidential actions, official administration policies, and court decisions.

As he did in so many areas, President Washington had a profound influence on the development of executive privilege because of the precedents he established. In the first controversy over the executive's withholding of information from Congress, the president decided that he indeed possessed such a power, but only if his actions were in the service of the public interest. Washington determined that he could not withhold information merely for the purpose of concealing politically damaging or embarrassing information.

The particular circumstance involved the disastrous November 1791 St. Clair military expedition against Native American Indians in which General Arthur St. Clair lost many of his troops and supplies. This was a huge embarrassment to the administration. The House convened an investigation and directed the president to turn over any documents or information germane to the decision to initiate the expedition. The political temptation for the president not to cooperate was clear.

With the unanimous advice of his cabinet, according to Thomas Jefferson's diaries, the president determined that he might exercise a discretion under the Constitution to withhold the information, as long as it was in the public interest to do so. Thomas Jefferson attended the cabinet discussion and later recorded in his notes that the cabinet members had determined "that the executive ought to communicate such papers as the public good would permit, and ought to refuse those, the disclosure of which would injure the public."[6] In the end Washington determined that there were no potentially serious public consequences to divulging the information, and he cooperated with the congressional investigation.

That Washington turned over all information requested by Congress in this controversy leads some to contend that this incident actually argues against the constitutional legitimacy of executive privilege.[7] The key point is that Washington first addressed the issue of the legitimacy of presidential withholding of information from Congress and concluded that the Constitution allows such an action. And equally important, Washington set the precedent for use of executive privilege to protect the public interest, not the president's own political interests. On other occasions Washington asserted a right to withhold information, and he followed through on those claims.

In 1794, for example, the U.S. Senate requested copies of diplomatic correspondence between U.S. officials and officials of the Republic of France. Washington believed that full disclosure of such correspondences was inappropriate. Again the president convened his cabinet, who agreed that he had the power to withhold the information from Congress. Washington replied to the Senate that he would direct that copies and translations of the correspondences be made available, "except in those particulars which, in my judgment, for public considerations, ought not to be communicated."[8] The Senate never challenged the president's decision to withhold portions of the correspondences.

In 1796 the House requested from the Washington administration information concerning the president's instructions to John Jay regarding treaty negotiations with Great Britain. President Washington refused the House request and replied that "the nature of foreign negotiations requires caution, and their success must often depend on secrecy."[9] The House reacted by passing a nonbinding resolution stating that Congress had a right to the information. During debate over the resolution, the primary author of the Constitution, Congressman James Madison, spoke on the floor of the House and declared "that the executive had a right, under a due responsibility, also, to withhold information, when of a nature that did not permit a disclosure of it at the time."[10] During the ratification stage, the Senate voted to keep the treaty secret, as Alexander Hamilton wrote, "because they thought it [the secrecy] the affair of the president to do as he thought fit."[11]

The secrecy decisions of other presidents from the constitutional period are germane to the debate over the origins and legitimacy of executive privilege. President John Adams withheld from Congress information pertinent to the 1798 XYZ Affair. In response to a House request that the president make public certain diplomatic correspondences from the French government, the president largely complied, although he omitted information that he deemed necessary to be kept secret.[12]

During his presidency Thomas Jefferson classified his correspondence as either public or secret, withholding from Congress that which he deemed secret.[13]

In 1807 Jefferson denied a congressional request for information about the Aaron Burr conspiracy. A House resolution requested that the president "lay before this House any information in the possession of the Executive, except such as he may deem the public welfare to require not to be disclosed."[14] It is significant that the House recognized the legitimacy of presidential withholding of information, when in furtherance of the public good. Jefferson responded that although Burr obviously was guilty of treason, it would be improper to divulge materials that would reveal the names of other alleged conspirators. The president wrote to the prosecutor in the case that it was "the necessary right of the President of the United States to decide, independently, what papers coming to him as President, the public interest permit to be communicated, and to whom."[15]

James Madison withheld information from Congress during his presidency, for example, about French trade restrictions against the United States, which eventually led to widespread support for war against Great Britain.[16] Madison, and then President James Monroe, withheld information from Congress regarding U.S. takeover of the Florida territory.[17] In 1825, the House requested from Monroe information about the "Steward incident," except, significantly, any details that the president determined it was not in the public interest to disclose.[18] Monroe did not provide the requested information and replied that doing so "would not comport with the public interest."[19]

These examples of presidential secrecy established precedents for the exercise of what we today call executive privilege. A common thread emerges in these early uses: these presidents and members of Congress accepted the legitimacy of such a power when exercised in the service of the public interest.

It is not possible here to recount all the instances of presidential withholding of information, but several prominent examples will suffice. In 1848, in response to a House request for documents pertaining to the return of President General Lopez de Santa Anna to Mexico, President James Polk released only those documents deemed "compatible with the public interest to communicate."[20] Polk cited the precedent of Washington's 1796 message to Congress that a president had the authority to refuse to release documents "improper to be disclosed."[21] Later that year Polk acceded to a separate House request for documents but made it clear that he retained the power to withhold information when in "the public interest" to do so.[22]

After President Theodore Roosevelt refused a Senate resolution requesting information from the attorney general, a Senate committee requested the same materials in the possession of the Bureau of Corporations. The president personally seized the documents and dared Congress to impeach him.[23] Roosevelt's objective, he said, was to ensure that the government's promise of secrecy to certain parties was upheld.

Presidents Franklin Roosevelt, Harry Truman, and Dwight Eisenhower, among others, refused on certain occasions to permit cabinet officers to testify before Congress about confidential matters. Most prominently, President Eisenhower holds the presidential record for assertions of executive privilege, at more than forty. Many of those assertions amounted to refusals to comply with congressional requests for testimony from White House officials. Eisenhower felt so strongly about the principle that at one point he stated, "Any man who testifies as to the advice he gave me won't be working for me that night."[24] A key event in the development of executive privilege was Eisenhower's May 17, 1954, letter to the secretary of defense, instructing department employees not to comply with a congressional request to testify about confidential matters in the Army-McCarthy Hearings. Eisenhower articulated the principle that candid advice was essential to the proper functioning of the executive branch and that limiting candor would ultimately harm "the public interest."[25]

Although many of Eisenhower's uses of executive privilege were clearly justified, the breadth of his understanding of that power disturbed many people. At one point he effectively declared that executive privilege belonged to the entire executive branch, when in fact over the course of history the practice had been to confine its use to the president and to high-level White House officials when directed by the president. He declared all advice to the president not subject to the compulsory powers of the other branches, although the development of executive privilege law more recently has resulted in a key distinction between discussions about official governmental matters and those about private matters.

Eisenhower's administration originated the use of the phrase "executive privilege" and expanded the actual practice of that power. Members of Congress, rightfully concerned about the expanded practice, sought to rein in Eisenhower's successors through the articulation of standards for the use of executive privilege. Congressman John Moss (D-Calif.), the chairman of the House Special Subcommittee on Government Information, led the effort. Beginning with the Kennedy administration, Moss sent letters to successive presidents requesting written clarification of their policy toward the use of executive privilege. President John Kennedy replied that executive privilege "can be invoked only by the president and will not be used without specific presidential approval."[26] President Lyndon Johnson responded similarly to a letter from Moss that "the claim of 'executive privilege' will continue to be made only by the president."[27]

Ironically, President Richard Nixon responded most forthrightly to Moss's inquiry when he wrote, "The scope of executive privilege must be very narrowly construed. Under this Administration, executive privilege will not be asserted without specific presidential approval. . . . I want open government to be a reality in every way possible."[28] Nixon issued the first detailed presidential memorandum specifically on the proper use of executive privilege:

> The policy of this Administration is to comply to the fullest extent possible with Congressional requests for information. While the Executive branch has the responsibility of withholding certain information the disclosure of which would be incompatible with the public interest, this Administration

will invoke this authority only in the most compelling circumstances and after a rigorous inquiry into the actual need for its exercise. For those reasons Executive privilege will not be used without specific Presidential approval.[29]

The memorandum outlined the procedure to be used whenever a question of executive privilege was raised. If a department head believed that a congressional request for information might concern privileged information, he or she would consult with the attorney general. They would then decide whether to release the information to Congress or to submit the matter to the president through the counsel to the president. At that stage, the president either would instruct the department head to claim executive privilege with presidential approval or request that Congress give some time to the president to make a decision.

The story of Nixon's vast abuse of executive privilege is well known and analyzed in detail elsewhere.[30] Nonetheless, Nixon's response to Moss and the executive privilege memorandum were important to the development of standard procedures on the scope and application of that doctrine.

Unfortunately, Nixon's practices gave executive privilege a bad name and had a profoundly chilling effect on the ability of his immediate successors either to clarify procedures or properly to exercise that power. President Gerald Ford began what became a common post-Watergate practice of avoiding executive privilege inquiries and using other constitutional or statutory powers to justify withholding information. Within a week of Ford's inauguration, Moss sent his usual inquiry to the president, requesting a statement on executive privilege policy.[31] Unlike Presidents Kennedy, Johnson, and Nixon, Ford ignored the letter. Other members of Congress weighed in with their own requests, and Ford ignored their letters, too. Numerous discussions took place within the White House over the need for the president to either reaffirm or modify Nixon's official executive privilege procedures. Ford took no action on the recommendations.

The associate counsel to the president summed up the dilemma nicely when he suggested three options: cite exemptions from the Freedom of Information Act as the basis for withholding information "rather than executive privilege"; use executive privilege only as a last resort—even avoid the use of the phrase in favor of "presidential" or "constitutional privilege"; or issue formal guidelines on executive privilege.[32] Ford chose to handle executive privilege controversies on a case-by-case basis rather than to issue general guidelines. He understood that for many people "executive privilege" and "Watergate" had become joined.

Neither did President Jimmy Carter respond to congressional requests for clarification of administration policy on executive privilege. It was not until the week before the 1980 election that the Carter administration established some official executive privilege procedures. On October 31, 1980, White House Counsel Lloyd Cutler issued an executive privilege memorandum to White House staff and heads of units within the Executive Office of the President. The memorandum established that those considering the use of executive privilege must first seek the concurrence of the Office of Counsel to the president. The memorandum also emphasized that only the president had the authority to waive executive privilege.[33] Cutler later became counsel to the president in the Clinton administration and wrote new procedures on the use of executive privilege in 1994.

On November 4, 1982, President Ronald Reagan issued an executive privilege memorandum to heads of executive departments and agencies. The Reagan procedures dovetailed closely with the 1969 Nixon memorandum. For example, Reagan's guidelines affirmed the administration's policy "to comply with congressional requests for information to the fullest extent consistent with the constitutional and statutory obligations of the executive branch." The memorandum reaffirmed the need for "confidentiality of some communications" and added that executive privilege would be used "only in the most compelling circumstances, and only after careful review demonstrates that assertion of the privilege is necessary." Finally, "executive privilege shall not be invoked without specific presidential authorization."

The Reagan memorandum developed greater clarity of procedures than preceding ones had. All congressional requests must be accommodated unless "compliance raises a substantial question of executive privilege." Such a question would arise if the information "might significantly impair the national security (including the conduct of foreign relations), the deliberative process of the executive branch or other aspects of the performance of the executive branch's constitutional duties." Under these procedures, if a department head believed that a congressional request for information might concern privileged information, he or she would notify and consult with both the attorney general and the counsel to the president. Those three individuals would then decide to release the information to Congress or have the matter submitted to the president for a decision if any one of them believed that it was necessary to invoke executive privilege. At that point, the department head would ask Congress to await a presidential decision. If the president chose executive privilege, he instructed the department head to inform Congress "that the claim of executive privilege is being made with the specific approval of the president." The Reagan memorandum allowed for the use of executive privilege, even if the information originated from staff levels far removed from the Oval Office.[34]

By avoiding the term "executive privilege," Presidents Ford and Carter actually succeeded more than Reagan did at protecting secrecy. Ford and Carter understood in the post–Watergate era the negative connotations of executive privilege. President Reagan tried to reestablish its legitimacy, only to be harshly criticized and fought every step of the way by the Democratic-led Congress. Reagan ultimately backed down from his several claims of executive privilege and did more to weaken the doctrine as a result.

President George H. W. Bush did not initiate any new executive privilege procedures. The 1982 Reagan memorandum remained in effect as official policy during the Bush years. Bush frequently withheld information without invoking executive privilege. Like Ford and Carter, he avoided the negative taint of executive privilege and generally used other bases of authority for withholding information. When his administration wanted to withhold information from Congress, it used a variety of other phrases to justify that action, among them "internal departmental deliberations," "deliberations of another agency," and the "secret opinions policy."[35] The chief investigator to the House Committee on the Judiciary during these years said that Bush "avoided formally claiming executive privilege and instead called it other things. In reality, executive privilege was in full force and effect during the Bush years, probably more so than under Reagan."[36]

EXECUTIVE PRIVILEGE: THE CLINTON LEGACY

In 1994, the Clinton administration issued its own executive privilege procedures. According to the memorandum from Special Counsel to the President Lloyd Cutler, "The policy of this Administration is to comply with congressional requests for information to the fullest extent consistent with the constitutional and statutory obligations of the Executive Branch. . . . Executive privilege will be asserted only after careful review demonstrates that assertion of the privilege is necessary to protect Executive Branch prerogatives." The memorandum further stated, "Executive privilege belongs to the President, not individual departments or agencies."

Cutler's memorandum described the formal procedures for handling executive privilege disputes, and these were not substantially different from earlier administrations. One sentence nonetheless stands out in light of later events: "In circumstances involving communications relating to investigations of personal wrongdoing by government officials, it is our practice not to assert executive privilege, either in judicial proceedings or in congressional investigations and hearings."[37]

According to the Cutler memorandum, the Clinton administration adopted the broad view that all White House communications are presumptively privileged. Furthermore, the administration's position was that Congress had a less valid claim to executive branch information when conducting oversight than when considering legislation.[38]

The administration made elaborate and mostly indefensible claims of executive privilege. Prior to the so-called Lewinsky scandal, it made several claims of executive privilege,[39] only one of which appeared designed to protect the constitutional prerogatives of the executive branch. The first claim involved a House committee investigation into the White House firings of Travel Office staffers in 1993. In response to a committee subpoena of Travel Office records and ultimately a vote to hold White House counsel Jack Quinn in contempt of Congress, the president claimed executive privilege.[40] Quinn had written to the committee that the requested documents included discussions between the president and legal counsel, among other confidential materials.[41] According to the general counsel to the committee, a "review of the documents proved that declaration to be erroneous."[42] The White House eventually released the documents, and the evidence supports the conclusion that Clinton's claim of executive privilege lacked merit. Documents for which Clinton had claimed executive privilege included those involving discussions between the First Lady and White House staff as well as White House talking points for sympathetic Democratic committee members, among other materials not traditionally covered by the privilege.[43]

In 1994 the Office of the Independent Counsel opened an investigation into allegations of wrongdoing by former Department of Agriculture secretary Mike Espy. The grand jury subpoenaed documents from a separate White House Counsel's office investigation of Espy. President Clinton claimed executive privilege and the deliberative process privilege in withholding eighty-four requested documents. The OIC challenged these claims, and in a key case, the D.C. Circuit upheld the constitutionality of executive privilege while ruling that the OIC's need for information outweighed the president's secrecy needs.[44]

In this decision, the court identified two forms of privilege: the presidential communications privilege and the deliberative process privilege. The former is rooted in separation of powers, pertains to "direct decisionmaking by the president," and concerns "quintessential and non-delegable" powers. The latter is easier to overcome because it belongs to executive branch officials generally, and it "disappears altogether when there is any reason to believe government misconduct has occurred." The key point is that the court defined the executive privilege more narrowly than did the administration. This precedent made it clear that the privilege is a direct presidential power, not a staff power, and that the privilege is specifically germane to the president's official Article 2 duties.

During the 1996 campaign, congressional Republicans sought access to a memorandum by FBI director Louis Freeh that apparently was critical of administration antidrug policy. Clinton claimed executive privilege, and Attorney General Janet Reno backed the president. Reno's argument in favor of executive privilege in this instance rested on the dubious assumption that in cases of investigations rather than legislation, Congress has a much weaker claim to access to executive branch information.[45]

Although there were allegations of a political motivation for seeking access to an embarrassing internal document in an election year, even if these were true, such a motivation does not validate an assertion of executive privilege. Absent a real threat to national security or to the public interest posed by revealing internal deliberations, the president's claim of privilege must be overridden by Congress's request for information unless it can be specifically demonstrated that Congress's actions were outside the scope of any legitimate investigation. As Louis Fisher points out, courts consistently have ruled that the congressional power of investigation is available, even for pursuit down "blind alleys."[46]

The burden is on the president to prove a compelling need to withhold information and not on Congress to prove that it has the right to investigate. Clinton never made a case that releasing the memorandum would cause any undue harm. It appeared that he stood to harm only his own political standing by releasing a document that contained embarrassing information. The president never proved that Congress's inquiry lacked any legitimate basis under the normal legislative power of investigation.

Clinton's one possibly defensible claim of executive privilege concerned a House committee request for White House documents on U.S.–Haiti policy. The White House refused, and in September 1996 the committee issued subpoenas. White House–congressional negotiations over certain sensitive documents stalemated and Clinton claimed executive privilege. Reno once again backed the president's claim.[47] In this case the House committee had pushed for memorandums from the national security adviser to Clinton, lending credibility to the president's position that releasing the documents would potentially compromise national security. The House committee did not fight the claim of executive privilege, making it impossible to judge at this time the actual seriousness of Clinton's use of that power in this controversy.

How does Clinton's use of executive privilege in the Lewinsky investigation measure up to the legal standards that have been developed to control its applications? There was obviously no national security justification to withholding information about presidential and staff discussions over how to handle that episode, although Clinton's White House counsel tried to make the argument that by harming "the president's ability to 'influence' the public," the investigation undermined his ability to lead foreign policy.[48] The White House case for executive privilege ultimately hinged on the claim that the president had the right to protect the privacy of internal deliberations. As correctly decided in the Mike Espy case (*In re: Sealed Case,* 1997), presidents are entitled to candid, confidential advice. The executive privilege extends to presidential advisers because they must be able to deliberate and discuss policy options without fear of public disclosure of their every utterance. Without that protection, the candor and quality of presidential advice would clearly suffer. The Clinton administration maintained that this decision justified any claims of privilege on behalf of discussions between the president and his aides, between and among aides, and even between the First Lady and an aide. As a general principle, it is correct that such discussions can be covered by the privilege, although extending such protection to the First Lady is controversial.[49]

Executive privilege for the First Lady is unprecedented and, regarding her deliberations during the Lewinsky investigation, quite likely a real stretch of the doctrine. To cover the First Lady properly with a claim of executive privilege, it would have to be established that she has an official position in her husband's administration; in such a capacity, she has played an active role in those matters and participated in some of those official discussions that led to a claim of executive privilege; and such discussions concern matters that actually deserve the protection of the privilege.

The key issue in these executive privilege debates is whether the White House discussions had anything to do with official governmental business as opposed to being merely deliberations over how to handle political strategy during a scandal. Judge Norma Holloway Johnson ultimately ruled against Clinton's use of executive privilege in the Lewinsky investigation, and although much of her reasoning gave credibility to some debatable White House arguments, she correctly determined that the balancing test weighed in favor of Independent Counsel Kenneth Starr's need for access to information that was crucial to a criminal investigation.[50]

For the White House position to have prevailed, Clinton had to make a compelling argument that the public interest would somehow suffer from the release of information about White House discussions over the Lewinsky investigation. Not only had he failed to do so, but also for months he even refused to answer basic questions as to whether he had formally invoked the privilege. Once Judge Johnson ruled against Clinton, the White House dropped its flawed claim of executive privilege. In an obvious face-saving gesture, White House counsel Charles Ruff declared victory because Judge Johnson, in ruling against the president, had nonetheless upheld the legitimacy of the principle of executive privilege and therefore had preserved this presidential power for Clinton's successors.

The doctrine of executive privilege certainly did not need this kind of help. Executive privilege already stood as a legitimate presidential power, although one clearly tainted in the public mind by the Watergate episode. Reestablishing the good reputation of executive privilege required a much more compelling circumstance for its exercise than a personal scandal—a military action, for example.

Furthermore, there is little evidence from this episode to suggest that the Clinton White House undertook this drawn-out battle merely to make a principled stand on executive privilege. All evidence to date suggests that Clinton used executive privilege to frustrate and delay the investigation, all the while successfully convincing most of the public that the blame for the inquiry's taking so long and costing so much belonged to the Office of the Independent Counsel.

Although the White House publicly claimed victory in protecting the principle of executive privilege and led people to believe that the issue was no longer germane to the investigation, additional claims of the privilege followed. In August 1998 a White House attorney and deputy White House counsel claimed executive privilege in testimony before the grand jury. Clinton told the grand jury that he merely wanted to protect the constitutional principal and did not want to challenge further the independent counsel's victory, yet the president several days later challenged one unfavorable court ruling and directed another aide to assert executive privilege.[51]

For months, the Clinton White House clearly did a masterly job of presenting its case before the court of public opinion. Due to a thriving economy, the president's approval ratings remained strong. Furthermore, most of the public had tired of the scandal and had become convinced that Starr lacked the objectivity necessary to conduct a fair investigation.

Many observers may ask, why did this dispute—and the politically motivated effort to delay its obvious resolution—matter? Because executive privilege embodies the principle that no one is above the law, not even the president—not even a president who might otherwise be seen as a great foreign policy leader (Nixon) or as contributing to a thriving economy (Clinton). White House efforts to obstruct and delay justice for the sake of some perceived political advantage cynically undermined both the privilege and the principle. Regarding executive privilege, Clinton's legacy appears not to be that of a president who reestablished this necessary power, but, like Nixon before him, as one who gave executive privilege a bad name.

RESTORING THE BALANCE

Because of the constitutional abuses of two presidencies, executive privilege remains tainted. In the post–Watergate era, Congress has shown little deference to presidential efforts to assert that power. Presidents with legitimate causes to assert executive privilege generally have avoided that power because of the negative connotations. And Bill Clinton, a president truly with something to hide, made elaborate and mostly bogus claims of executive privilege.

Is it any longer possible to restore the proper balance to the exercise of executive privilege? Because of the Watergate taint and Clinton's more recent abuses, that may take years to happen.

One approach is to establish a statutory definition of executive privilege with specific guidelines for its future exercise. The appeal of that approach is to make the exercise of this power less subject to the whims of the occupants of the White House. Another approach is to concede the whole debate to such critics of executive privilege as Raoul Berger, who argue that the president simply lacks that power. The appeal of this approach is that there is no ambiguity at all: executive privilege simply does not exist; and those with compulsory power, especially Congress, have access to any and all executive branch information.

Both of these solutions are worse than the problem they seek to overcome. It is impossible to establish in advance all the circumstances that may call for presidential exercise of secrecy. Statutory guidelines would simply take away too much of the discretion that presidents have to exercise this power on behalf of the public good. Presidential prerogatives should not be confined by statutory limits.

One way indeed to eliminate the potential abuse of power is to eliminate the source of authority altogether. That is true for any power given to presidents. Yet to eliminate a source of occasional abuses of power is also to strip away the ability of presidents to do good for the country. Any source of authority can be used for good or ill. At a certain level, we have to trust that those individuals endowed with the powers of the presidency will conduct themselves properly and in accordance with the public interest. If they fail us in that regard, we must resort to the constitutional constraints provided by the separation of powers system.

The solution to the potential abuse of executive privilege is not to eliminate that power, and it is not found in some future congressional statute. The solution is to rely upon the constitutional Framers' notion of the separation of powers. The coordinate branches have the ability to challenge presidential exercise of executive privilege through various sources of power. These sources include not only the more obvious use of the power of investigation, litigation, and impeachment but also of confirmation, lawmaking, and budgetary authorization, among others. Thus, Congress can challenge executive privilege, for example, by withholding support for presidential nominations or initiatives or withholding funding for an administration's favored programs. The judicial branch can certainly arbitrate constitutional disputes between the political branches, such as over the exercise of executive privilege.

Under the separation of powers, the president's options are quite clear: if, indeed, withholding certain information is crucial to the national security or for protecting the confidentiality of executive branch deliberations, the president should be willing to withstand congressional inquiries or policy and political threats. The president should have to weigh the importance of secrecy against the prospect of a drawn-out battle with Congress and make the decision that he believes his duties and the national interest require. In a democratic republic, the presumption generally should be in favor of openness, but it is also important to recognize that presidents sometimes have legitimate needs for secrecy.

NOTES

1. Raoul Berger, *Executive Privilege: A Constitutional Myth* (Cambridge: Harvard University Press, 1974); letter from President Richard M. Nixon to Judge John Sirica, July 25, 1973, White House Central Files, FE4-1 (May 1, 1973–September 30, 1973), Nixon Presidential Materials Project, Alexandria, Virginia.

2. Judge Johnson's Order on Executive Privilege, May 26, 1998, Available online: <washingtonpost.com/wp-srv/politics/special/Clinton/stories/order052898.htm>.

3. "Referral to the U.S. House of Representatives Pursuant to Title 28, U.S. Code 595C," submitted by the Office of Independent Counsel, September 9, 1998.

4. See Berger, *Executive Privilege*, p. vii, and Saikrishna Prakash, "A Critical Comment on the Constitutionality of Executive Privilege," *Minnesota Law Review* 83 (May 1999): 1143.

5. Louis Fisher, "Raoul Berger on Public Law," *Political Science Reviewer* 8 (1978): 181.

6. Thomas Jefferson, *The Writings of Thomas Jefferson*, ed. Paul Ford (New York: Putnam, 1892–1905), 1: 189.

7. See Berger, *Executive Privilege,* pp. 167–171, and Prakash, "Critical Comment," pp. 1177–1179.

8. *Annals of Congress* 4 (1794): 56.

9. James Richardson, *A Compilation of Messages and Papers of the Presidents,* 20 vols. (New York: Bureau of National Literature, 1897), 1: 186.

10. *Annals of Congress* 5 (1796): 773. To be sure, the House rejected Madison's motion. I find the view of Madison on constitutional questions far more compelling than what the majority of the House decided.

11. Alexander Hamilton, *The Works of Alexander Hamilton,* ed. Henry Cabot Lodge, 12 vols. (New York: Putnam, 1904), 10: 107.

12. *Annals of Congress* 8 (1798): 1374–1375.

13. Abraham Sofaer, "Executive Power and Control over Information: The Practice Under the Framers," *Duke Law Journal* (1977): 16–17.

14. *Annals of Congress* 16 (1806–1807): 336.

15. Ford, ed., *Writings,* 1: 55.

16. Sofaer, "Executive Power," pp. 19–24.

17. Ibid., pp. 28–45.

18. *House Journal,* 1825, p. 102.

19. Richardson, *Compilation,* 2: 847.

20. Ibid., 5: 2415.

21. Ibid., 5: 2416–2417.

22. Ibid., 6: 2529–2537.

23. Edward Corwin, *The President: Office and Powers, 1787–1957* (New York: New York University Press, 1957), pp. 429–430.

24. Fred Greenstein, *The Hidden-hand Presidency: Eisenhower as Leader* (New York: Basic Books, 1982), p. 205.

25. *Public Papers of the Presidents,* 1954 (Washington, D.C.: U.S. Government Printing Office, 1954), pp. 483–484.

26. Clark Mollenhoff, *Washington Cover-Up* (Garden City, N.Y.: Doubleday, 1962), p. 239.

27. U.S. Senate, *Executive Privilege: Hearings Before the Subcommittee on Separation of Powers of the Committee on the Judiciary,* 92nd Cong., 1st sess., 1971, p. 35.

28. Letter from President Richard M. Nixon to Congressman John E. Moss, April 7, 1969, Executive Privilege Folder (2), Box 13, Edward Schmultz Files, Gerald R. Ford Library (GRFL), Ann Arbor, Michigan.

29. Memorandum from President Richard M. Nixon to Executive Department Heads, March 24, 1969. Executive Privilege Folder (1973), White House Staff Files, Ronald Ziegler Files, Nixon Presidential Materials Project, Alexandria, Virginia.

30. See Michael Genovese, *The Watergate Crisis* (Westport, Conn.: Greenwood Press, 1995).

31. Letter from Congressman John E. Moss to President Gerald R. Ford, August 15, 1974, Executive Privilege Folder (2), Box 13, Philip Buchen Files, GRFL.

32. Memorandum from Dudley Chapman to Philip W. Buchen et al., November 5, 1974, Executive Privilege Folder, General (1), Box 13, Edward Schmultz Files, GRFL.

33. Memorandum from Lloyd Cutler to heads of all units within the Executive Office of the President and Senior White House Staff, October 31, 1980, Executive Priv-

ilege File, June 1977–November 1980, Box 74, Lloyd Cutler Files, Jimmy Carter Library, Atlanta, Georgia.

34. Memorandum from President Reagan to heads of Executive Departments and Agencies, procedures governing responses to congressional requests for information, November 4, 1982 (on file with author).

35. See Mark J. Rozell, *Executive Privilege: The Dilemma of Secrecy and Democratic Accountability* (Baltimore: Johns Hopkins University Press, 1994), chap. 5. See also Rozell, "Executive Privilege and the Modern Presidents: In Nixon's Shadow," *Minnesota Law Review* 83 (May 1999):1069.

36. Author's interview with James Lewin, November 19, 1992.

37. Memorandum from Lloyd Cutler to all Executive Department and Agency General Councils, September 28, 1994 (on file with author).

38. See letter from Attorney General Janet Reno to President Bill Clinton, September 20, 1996; Letter from Attorney General Janet Reno to President Bill Clinton, September 30, 1996 (on file with author). The administration draws its view that Congress lacks a compelling need for executive branch information in cases of oversight from a dubious interpretation of the D.C. Circuit court's 1974 ruling in *Senate Select Committee on Presidential Campaign Activities v. Nixon* (498 F. 2d 725). Although the court did not explicitly acknowledge Congress's need for information in cases of oversight, that does not mean that the court thereby overruled the well-established investigative powers of legislative committees. The Reagan and Bush administrations also made such broad claims in this regard. See letter from Attorney General William French Smith to President Ronald Reagan, October 31, 1981; memorandum from Attorney General William Barr to Counsels' Consultive Group re congressional requests for confidential executive branch information, June 19, 1989.

39. Clinton made several unfounded claims of executive privilege that he eventually dropped. For example, in 1993, in response to a House inquiry into allegations of abuses of FBI background files, he claimed executive privilege; his own Justice Department would not support the claim and he backed down. In 1996 Clinton claimed executive privilege to shield from the Office of Independent Counsel access to records of the First Lady's conversations with White House attorneys; the OIC challenged the claim and he backed down, using instead the attorney-client privilege. In 1997 Clinton claimed executive privilege to prohibit OIC from questioning Chief of Staff Thomas McLardy; Clinton withdrew the claim as the OIC prepared a motion to compel. See "Referral to the U.S. House of Representatives Pursuant to Title 28, U.S. Code 595C," submitted by the Office of the Independent Counsel, September 9, 1998.

40. See House, *Report of the Committee on Government Reform and Oversight Citing John M. Quinn, David Watkins, and Matthew Moore Together with Additional and Dissenting Views*, 104th Cong., 2d sess., May 29, 1996.

41. See letters from Jack Quinn to Congressman William F. Clinger, May 2, 3, 9, 30, June 25, and August 15, 1996. The attorney general backed the president's assertion of privilege in this case (see letter from Attorney General Janet Reno to President Bill Clinton, May 8, 1996). For the complete record of White House and congressional correspondence over privilege and other issues in the Travel Office controversy, see House, *Correspondence Between the White House and Congress in the Proceedings Against John M. Quinn, David Watkins, and Matthew Moore as Part of the Committee Investigation into*

the White House Travel Office Matter, 104th Cong., 2d sess., May 1996. Indeed, the committee reported that Quinn's category of privileged documents was so broad that it was tantamount to the breadth of privilege claims rejected in *U.S. v. Nixon,* 418 U.S. 683 (1973). See House, *Report of the Committee on Government Reform and Oversight Citing John M. Quinn, David Watkins, and Matthew Moore Together with Additional and Dissenting Views,* May 29, 1996, p. 9 n. 13.

42. Kevin Sabo, "Scandal Retardant," *Legal Times,* October 28, 1996, p. 27.

43. Ibid., pp. 27–28.

44. *In re Sealed Case,* 124 F. 3d 230 (D.C. Cir. 1997).

45. Attorney General William French Smith first drew this distinction from his erroneous interpretation of *Senate Select Committee on Presidential Campaign Activities v. Nixon,* 498 F. 2d 725 (1974), and his successors, including Reno, have repeated the mistake. For a clear refutation of this "extraordinary misconception," see Louis Fisher, *Constitutional Conflicts Between Congress and the President,* 4th ed., rev. (Lawrence: University Press of Kansas, 1997), p. 187.

46. Fisher, *Constitutional Conflicts,* p. 187.

47. Letter from Attorney General Janet Reno to President Bill Clinton, September 20, 1996 (on file with author).

48. Ruff's Argument for Executive Privilege," unsealed May 27, 1998 <*www.washingtonpost.com/wp-srv/politics/special/clinton/stories/ruff052898.htm*>.

49. "White House Motion Seeking Privilege," filed March 17, 1998 <*www.washingtonpost.com/wp-srv/politics/special/clinton/stories/whitehouse052898.htm*>.

50. "Judge Johnson's Order on Executive Privilege," issued May 26, 1998 <*www.washingtonpost.com/wp-srv/politics/special/clinton/stories/order052898.htm*>.

51. "Referral to the U.S. House of Representatives Pursuant to Title 28, U.S. Code, 595C," submitted by the Office of the Independent Counsel, September 9, 1998.

4

The Pardon Power Under Clinton: Tested but Intact

Michael A. Genovese and Kristine Almquist

The literature on presidential power is littered with references to limits, checks, and roadblocks; power is shared and overlapping. Presidents often (less so in foreign policy and war issues) appear as Gullivers, enchained by thousands of others, and seem unable to muster enough energy to act. There are, critics charge, too many checks and not enough powers.[1]

The view from the White House frequently reinforces this refrain. Teddy Roosevelt lamented, "If I could be both president and congress for five minutes . . . ." And so it goes. Presidents feel bound and chained, and in many ways they are. That is at once the strength and weakness of the Madisonian system of checks and balances.[2]

In contrast to the sharply limited character of most presidential powers, the pardon power stands alone in its capaciousness. The president's authority to grant pardons and reprieves is subject to few checks and balances, and even then, they are not primarily legal but political in nature. And the sheer breadth of this discretionary power, coupled with a largely judicious historical usage, has served to quiet debate and to still criticism. But on those relatively few occasions when the grant of executive clemency has provoked controversy, as in Gerald Ford's pardon of Richard Nixon and George Bush's pardon of Caspar Weinberger, and now with a panoply of eleventh-hour pardons issued by Bill Clinton, academics and the public-minded have been moved to reexamine the origins of the pardon authority and the purposes of the Framers in vesting such an expansive power in the presidency. Our aim here is twofold: to conduct an inquiry into the nature and scope of the pardon power, and to evaluate Clinton's exercise of the pardon authority.

ENGLISH ROOTS

The concept of executive clemency was not created in the Constitutional Convention but found its way into American law through English practice, beginning in the seventh century.[3] This was during the time of King Ine of Wessex, and section 6 of Ine's law stated, "If any one fight in the king's house, let him be liable in all his property, and be it in the king's doom whether he shall or shall not have life." The law was expanded later by others such as Ethelred:

> And he who oft before has been convicted openly of theft, and shall go to the ordeal, and is there found guilty; that he be slain, unless the kindred or the lord be willing to release him by his "wer" and by the full "ceap-guild," and also have him in "borh" that he thenceforth desist from every kind of evil. If after that he again steal, then let his kinsmen give him up to the reeve to whom it may appertain, in such custody as they before took him out of from the ordeal, and let him be slain in retribution of the theft. But if any one defend him, and will take him, although he was convicted at the ordeal, so that he might not be slain; then he should be liable in his life, unless he should flee to the king, and he should give him his life.[4]

This passage illustrates that a criminal should receive punishment, but it also shows that the criminal could "flee to the king," who could give him his life back if he felt it was deserved.

Over time, the power to pardon was expanded. King Cnut issued a proclamation guaranteeing that if one desired to return from lawlessness and to observe the law, he would be shown mercy. The pardon power was extended in the codes of William the Conqueror, and his son, Henry I, used the power to hear "pleas concerning serious offenses that merited heavy punishment."[5] Henry I wanted more pardons for those seeking them, and it is here that compensation for a pardon is introduced, leading to accusations of the abuse of the pardon power. Pardons were intended as an act of grace, used in cases where the king could employ his royal prerogative of mercy in any way he chose. Yet the record suggests that the pardon power was often bought or used for the good of the king, instead of as an act of grace. Pardons were often sold for a fee and were used to lure convicted felons into military service if they accepted the terms of the pardon.[6] Edward I was the first king to employ this tactic of using the pardon power to release felons for service in times of war. "As soon as war was declared, it was the custom to issue a proclamation, in which a general pardon of all homicides and felonies was granted to anyone who would serve with the military for a year at his own cost."[7]

The abuse of the pardon power by kings did not go unnoticed by Parliament, which in turn made several complaints and suggested that the king use more restraint when issuing pardons. Parliament tried but did not succeed in restraining the king until 1389, when an important victory was achieved. Parliament enacted a statute that prevented the issuance of a pardon in the case of serious crimes unless it specified the exact nature of the crime and contained the name of the culprit.[8] Even though this statute was a victory for Parliament, the king did not follow the law. Serious abuses continued to occur, and Parliament again tried to curtail them. Statutes were enacted but were rarely, if ever, followed. It was not until the controversial case of the Earl of Danby that constraints on the pardon power were effectuated. This case gave form to the pardoning power for almost three centuries.[9]

Thomas Osborne, earl of Danby and lord high treasurer of England from 1673 to 1679, was to be impeached after it was learned that he had written a letter to the English minister in the Court of Versailles, empowering him to make decisions beyond his authority. Charles II came to Danby's rescue to explain that Danby had written the letter at his direction and that Danby had merely played the role of a faithful servant. But Charles II's explanation was not entirely truthful, and Parliament was upset with Danby for "blindly following the commands of a king whose policies were incongruent with the notion of 'constitutional balance.'"[10] On the same day that Charles II claimed that he had instructed Danby to write the letter, he also issued him a pardon. The question arose: could an impeachment be prevented by a pardon? For many members of Parliament, this exercise of the pardon power could not be taken lightly because they saw the impeachment process as being the only means of bringing corrupt ministers to heel. Charles did not want to lose Danby, but he also did not want to cause a civil war. Thus the king withdrew the pardon, and Danby was sentenced to the Tower of London for five years without trial.[11]

The Danby episode so influenced Parliament that in 1700 with the Act of Settlement it was declared "that no pardon under the great seal of England [shall] be pleadable to an impeachment by the Commons in Parliament."[12] The right of the king to grant pardons after sentencing was still intact, but this episode established that the pardon power could not reach cases of impeachment. The Act of Settlement exercised considerable influence on the American Framers, who embraced the concept and included it in their drafting of the pardon clause.

FRAMERS OF THE CONSTITUTION

During the colonial period, the Crown had delegated broad authority to the royal governors. For example, the Virginia Charter of 1609 granted the governor "full and absolute Power and Authority to correct, punish, pardon, govern, and rule all such the Subjects of Us, our Heires, and Successors as shall from Time to Time adventure themselves into the colony." Over time, the various charters changed, from the Virginia Charter to the Charter of New England and the charter of the Massachusetts Bay Company, but the power to grant pardons remained in the royal governors of the colonies. Around 1635 this changed, and under Governor John Winthrop of the Massachusetts Bay Company, the General Court was granted the exclusive power to issue pardons. At this juncture, the governor enjoyed only the power to grant reprieves until the next quarter of the General Court, but even though he could still grant reprieves, he could not do so without the consent of the deputy governor or any of his three assistants.[13]

During the Revolutionary War period, almost every state constitution made some mention of the pardon power. For example, the Georgia Constitution of 1777 strictly forbade the governor from issuing pardons. The Massachusetts Constitution of 1780 permitted pardons only after conviction. The Pennsylvania Constitution of 1776 and the New York Constitution of 1777 did not permit pardons in cases of treason and murder. The New Hampshire Constitution of 1784 gave the pardoning power to the legislature.[14] The limited scope of the pardon authority in these new state constitutions obviously reflected the founders' concerns about executive abuse of power, a natural inclination, considering their recent difficulties with the British king.

These concerns and suspicions shadowed the Framers' debate on the pardon power. Neither the Virginia nor the New Jersey Plan mentioned the pardon power, but Charles Pinckney of South Carolina introduced a proposal that the executive "shall have power to grant pardons and reprieves except in impeachments."[15] Pinckney's proposal was similar to the English Act of Settlement of 1700, which vested the pardoning power in the executive, except in cases of impeachment. A rather limited debate ensued before the convention embraced a presidential pardon power. Edmund Randolph thought the pardon power was too great to be vested in one man and moved to insert "except cases of treason." He argued that the power to pardon, "in these cases was too great a trust. The President may himself be guilty. The Traytors may be his own intruments." James Wilson did not agree, stating, "Pardon is necessary for cases of treason, and is best placed in the hands of the Executive. If he be himself a party to the guilt he can be impeached and prosecuted." Some members thought the power should be vested in the legislature, but that argument was countered by Rufus King, who stated that "a Legislative body is utterly unfit for the purpose. They are governed too much by the passion of the moment." He then invoked the mixed reaction to Shays's Rebellion by members of the Massachusetts Assembly, of which he said, "One would have hung all the insurgents in that State: the next was equally disposed to pardon them all."[16]

Although the decision to include treason in the power to pardon was a difficult one, Alexander Hamilton provided some measure of assurance. In *Federalist* no. 74 he explained that the principal reason for including treason was to give the president the power to halt rebellions: "In seasons of insurrection or rebellion, there are often critical moments, when a well-timed offer of pardon to the insurgents or rebels may restore the tranquility of the commonwealth; and which, if suffered to pass unimproved, it may never be possible afterwards to recall."[17] The Framers believed such inclusion would make it possible to end rebellions and to prevent the outbreak of civil war. Even with these convincing arguments, it is difficult to understand why the Framers would give one man so much power, given their fear of the potential for abuse of the power. According to David Gray Adler, three factors illuminate the Framers' decision to vest the power in the president: a timely pardon may be used to quell a rebellion, a pardon may be used to correct injustices of the criminal justice system, and the threat of impeachment and removal from office would prevent the president from abusing the power.[18]

DEFINING THE PARDON POWER

The language of the Constitution seems to leave room for interpretation in many areas, and the Article 2, section 2 provision that the president may "grant reprieves and pardons" is no exception. We often look to the courts to interpret this language and to define the president's power, including the pardon power. In 1833, in *United States v. Wilson,* Chief Justice John Marshall defined the power as an "act of grace."[19] In 1855, in *Ex parte William Wells,* the Court declared that a pardon implies "forgiveness, release, remission."[20] For a long time, mercy was seen as the principal reason for granting a pardon. But in *Biddle v. Perovich,* in 1927, the Court, according to Justice Oliver Wencell Holmes, regarded the decision to issue a pardon as "the determination of the ultimate authority that the public welfare will be better served by inflicting less than what the judgment fixed."[21]

Both rationales may be applicable in the grant of a pardon. President Gerald Ford drew upon both in the explanation of his decision to pardon Richard Nixon. Moreover, it has been established that a pardon may be "conditioned" by particular requirements or duties, so long as the conditions themselves are not unconstitutional. The pardon clause also includes amnesties and commutations. Amnesties are general pardons that are either full or conditional in nature, they may be granted by the president or by Congress to exempt from prosecution or punishment as entire class of citizens. A commutation is a reduction of judicial sentence. Thus a president may substitute a milder punishment for the one imposed by the court. For example, a president might commute a death-penalty sentence for one of life imprisonment.

Amnesties were not usually an issue of controversy prior to the Civil War. For example, in 1795 President George Washington issued a Proclamation of Amnesty to the Whiskey Rebels. President John Adams granted general amnesty to Pennsylvania insurgents in 1800, and James Madison granted a general pardon to pirates in 1815.[22] The act of treason posed a particular problem during the Civil War, for it carried the death sentence. The power to pardon in cases of treason has always been a controversial subject, and in the time of Lincoln and the Civil War, it was no different. Nevertheless, Lincoln granted amnesties to those who "participated in the existing rebellion," with the understanding that "a full pardon is hereby granted to them and each of them, with restoration of all rights of property."[23] A reprieve is a temporary postponement of a sentence that is to be handed down by the court. This is usually granted in order to give the executive branch more time to investigate the person or people involved in the request of a pardon.

PROCESS

The pardon process begins with the administration of the pardon authority, which includes the attorney general and the pardon attorney, in the Department of Justice.[24] The president looks to the attorney general for advice when deciding on executive clemency. The attorney general goes to the Office of the Pardon Attorney for information, where cases are prepared for the president to hear. In 1865 a pardon clerk was established to manage this part of the administration and requests for clemency. The pardon clerk was replaced by the pardon attorney in 1892. The current Office of the Pardon Attorney is staffed by about fourteen employees, including attorneys, paralegals, and support personnel.[25] Federal code requires the satisfaction of eligibility and requirements for petitioners of a pardon, including, usually, a five-year waiting period after an individual has served his sentence, or if he is still serving a sentence, before filing a request for a presidential pardon.[26]

There are five stages to the pardon process, each one supervised by the pardon attorney: application, investigation, preparation, consideration and action, and notification. When one requests a presidential pardon, the office of the pardon attorney goes to work investigating the request. The office receives information from the prosecuting attorney, the sentencing judge, the probation department, employers, and friends and also examines all documents.[27] The FBI usually conducts a background check on the applicant as well. With all this information the pardon attorney can make a recommendation to the attorney general, who in turn makes a recommendation to the president. It is noteworthy that not all presidents follow the code or the process all the time. It is up to the president to determine when, and to whom, he wants to grant a pardon. However, this process is typically followed. Approximately 74,000 pardon and commutation requests have been processed by the Office of the Pardon Attorney since 1900, and 20,000 of those requests have been granted.[28]

HISTORICAL PRACTICE

Pardons have been granted since the early years of George Washington's administration to, among others, participants in the Whiskey Rebellion, pirates, convicted federal officials, confederate soldiers, and polygamists.[29] Presidents have issued pardons for numerous reasons, including political factors, policy concerns, and principles of justice.

Wars have provided a basis for the frequent exercise of the pardon power. Some 200,000 people were the beneficiaries of amnesty programs under Abraham Lincoln and Andrew Johnson. President Franklin Roosevelt restored the rights of about 1,500 people who had already served their time in prison for violating the Espionage Acts during World War I. There were 10,000 beneficiaries of the clemency and amnesty programs of Presidents Ford and Carter after the Vietnam War.[30]

The pursuit of justice perhaps best explains President Warren G. Harding's pardon of Eugene Debs, a prominent labor organizer and socialist. Along with those of twenty-four other political prisoners, Debs's sentence was commuted in 1921. President Truman granted pardons in 1946 to at least 1,500 people who had violated the Selective Service Act, and he also restored civil rights in 1952 to more than 9,000 people who had deserted during peacetime. In 1971 President Nixon commuted the sentence of labor leader James Hoffa, an act quite controversial at the time.[31] More recently President Clinton pardoned tax dodgers, a man convicted of mail fraud, and various military convicts, among others.[32]

CONTROVERSIAL EXAMPLES

Few pardons attract media attention, but those that do usually carry political baggage. For example, President Ford's pardon of Richard Nixon in 1974 provoked a storm of controversy, and it elicited tales of a possible conspiracy between Nixon and Ford. It had been alleged that Ford was chosen to be vice president because Nixon could rely on him for a pardon. Did Nixon and Ford have a pre-resignation deal worked out? Ford and other principal members of the administration denied the existence of a deal, and no evidence has surfaced to prove such an arrangement. However, as Nixon's resignation approached, some observers feared a pardon might be in the works.[33]

After Nixon's resignation there was a great deal of discussion concerning a pardon by President Ford. Some individuals, such as the special prosecutor, were still building a case against Nixon, but others suggested a pardon or immunity. A Gallup poll conducted between August 16 and 19, 1974, revealed that 56 percent of the public favored a criminal trial for Nixon.[34] However, others thought Nixon had already paid a heavy price by resigning. On September 8, 1974, President Ford made official and public his decision to grant Nixon a pardon. In defense of his decision, Ford offered several reasons, which included the assertion that the former president would not get a fair trial and the contention that the lengthy and drawn-out process would disrupt the nation's tranquillity. Therefore, President Ford granted Richard Nixon "a full, free, and absolute pardon, . . . for all offenses against the United States, . . . that he, has committed, or may have committed or taken part in during the period from January 20, 1969 through August 9, 1974."[35] In the aftermath of the Nixon pardon the White House received 270,000 written communications; almost all of them condemned the pardon. A week after the pardon was issued President Ford's Gallup poll approval rating was only 49 percent, and it was to sink even lower.[36]

The exercise of the pardon power excited further controversy on December 24, 1992, when important figures in the Iran-Contra Affair were pardoned by President George H. W. Bush, who had served as vice president under President Reagan when news of the scandal broke. The Iran-Contra scandal began after it became public that high-level government officials who were close to Ronald Reagan had sold arms to Iran, a nation the United States acknowledged had been sponsoring international terrorism, in an arms-for-hostages deal. Profits from the arms sales went to fund the Contras in Nicaragua, an act made illegal by the Boland amendments. In the Iran portion of the scandal, the president ignored advice from his top advisers against such an action as well as his own stated foreign policy when he decided to negotiate with the terrorists. Reagan decided to sell arms to Iran, which was at war with Iraq, and in turn the Iranians, he thought, would persuade the kidnappers to release American hostages. Weapons were transported through Israel from their own supply, with the promise from the United States that the Israelis' weapons would be replaced. Not only was Reagan violating his own stated foreign policy, but he was also violating the Arms Export Control Act, which prohibits transport of weapons to another country without giving Congress notification. Soon after this, the CIA started selling weapons directly to Iran, and by inflating the prices, diverted the extra money to fund the Contras in Nicaragua. In 1986 a Lebanese magazine article was published that exposed this project, and the secret dealings were blown wide open. After this initial discovery, those involved continued to deceive Congress and the American public about what really had occurred at the highest levels of government.[37]

This scandal led to an investigation by an independent counsel, Lawrence E. Walsh. In March 1988, Iran-Contra principals Oliver North, John Poindexter, Richard Secord, and Albert Hakim were indicted by a grand jury. In the same month, Robert McFarlane pleaded guilty to four misdemeanor counts of withholding information from Congress.[38] Other Iran-Contra participants were convicted, including Elliott Abrams, Alan Fiers, and Clair George for withholding information from Congress. When Bush decided to pardon former secretary of defense Caspar Weinberger and Duane Clarridge, they had not yet been tried. At this time he also decided to grant commutations to Abrams, Fiers, George, and McFarlane. The immediate impact of President Bush's announcement on Christmas Eve of his decision to grant clemency was muted by the holiday. Moreover, his lame-duck status as president protected him from the wrath of public opinion. Bush said that Weinberger was "a true patriot, who had rendered long and extraordinary service," and, he continued, "I am pardoning him not just out of compassion or to spare a seventy-five-year-old patriot the torment of a lengthy and costly legal proceeding, but to make it possible for him to receive the honor he deserved." Bush offered a broad rationale for the acts of clemency: "Now the Cold War is over. When earlier wars have ended, presidents have historically used their power to pardon, to put bitterness behind us and look to the future." And thus President Bush issued pardons to men he believed to be American patriots but who might also have implicated Bush in criminal wrongdoing.[39]

Although there were some supporters, including Senate Majority Leader Bob Dole, who hailed the pardon as "a Christmas Eve act of courage and compassion," there was also considerable opposition to Bush's actions.[40] In the *National Law Journal,* James Brosnahan outlined ten reasons why the Bush pardon was harmful to the country. First, the president had a direct conflict of interest because he was personally involved in the Iran-Contra cover-up, and his action only heightened suspicions that he was more involved than he had stated. Second, the pardon was granted before trial, and by preventing it President Bush blocked an investigative resolution of the scandal. Third, the president pardoned people who had lied to Congress, which sent the wrong message to everybody. Fourth, Brosnahan believed Iran-Contra involved constitutional violations, and therefore those involved should not have been pardoned. Fifth, it was asserted that President Bush did not follow the procedures that were supposed to be followed when deciding on a pardon. Sixth, the pardon sent an elitist message to the American public, saying that the most powerful will not be punished no matter what crimes they commit. Seventh, the pardon set a poor precedent for future cover-ups in government. Eighth, it undermined the work of the independent counsel by shutting down the Weinberger trial. Ninth, some individuals such as Bob Dole attacked the independent counsel and blamed the prosecutor for being too zealous. Finally, President Bush left the office of the president under the cloud of the unresolved scandal.[41]

CLINTON'S USE OF THE PARDON POWER

President Clinton's exercise of the pardon power generally rivaled the controversy that surrounded Ford's pardon of Nixon and Bush's pardon of six Iran-Contra figures. One of his more controversial and early uses of it occurred in 1999 when he granted clemency to sixteen members of the Armed Forces of National Liberation (FALN), a Puerto Rican liberation organization implicated in acts of terrorism. They had been convicted of seditious conspiracy for planting more than 100 bombs in restaurants and shopping malls. Some seventy persons were injured and six were killed. Clinton's exercise of the pardon power, as with Ford's pardon of Nixon and Bush's pardon of the six Iran-Contra figures, circumvented the Justice Department's regulations and procedures in the clemency process. One who seeks a presidential pardon "shall execute a formal petition."[42] In fact, FALN members submitted no petition for clemency. Moreover, it is provided that the pardon attorney in the Justice Department "shall exercise such discretion and authority as is appropriate and necessary for the handling and transmittal of such recommendations to the President."[43] Other regulations provide that the attorney general "shall review each petition and all pertinent information developed by the investigation and shall determine whether the request for clemency is of sufficient merit to warrant favorable action by the president." Further, the attorney general "shall report in writing his or her recommendations to the president, stating whether in his or her judgement the president should grant or deny the petition."[44] These procedures were ignored by the White House. There was no formal review by the pardon attorney, the deputy attorney general, or the attorney general. Clinton did not request FBI background checks. Indeed, the FBI was on record as opposing a pardon for FALN members. The pardon power clearly belongs to the president alone, but the Justice Department's procedures serve the purpose of protecting the president from granting pardons without the benefit of accurate and adequate information. The pardons were met with a chorus of protests from members of Congress and the public. Some observers believed the pardons were politically motivated and calculated to promote the candidacy of Hillary Clinton, who was seeking a U.S. Senate seat in New York. Given these circumstances, it is hard to believe that politics did not play a prominent role in the president's decision. But even under such suspicious circumstances, Clinton felt free to engage in highly questionable acts without fear of political retribution. So widely accepted is the president's unilateral pardon power that even in highly politicized cases such as the Ford pardon of Nixon, the Bush pardon of Weinberger, or the Clinton pardon of the FALN members presidents feel immune from criticism or punishment.

Another Clinton pardon that gained media attention was his February 21, 2000, pardon of the political scientist Preston King, who went into self-imposed exile nearly forty years ago "after his draft board in Georgia, learning that he was black, refused to address him as 'mister.'" Clinton's pardon of King, a professor at the University of Lancaster in England, overturned a 1961 conviction for draft evasion.[45] This act of clemency met only mild criticism. Ironically, a *Washington Post* editorial of December 27, 1999, accused Clinton of "under-utilizing the pardon authority. It was contended that "given the desultory use of this constitutional power . . . there seems to be no danger" that Clinton or his immediate predecessors have been excessive in issuing pardons. Indeed, "The danger . . . is that a valuable check on the justice system has wilted into symbolism."

As is the presidential custom, President Clinton issued a number of eleventh-hour pardons before leaving office. Pardons were granted to Patricia Hearst, the heiress kidnapped in 1970 who was later a party to a bank robbery; to Roger Clinton, the president's half-brother, convicted of drug charges; to Susan McDougal, who spent eighteen months in jail for refusing to testify against the Clintons in the Whitewater investigation; to former housing secretary Henry Cisneros, who lied to the FBI; to John Deutch, the former CIA director, who was under investigation for mishandling classified information; and to Arizona governor Fife Symington. Not pardoned, in spite of heavy lobbying and much speculation, were Michael Milken, the convicted financier; the convicted spy Jonathan Pollard; the Native-American political activist, Leonard Peltier; and a former law partner of Hillary Clinton, Webster Hubbell. At the last minute, Clinton issued 456 pardons, about as many as Ronald Reagan issued in his eight years in office. Herbert Hoover, in just four years, granted nearly 1,400 pardons. In roughly two years, Gerald Ford issued 409 pardons and commutations, and President Carter issued 566 in four years; George Bush issued only 77. Franklin Roosevelt, in over twelve years in office, granted 3,687 pardons.

One of the more controversial of the eleventh-hour pardons was made on behalf of the white-collar fugitive Mark Rich. Charged with an illegal oil-pricing scheme, Rich hid in Switzerland to avoid U.S. prosecution. Rich's former wife, a prominent Democratic fund-raiser, along with other well-known Democrats and officials from the Israeli government, lobbied Clinton, who, in granting the Rich pardon, circumvented the normal Justice Department procedures. Many Democrats and Republicans were dismayed by his action. The Rich pardon, and several others, attracted a tremendous amount of attention and criticism. A political firestorm broke out as questions of trading pardons for favors and contributions were raised. When it was revealed that roughly one in three of the eleventh-hour pardons did not follow Justice Department procedures, further suspicions were raised. And it only went from bad to worse when news surfaced that the president's brother-in-law, Hugh Rodham, had accepted nearly $400,000 to plead the cases of Glen Braswell and of a man convicted of drug dealing.

Republicans immediately smelled blood and went on the attack. House Government Reform Committee chair (and long-time Clinton hater) Dan Burton (R-Ind.) began hearings and investigations. The Justice Department designated a special team of prosecutors to investigate the pardons. And Attorney General John Ashcroft empowered U.S. Attorney Mary Jo White of New York with broad powers to investigate all the Clinton pardons and commutations and assured her nearly limitless subpoena power.

These challenges to Clinton's (and to the president's) pardon power were both politically motivated (the Republicans seem intent on "getting" Clinton, even in his retirement) and driven by a real sense of moral outrage over the ethical questions raised by this scandal. It was typically Clintonian in scope: he pushed the envelope of propriety and may have engaged in unethical behavior, and his critics overreacted and pounced even before the facts were in. The problem with these investigations is that it is exceedingly difficult to convict in cases involving alleged bribery or violations of federal gratuity statutes. Added to this hurdle is the presumption that a president can give a pardon to just about anyone for just about any reason. Much ado about nothing? Perhaps.

President Clinton is by no means alone in issuing questionable pardons. From Nixon's pardon of Jimmy Hoffa, to Ford's pardon of Nixon, to Reagan's pardon of George Steinbrenner, to Bush's pardon of Caspar Weinberger and others such as Aslam Adam (serving a fifty-five-year sentence for heroin trafficking), each one could have raised significant political and perhaps legal problems. So why the outcry against Clinton?

Apparently there are several reasons why the Clinton pardons caused such an outcry. Many of the pardons did raise legitimate questions of propriety. Further, Clinton, given his past activities, invites cynicism. Moreover, his political enemies seem never to tire of trying to destroy him. Such reasons produce a volatile combination of combustible components.

The attacks on Clinton reached such a fever pitch that in a February 18, 2001, *New York Times* editorial, the former president defended his pardons to a skeptical public. After explaining that Article 2 of the Constitution granted "the president broad and unreviewable power to grant" pardons, and after arguing that the pardon power is "granted without limit," Clinton insisted that he believed his decision "was in the best interests of justice" and that any suggestions that the pardons were granted in exchange for favors or contributions were "utterly false. There was absolutely no quid pro quo."

But the attacks and investigations continued, even intensified. Republicans in Congress sought ways to punish Clinton. Recognizing that indeed there was little they could do about the pardons themselves—except embarrass the former president—they explored ways either to punish him, by reducing his government pension, or even, as Senator Arlen Spector (R-Pa.), a senior member of the Judiciary Committee, suggested, to "reimpeach" him (a suggestion of dubious credibility, at best). Other Republican legislators attempted to push for a constitutional amendment to limit the president's pardoning power.

The Framers of the Constitution vested this powerful tool, the pardon power, solely in the executive because they believed that in some situations it not only could prevent rebellions and civil war but also could intervene when justice or the public welfare required it. Though good may come from the exercise of clemency, there is also the danger of abuse. Yet the Framers were confident that the impeachment exception would deter any president from using the pardon power in a corrupt manner. In general, presidents have exercised it quite judiciously. Yet several controversial pardons—especially the Bush pardon of Caspar Weinberger—raise unsettling questions about the potential abuse of this power and suggest the need for reform. To anyone serious about reforming the pardoning power, the starting point remains Senator Walter Mondale's 1974 proposal: "No pardon granted to an individual by the President under Section 2 Article II shall be effective if Congress by resolution, two-thirds of the members of each House concurring therein; disapproves the granting of the pardon within 180 days of its issue."[46] Mondale's proposal could go far in affording the nation meaningful protection against a presidential abuse of the pardon power. While such a congressional veto would be seldom utilized, perhaps its availability alone would serve to deter executives from granting pardons under suspicious circumstances.

Although underused in recent years, the power to grant pardons remains a well-established and (surprisingly) independent power of the president. On rare occasions, presidential pardons grab the headlines and spark debates. Clinton's controversial exercise of the clemency authority was not the first. President Bush's eleventh-hour pardon of Weinberger effectively ended the Iran-Contra investigations and may have protected Bush from criminal charges. President Ford's pardon of Richard Nixon saved the former president from possible criminal indictments and diminished Ford in the eyes of the public.

The Framers of the Constitution relied heavily on English law and tradition, as well as on the royal pardoning power, in devising the pardon power for the newly invented American presidency. The Framers institutionalized an impeachment exception, but they otherwise gave the president virtually unlimited powers to grant pardons. True, this power has on occasion been abused, but there have been no serious challenges to this presidential power; and today, presidents maintain nearly limitless power to grant pardons.

NOTES

1. See, generally, Michael A. Genovese, *The Presidential Dilemma* (New York: Harper Collins, 1995).

2. See the discussion in Thomas E. Cronin and Michael A. Genovese, *The Paradoxes of the American Presidency* (New York: Oxford University Press, 1998).

3. Quoted in David Gray Adler, "Pardon Power," in *Encyclopedia of the American Presidency*, ed. Leonard W. Levy and Louis Fisher, 4 vols (New York: Simon and Schuster, 1944), 3: 1145.

4. Quoted in William F. Duker, "The President's Power to Pardon: A Constitutional History," *William and Mary Law Review* 18 (1977): 476.

5. Ibid., p. 478.

6. Adler, "Pardon Power," p. 1145.

7. Duker, "President's Power," p. 479.

8. David Gray Adler, "The President's Pardon Power," in *Inventing the American Presidency*, ed. Thomas E. Cronin (Lawrence: University Press of Kansas, 1989), p. 213.

9. Duker, "President's Power," p. 488.

10. Ibid.

11. Adler, "President's Pardon," p. 214.

12. Quoted in ibid.

13. Duker, "President's Power," p. 498.

14. Adler, "President's Pardon," p. 215.

15. Ibid., p. 215.

16. James Madison, *Notes of Debates in the Federal Convention of 1787*, ed. Adrienne Koch (New York: W. W. Norton, 1987), p. 646.

17. Hamilton, *Federalist* no. 74, in Alexander Hamilton, James Madison, and John Jay, *The Federalist,* ed. Edward M. Earle (New York: Modern Library, 1937), p. 483.

18. Adler, "President's Pardon," p. 217.

19. 7 Pet. 150, 161 (1833).

20. 59 U.S. 307, 311 (1855).

21. 274 U.S. 480, 486 (1927).

22. Duker, "Presidents's Power," p. 516.

23. Ibid., p. 511.

24. Adler, "President's Pardon," p. 212.

25. Jody C. Baumgartner and Mark H. Morris, "Presidential Power Unbound: A Comparative Look at Presidential Pardon Power," paper, Annual Meeting of the Western Political Science Association, Seattle, Washington, March 25–27, 1999, pp. 5–6.

26. Congressman Curt Weldon, House, "President Continues Pardon Polka," Congressional Press Release, Tuesday, October 8, 1996, p. 1.

27. Adler, "President's Pardon," p. 212.

28. Baumgartner and Morris, "Presidential Power Unbound," p. 6.

29. Adler, "President's Pardon," p. 218.

30. Ibid., pp. 218–220.

31. Ibid., p. 226.

32. Kalpana Srinivasan, "On Christmas Eve Clinton Gives Pardons to 33 Criminals," *Nando Media, <www.nandotimes.com>* December 1998, p. 1.

33. Stanley Kutler, *The Wars of Watergate* (New York: Knopf, 1990), pp. 555, 541.

34. Ibid., pp. 557, 558.

35. Arthur M. Schlessinger Jr., Introduction, in *The Growth of Presidential Power: A Documented History,* vol. 3, *Triumph and Reappraisal,* ed. William M. Goldsmith (New York: Chelsea House, 1974), p. 2279.

36. Kutler, *The Wars,* pp. 564, 566.

37. Lawrence E. Walsh, *Firewall: The Iran-Contra Conspiracy and Cover-up* (New York, London: W. W. Norton, 1997), p. xiv.

38. See the discussion in William S. Cohen and George J. Mitchell, *Men of Zeal: A Candid Inside Story of the Iran-Contra Hearings* (New York: Penguin Group, 1989), pp. 295, 296.

39. Walsh, *Firewall,* pp. 494–496.

40. Quoted in ibid., p. 497.

41. James J. Brosnahan, "Pardoning Weinberger Belittles Democracy," *National Law Journal* 18 (January 1993): 17.

42. 28 C.F.R. sec. 1.1 (July 1, 1999).

43. Ibid., at sec. 0.36.

44. Ibid., at sec. 1.6(b).

45. Phillip Shenon, "Pardon Lets Black Exile Come Home," *New York Times,* February 21, 2000, p. A12.

46. Quoted in Adler, "President's Pardon," p. 230.

5

The Independent Counsel
and the Post-Clinton Presidency

Robert J. Spitzer

The link between law and politics is close and almost always closer than those who study the law claim. The brief and turbulent history of the independent counsel law, and its relationship to the presidency, is surely an exemplar of intertwining law and politics. The independent counsel law was the product of a specific political event, Watergate. Independent counsel prosecutions have issued forth in accordance with the terms of the enabling legislation. Yet these prosecutions have always contained, and have operated within, political context.

I shall examine here the politics of the independent counsel law and the law of independent counsel politics, as these have climaxed during the Clinton presidency, in order to understand what this means for the presidency after Clinton. The former refers to the escalating political storm surrounding independent counsel actions; the latter refers to the meaning of this politics. The narrow constitutional question concerning the legality of the independent counsel law was settled by the Supreme Court in 1988, when it upheld the law in a seven to one decision. The growing chorus of the law's critics have extolled Justice Antonin Scalia's lone dissent in this case with ever greater fervor, but that does nothing to alter the Court's emphatic pronouncement.

For all the abundant debate over the independent counsel's constitutional and legal status, and how it might be altered or amended,[1] the legal questions explain relatively little about the law's rocky history. Therefore, the main focus here will be on the politics that have arisen from and swirled around the law. I first consider the background of the independent counsel law, then its actual operation since its enactment in 1978. These investigations cannot be separated from an essentially unexamined feature of the office of the presidency: its susceptibility to scandal. I argue here that this trend has largely escaped notice by students of the presidency because of two traits: the compartmentalization of scandal and the veneration of the presidency. The partisan cloud that has overshadowed independent counsel investigations is examined closely, primarily that surrounding the Kenneth Starr investigation of the Clinton administration, as this was key to the statute's lapse without renewal in 1999. The heightened partisanship of the Starr inquiry had the unintentional effect of solidifying bipartisan opposition to renewal of the independent counsel law. The continued need for some kind of independent prosecuting office is supported by the precarious political position of the attorney general. The structural, as opposed to political, feasibility of independent counsel renewal is recognized by the various reform proposals that have been discussed in the press and elsewhere.

BACKGROUND

The independent counsel (IC) law was first enacted in 1978 as Title VI of the Ethics in Government Act (28 U.S.C. sec. 591–599) and renewed by Congress in 1982, 1987, and, after a two-year lapse, again in 1994. On June 30, 1999, the law again lapsed, with little prospect that it will be revived any time in the near future and certainly not in its preexisting form.

The IC law arose from the ashes of the Watergate scandal. In brief, the act, as amended, allowed the attorney general to request a special division of the Court of Appeals for the District of Columbia (the membership of this three-judge panel is appointed by the chief justice of the Supreme Court) to appoint an IC if the attorney general believed that "specific and credible" evidence of wrongdoing involving senior members of the executive branch required such a step. Such a recommendation followed a 90-to-120 day review of evidence and allegations by the attorney general. The IC's jurisdiction, including subsequent requests to alter the scope of an ongoing investigation, was determined by the attorney general and the judicial panel.[2] For example, during Kenneth Starr's investigation into Whitewater, Starr obtained permission from Attorney General Janet Reno to expand the scope of the investigation from Whitewater and the Madison Guaranty Savings and Loan to include the Monica Lewinsky matter. This was done with a favorable recommendation from Reno transmitted to the three-judge panel, which also approved the expansion of the investigation.[3] The IC was to operate in compliance with Justice Department regulations and guidelines, with spending audited by the General Accounting Office. Further, the IC served until the investigation was completed. Aside from impeachment, the IC could be removed only by the attorney general, for cause. Congress could also summon the IC for questioning in a public hearing to question conduct.[4]

The IC law was enacted in order to address a relatively simple, if intractable, constitutional/legal problem and a more complex political problem. While "special prosecutors" had been employed to investigate such executive branch misdeeds as the Teapot Dome scandal of the Harding administration,[5] a tax scandal during the Truman administration,[6] and Watergate, they reported directly to the attorney general. The constitutional/legal problem was to provide a formal, independent, and impartial mechanism for investigations of alleged wrongdoing among high executive branch officers (about seventy-five in all), including the president, cabinet secretary–level positions, or top Justice Department officials, any of whom might face conflict of interest problems if charged with violations of federal criminal law. The existing constitutional remedy for executive misdeeds, impeachment, was viewed as too blunt and cumbersome a mechanism to deal with the full range of possible executive misbehaviors, a conclusion reflected in the fact that only one cabinet secretary has ever been impeached (Secretary of War William W. Belknap in 1876; he was acquitted). Most observers agree that impeachment is "to be exercised with extreme caution," in "extreme cases."[7] Looming questions concerning the constitutionality of the IC statute were resolved in 1988, in *Morrison v. Olson,* when the Supreme Court upheld the law's constitutionality.[8]

The political problem giving rise to the IC law was twofold. First, the government faced a crisis of public confidence after Watergate, and the independent counsel mechanism provided a political salve to heal the wound left by that scandal. The second, more specific political problem centered on the key law enforcement official of the executive branch, the attorney general. By long tradition, presidents have appointed close political associates to this sensitive position, making the post the one most likely to be occupied by a partisan politico and presidential confidant, next to the now-defunct office of postmaster general.[9] "By the early 1970s the designation of a leading campaign official as attorney general had become a standard feature of the twentieth century presidency."[10]

Thus, for example, Warren G. Harding's attorney general (AG) was Harding campaign manager Harry Daugherty; Franklin D. Roosevelt's first AG was Democratic National Chairman Homer Cummings; Harry Truman's was Democratic National Chairman J. Howard McGrath; Dwight D. Eisenhower's was former Republican National Chairman and campaign manager Herbert Brownell; John F. Kennedy's AG was his campaign manager and brother Robert Kennedy; Nixon's AG was his campaign manager and law partner John Mitchell, followed by the longtime Republican Party activist Richard Kleindienst; Carter's AG, Griffin Bell, was a longtime political supporter, adviser, and friend from Georgia; Reagan's first AG was his personal lawyer, William French Smith, followed by his campaign strategist, Edwin Meese. Under these circumstances, it is all but inevitable that investigations of executive branch wrongdoing may be compromised in the public mind, if not in fact. In the notable case of Watergate, the initial investigation conducted first by Attorney General John Mitchell was indeed a sham, as was that of his successor, Richard Kleindienst.[11]

Recent presidents not listed here, including Johnson, Ford, Bush, and Clinton, do share credit for seeking AGs with fewer or no political ties to the president. Nevertheless, the political tradition and its temptations remain. This point aside, heated charges of politically motivated AG decisions persist, regardless of the AG's background, as the case of Janet Reno illustrates.

As a Florida prosecutor with no prior connections to Clinton, Reno was the paradigm of an independent AG appointment. By all accounts, Reno and Clinton have never had a close relationship, and many of her actions and decisions have angered the White House, from her acceptance of blame for the 1993 Waco incident to her several IC recommendations. Indeed, Clinton wanted her to resign after the 1996 elections. That Clinton did not fire her after she failed to do so reflected the administration's fear that forcing her out would be politically risky for the administration.[12] It was thus even more ironic when Reno was accused of seeking to protect Clinton when she decided in 1997 against recommending an IC to investigate fund-raising phone calls made by Clinton and Vice President Al Gore. Republican House Judiciary Committee Chair Henry Hyde (Ill.) accused Reno of "circling the wagons around the President," and Republican Senator Fred Thompson (Tenn.) said that Reno was using the IC law "as a shield to prevent investigations."[13] Reno's independent political credentials and actions failed to insulate her from the usual charges of partisanship.

THE IC IN OPERATION

Once enacted, the IC provision has been applied with regularity and increasing vigor. From 1978 to 2000, twenty-one ICs (actually, twenty-five prosecutors working on twenty-two cases) have been appointed to investigate charges of wrongdoing in the Carter (two), Reagan (seven), Bush (four), and Clinton (seven) administrations (see Table 5.1). Independent Counsel John C. Danforth, who investigated the 1993 government raid on the Branch Davidian compound in Waco, Texas, was appointed after the IC law had expired. Spending for these investigations has increased dramatically. Of the first ten ICs, only four spent over $1 million; of the second ten, nine spent over $1 million.

The persistent and central controversy concerning the IC has been political. Every IC appointment has been accompanied in varying degrees by charges of political or partisan inspiration or manipulation. On the other hand, critics have also charged that ICs are inadequately controlled. Since no preset spending or time limits are imposed, investigations often span years, running to tens of millions of dollars, although it is important to note that eleven of the twenty investigations listed in Table 5.1 resulted in no charges. Larger and lengthier investigations are, to some observers, little more than prosecutorial fishing expeditions. The accountability–independence problem has hung like a cloud over ICs and has therefore been a central issue concerning possible revival of the IC law. Like gasoline on fire, these allegations have accelerated because of the Kenneth Starr investigation of Bill Clinton. Before discussing the Clinton case, and its consequences for the presidency after Clinton, we need to consider more closely the institutional quandary behind the IC—the nature of presidential scandal.

Table 5.1. Independent Counsel Investigations, 1978–2000

President, Independent Prosecutor	Subject of Investigation, Charges	Results	Cost
Carter			
1. Arthur H. Christy (1979)	Hamilton Jordan (cocaine use)	no charges	$182,000
2. Gerald Gallinghouse (1980)	Tim Kraft (cocaine use)	no charges	$3,300
Reagan			
3. Leon Silverman (1981)	Ray Donovan (bribery, perjury)	no charges	$326,000
4. Jacob Stein (1984)	Edwin Meese (financial improprieties)	no charges	$312,000
5. Alexia Morrison (1986)	Theodore Olson (perjury)	no charges	$1.5 million
6. Whitney N. Seymour (1986)	Michael Deaver (perjury)	convicted	$1.5 million
7. Lawrence Walsh (1986)	Iran-Contra arms deals	7 guilty pleas, 4 convictions, 6 presidential pardons	$47.9 million
8. James McKay (1987)	Lyn Nofziger, Edwin Meese (conflict of interest)	Nofziger, conviction over-turned; Meese, no charges	$2.8 million
9. Carl Rauh, James Harper (1987)	W. Lawrence Wallace (finances)	no charges	$50,000
Bush			
10. sealed (1989)	confidential	confidential	$15,000
11. Arlin Adams (1990); Larry Thompson (1995)	Samuel Pierce et al. (defraud United States)	16 convictions	$25.8 million*
12. sealed (1991)	confidential	no charges	$93,000
13. Joseph diGenova (1992)	Janet Mullins, Margaret Tutwiler (State Dept. passport file search)	no charges	$2.8 million
Clinton			
14. Robert Fiske (1994)	Clinton (Whitewater)	3 plea agreements	$6.1 million
15. Kenneth Starr (1994)	Clinton (Whitewater, White House Travel, Vince Foster, Monica Lewinsky)	3 convictions, 6 pleas, 2 acquittals	$50 million*
16. Robert Ray (1999)	Monica Lewinsky	no charges	
17. Donald Smaltz (1994)	Michael Espy (bribery)	1 conviction, 1 guilty plea	$23 million*

Table 5.1. *Continued*

President, Independent Prosecutor	Subject of Investigation, Charges	Results	Cost
Clinton, *continued*			
18. David Barrett (1995)	Henry Cisneros (lying in background check)	guilty plea	$10 million*
19. Daniel Pearson (1995)	Ron Brown (financial improprieties)	ended after Brown's death	$3.3 million*
20. Curtis von Kann (1996)	Eli Segal (conflict of interest)	no charges	$244,822*
21. Carol Bruce (1998)	Bruce Babbitt (lying to Congress)	no charges	$3.9 million*
22. Ralph Lancaster (1998)	Alexis Herman (influence peddling)	ongoing	$1.4 million*

Sources: "Special Prosecutor Investigations," *National Journal,* February 1, 1997, p. 218; "Ex-Special Counsels Would Overhaul Law," *New York Times,* August 11, 1998; "Independent Counsels at a Glance," *Washington Post,* October 14, 1999.
*These investigations still reported expenditures as of September 30, 1999, to the General Accounting Office: "Independent Counsel Expenditures for the Six Months Ended September 30, 1999, GAO, March 2000, AIMD-00-120.

WHY AN INDEPENDENT COUNSEL?

When one considers the prolific history of executive wrongdoing, it is more than a little surprising that no similar, special office was created long before 1978. From George Washington's presidency, when Attorney General Edmund Randolph was accused of treason and bribery,[14] to Bill Clinton and the Monica Lewinsky matter, scandal has been a nearly inextricable component of the presidency.[15] Clearly, not all presidential activities that fall under the rubric of scandal warrant criminal investigation. For example, the fact that Grover Cleveland fostered an illegitimate child amounted to a scandal of considerable proportions, but it did not necessitate prosecutorial action then, any more than it would now. Further, many executive branch actions fall within a large gray area where the law, or precedent, provide no clear guidance as to legality or even propriety. Our concern is with the subset of presidential and executive branch criminal misdeeds of the sort that the independent counsel law was designed to investigate. Even by this narrower standard of presidential scandal, few presidential administrations have concluded without having been tarred by some kind of scandal. That most people do not think of the presidency as a scandal-plagued institution is attributable to two factors: the compartmentalization of scandal and the veneration of the presidency.

The Compartmentalization of Scandal

The onus of scandal is closely associated with the presidential administrations most riddled with, and scrutinized for, scandal: Ulysses S. Grant, Warren G. Harding, and Richard Nixon. These presidencies came to be defined by Credit Mobilier and Belknap (Grant), Teapot Dome (Harding), and Watergate (Nixon). Other presidencies failed to be defined by scandal problems for three reasons: their scandals were of a lesser nature, they did not touch the president directly, and these presidencies were defined in the eyes of history by other, affirmative accomplishments. Harry Truman's administration illustrates these factors.

Although Truman was considered personally and scrupulously honest throughout his presidency, his administration was plagued by financial conflicts of interest, improper gift giving, and influence peddling. This extensive graft reached from the White House staff to entire executive departments.[16] Truman himself bore at least partial responsibility because many of his appointees were inexperienced or unqualified personal friends, considered "banal and second-rate."[17] The problem was compounded by Truman's dogged, unquestioning loyalty to these friends. As one historian has noted, "Truman found it hard to censure friends and harder still to break with them."[18] These events undoubtedly contributed to his plummeting popularity and therefore to the ending of his presidency, and to the elevation of corruption as a primary issue in the 1952 presidential elections. Dwight D. Eisenhower made cleaning up the "mess in Washington" a foundation theme of his campaign.[19] Truman concluded his presidency with a popularity rating of just over 20 percent, the lowest of any president until Nixon at the time of his resignation. Yet Truman's standing among historians and the general public has rocketed since then.[20] His rehabilitation illustrates how his personal integrity, the banal nature of the scandals of his administration, and the importance of his leadership in adjusting the country to the post–World War II, cold war era, helped eradicate the stain of scandal from history's overall evaluation.

Any detailed treatment of the Truman presidency includes coverage of administration scandals. Yet one searches writings on the presidency mostly in vain for systematic treatment of presidential scandal as it might be connected to the institution itself—a startling scholarly lapse, considering the relative commonness of presidential scandals and the almost desperate search by scholars of the presidency to uncover trends and patterns that transcend particular presidencies. An exception to this is Charles W. Dunn's recent book, *The Scarlet Thread of Scandal,* which provides a descriptive chronology of presidential scandals. This chronology, while useful, intermixes a variety of moral concerns related to the presidency, well beyond the subset of scandal problems that connect with the topic of criminal wrongdoing in the executive branch.[21]

A good example of the profession's lapse in systematic treatment of presidential scandal is the absence of encyclopedic or index references to presidential "scandal" or "corruption" in the three most significant and comprehensive reference works on the presidency published in the last ten years: the *Encyclopedia of the American Presidency*,[22] *Congressional Quarterly's Guide to the Presidency*,[23] and *Vital Statistics on the Presidency*.[24] By treating episodes of scandal as idiosyncratic, little to no attention is focused on the fact that it is a nearly ubiquitous feature of the institution. Scandal is thus "compartmentalized" within respective presidential administrations.

The Veneration of the Presidency

Despite the "shrinkage" the presidency seems to have undergone in recent years, owing to seemingly endless investigative probes, the rise of cynicism, and the escalation of partisan fury, Americans continue to venerate the institution of the presidency. Even if, as Michael Genovese has noted, recent presidents constitute "a period of failure or disappointment,"[25] the institution itself continues to be treated in hallowed, even reverential, terms. Thomas Cronin noted two decades ago that the presidency tends to be thought of as "benevolent, omnipotent, omniscient, and highly moral."[26] A revealing study of the coverage of the presidency in precollege texts by Harold Barger found that these books emphasize mythical, heroic images of the presidency and uniformly ignore scandal and corruption in the White House.[27] Even attempts by serious scholars to demythologize and inform fall into the myth trap.

A recent, archetypal case in point is the coffee-table book *The American President*.[28] Aimed at a mass audience, the book is organized thematically rather than chronologically, a bow to the scholarship of the two respected presidential scholars, Stephen Skowronek and Richard Neustadt, brought in to participate in the project by the three authors. In the foreword and the introduction, Skowronek and Neustadt seek to lay out a more analytical and probing view of the presidency. Yet despite this brief effort, the book's lapses into the rosily reverential are more than occasional. The reader encounters this almost immediately in the journalist Hugh Sidey's prefatory commentary, which expresses the hope that readers will "hear the voices and the bugle calls and the church bells, and then feel the excitement of these men calling their nation to the most magnificent efforts in war and peace that humankind has ever known."[29] The reverential all but overwhelmed the analytical in the ten-hour, multipart companion series broadcast in spring 2000 on the Public Broadcasting System. While duly noting at least some presidential scandals and misdeeds, the series was otherwise filled with worshipful commentary that is utterly typical of the institution's treatment for mass audiences. Further, presidential failings are often glossed over by the book (for example, in the case of John Tyler's habitually artless political style) or are missing entirely (for example, the chapter on Truman makes no mention whatsoever of his administration's serious scandal problems). Even more conventional scholarly efforts succumb to "our selective memories about the past glories and

victories under our favorite presidents."[30] The microscopically examined misdeeds of recent presidents, such as Reagan and Clinton, only serve to fortify the
veneration of past presidents and the institution of the presidency precisely
because these flawed recent presidencies make many people wish even more fer-
vently for the hallowed presidencies of the past. Further, this pattern of denigrat-
ing new presidents by implicit comparison to old presidents strongly suggests
that the Reagans and Clintons of today will be the object of the same penchant
for veneration fifty years hence.

Perhaps we should venerate past presidents and the institution itself. Perhaps
America and Americans need this as a kind of historical and cultural anchor. But
regardless of its rightness, a consequence of presidential veneration is a kind of
selective amnesia that minimizes and marginalizes the fact that scandal is very
much in the fabric of most presidential administrations. I do not offer this conclusion to argue somehow that the presidency is a failed or contemptible institution—far from it. It is offered, instead, to recognize that presidents are mortal
political figures who operate in a political environment no less than that of governors, mayors, and other officeholders. It is right for the country to ask the president to set a high standard for official conduct, but it is equally right to
remember what James Madison knew, expressed in *Federalist* no. 51. "In fram-
ing a government which is to be administered by men over men, the great diffi-
culty lies in this: you must first enable the government to control the governed;
and in the next place oblige it to control itself."[31] The temptations that give rise
to corruption arise inherently from the junction of money, position, and power.
The growth of executive-centered governance since the New Deal makes the
need to control executive excesses greater because the opportunities and temptations are also greater.

THE PARTISAN CLOUD

Every IC investigation, including the Watergate special prosecutor investigations, has prompted claims that the investigations were, at least to some degree,
partisan witch-hunts. Such allegations are predictable, whether true or not. Even
if true, a partisan-tinted investigation can still be fair on its merits, if the charges,
and the evidence, are persuasive. Nevertheless, fairness and the appearance of
fairness turn substantially on the sense that a case moves ahead based on its merits, not on partisanship.

Support for the IC in Congress tended to split along party lines, a fact vividly
seen in the law's lapse in 1992, when congressional Republicans succeeded in
preventing the law's renewal. Republicans were sharply critical of IC Lawrence
Walsh's lengthy and expensive investigation of the Iran-Contra scandal during
the Reagan administration, considering it a politically inspired witch-hunt. The
argument on behalf of Walsh's investigation, as seen in the misdeeds surround-

ing the Iran-Contra scandal, is indeed compelling.[32] But the size and scope of Walsh's investigation dwarfed every one preceding it, lending credence to the Republican outcry (see Table 5.1). Senate Republican Leader Bob Dole (Kans.) charged that "Mr. Walsh and his army of lawyers have destroyed reputations, harassed families and run up a tab of more than $40 million billed directly to the taxpayers."[33]

In 1994, however, bipartisan support for IC renewal was rallied because of ethics questions raised about the Clinton administration (although Clinton actively supported renewal of the law).[34] As the *Los Angeles Times* noted, "With a Democrat in the White House, leading Republicans dropped efforts to delay passage of the measure."[35] As early as 1993, Republicans were urging independent investigations of Commerce Secretary Ron Brown and of the Arkansas savings and loan failure to which the Clintons were connected.[36] Both investigations went ahead after the IC law was revived.

This partisan buzz escalated to ear-splitting levels as the result of Kenneth Starr's investigation of the Clinton administration. Two sets of partisan-related charges were leveled at the Starr investigation. First, critics charged that Starr's appointment was a mistake because of his political ties, background, and subsequent prosecutorial behavior. Second, critics charged that the three-judge panel was politically tainted and politically motivated, as seen in suspicions regarding Starr's appointment and in the three-judge panel's pattern of IC appointments.

The Tainted Prosecutor

Kenneth Starr's career was marked by close association with the Reagan and Bush administrations and with conservative political organizations squarely opposed to the Clinton administration and its policies, such as the Bradley Foundation. Starr also accepted, then rejected, an invitation to serve as dean of the Pepperdine Law School, an institution heavily financed by conservative financier Richard Mellon Scaife, who has spent millions of dollars to underwrite investigations of Clinton, including a protracted and failed effort to prove that the White House aide Vince Foster was murdered, despite repeated findings that he committed suicide.[37] Starr's experience as a member of Reagan's Justice Department, as a federal judge appointed by Reagan, and as solicitor general under Bush represented solid experience, but he had no experience as a prosecutor, and other prosecutors with similar legal experience but fewer directly partisan ties could surely have been found. Indeed, five former heads of the American Bar Association objected to the political taint surrounding Starr's appointment.[38]

Those who were suspicious of Starr's impartiality found support in some of his actions. For example, Starr persuaded Monica Lewinsky's then-friend, Linda Tripp, to wear a wire in order to obtain incriminating information from Lewinsky on tape before he had permission to expand his investigation into this area.[39] Ethical questions were also raised when Starr questioned Lewinsky without her lawyer present, even though she had already retained counsel and had requested that her lawyer be present during the questioning, and again when Starr forced Lewinsky's mother to testify.[40] In his report to Congress recommending that Clinton be impeached, Starr argued aggressively and strenuously on behalf of articles of impeachment, going beyond the simple presentation of evidence and information.[41] Nancy Kassop has identified Starr's behavior as "his political choice to become an advocate for impeachment," a decision that "was to overwhelm and swallow up the constitutional requirement of Article 1 that 'the House of Representatives shall have the sole Power of Impeachment.'"[42] Michael J. Gerhardt has referred to Starr's "aggressive efforts . . . to influence the course of the impeachment proceedings," which "undermined Starr's claims of impartiality or neutrality."[43]

While serving as IC, Starr refused to withdraw from his other professional obligations. He taught a course at New York University Law School and gave talks before groups hostile to Clinton. He continued his association with the law office of Kirkland and Ellis, arguing cases in court and representing various corporations.[44] Notably, he defended tobacco interests in court against the Clinton administration's legal action. He also advised the lawyers for Paula Jones, in connection with her private sexual harassment suit against Clinton. Both actions raised obvious conflict of interest questions.[45]

A Political Panel?

Shortly after Starr's appointment by the three-judge panel in August 1994, news stories reported that the chief judge of the panel, David Sentelle, had had lunch with North Carolina Republican senators Jesse Helms and Lauch Faircloth about a week before Starr's appointment. The three men were political and social friends; Helms and Faircloth were among Clinton's staunchest foes; and Faircloth had been highly critical of Starr's predecessor, Robert Fiske, arguing that Fiske had been insufficiently zealous in prosecuting Clinton. Sentelle himself was known for his lifelong enthusiastic partisanship, having served as a North Carolina Republican Party county chair. Critics alleged improper political meddling, and a partisan agenda on the part of Sentelle, who had been appointed to the federal bench by Reagan. After earlier denying that Starr's appointment had been discussed at the luncheon, Sentelle later admitted that Starr's possible appointment indeed had been discussed.[46] The other two judges, both retired, were Peter Fay, a Nixon appointee, and John Butzner, a Johnson appointee.

Critics further contended that other IC appointments by this panel had been more expressly partisan, including David Barrett, chosen to investigate former HUD secretary Henry G. Cisneros; Joseph diGenova, appointed to investigate the Bush administration; Donald Smaltz, chosen to investigate Agriculture Secretary Mike Espy; and Daniel Pearson, chosen to investigate Commerce Secretary Ron Brown. This point was amplified by an analysis finding that most IC appointments have been "significantly skewed" toward Republicans, perhaps because the judges who have picked ICs were themselves Republicans.[47]

The Clinton Counterattack

The numerous criticisms leveled at the Starr prosecution do not sweep away the Clinton administration's behavior. Predictably, it charged that the prosecution was part of a right-wing political vendetta, and it launched a furious political and legal counterassault. The political attacks centered on Starr's political past and the other criticisms just summarized. The legal attack centered on executive privilege and immunity claims that played themselves out in several courts. For the most part, Starr prevailed in these court challenges.[48] And though Clinton was acquitted of the two impeachment counts he faced in the Senate, most senators conceded that he indeed had erred.[49] The failure to convict, however, lay in the belief among many in Congress, and most in the country, that these misdeeds did not rise to the level of impeachment.[50]

Clinton's political counterattack only served to further delegitimize the already clouded future of the IC office. Yet it logically followed the political counterattacks of the Reagan and Bush presidencies on IC investigations of those administrations. The difference in the Clinton case was twofold: Clinton was the first Democratic president to face IC allegations, thereby solidifying bipartisan criticism of IC actions; and Starr's singularly maladroit handling of the prosecution of what was a relatively minor legal matter (perjury and obstruction of justice in a civil matter arising from embarrassing sexual behavior connected with a case that was dismissed) lent legitimacy to Clinton's countercharges.

PROSECUTORS WILL BE PROSECUTORS

Another kind of criticism of Starr's investigation arises not from politics but from the nature of the job—that is, the very nature of prosecutorial behavior in a criminal investigation and prosecution. Even prosecutors who were critical of Starr for being overzealous, especially given that the most serious crimes being investigated were charges of perjury and obstruction of justice in a civil action, admitted that his tactics were part of the typical prosecutor's arsenal.[51] Katy Harriger has raised the critical point that independent counsels have operated very much in the mold of other prosecutors, not only in the tactics employed but also in the degree of discretion they possess—and, therefore, in the high potential for abuse of power. That independent counsels may push the limits of this power also reflects the fact that "the courts have permitted prosecutorial discretion to grow virtually unchecked."[52] Moreover, prosecutors invariably mark their degree of success by the number of cases brought and convictions obtained. Thus, the incentive to win prosecutorial notches is great, just as the failure to prosecute or convict may be seen as a sign of professional weakness or failure.[53]

One key difference between regular prosecutors and ICs is that the former's practices are rarely subject to public scrutiny whereas those of the latter are. This does not mean that Starr did not overreach or mishandle the case; rather, it means that his actions, whether justifiable or not, would seem to be the logical consequence of the job. Yet the widespread disdain for Starr's handling of the Clinton investigation underscores a second important difference between ICs and regular prosecutors. ICs are charged with investigating the highest political officers in the executive branch, including the president, and it is therefore reasonable to try to strike a different balance between politics and law. This does not mean holding the president and other executive branch officials above the law; rather, it means tailoring the position to make it more responsive to the particular scandal concerns that have dogged the executive branch.

REFORM

Had there been no Watergate scandal, it is unlikely that the IC law would have been enacted. The fact that a Republican president, Nixon, was forced from office for serious constitutional misdeeds, and that two subsequent Republican presidents, Reagan and Bush, came under close IC scrutiny at a time when Congress was dominated by Democrats, helped ensure that many Democrats would become IC advocates and many Republicans suspicious opponents. Multiple IC investigations against a Democratic president in the 1990s led to many Republican I-told-you-sos to Democrats, who began to voice doubts about the IC law. Most notably, the Clinton administration reversed positions on the issue. In 1993 Attorney General Janet Reno testified before Congress in a vigorous defense of IC law renewal, which Clinton also strongly supported. By 1999 Reno and the Justice Department reversed this stand, considering the law "fundamentally flawed" and beyond repair.[54] These changes, plus the ill-fated Starr investigation, ensured that the IC law would not be renewed in 1999 or any time in the near future.

Nevertheless, the executive branch scandal problem remains, as does the political nature of the Department of Justice.[55] Both factors, I argue, support the wisdom of reviving the independent counsel office in the future, and many commentators have proposed ways in which the office could be reformulated.[56] The most sensible reform ideas include limiting IC investigations to crimes committed in office. Criminal allegations concerning prior behavior can be handled through regular federal or state channels. In 1973 Vice President Spiro Agnew resigned his office because of a state criminal investigation conducted in Maryland concerning improprieties on his part while he was governor. Had Agnew refused to relinquish his vice presidency in the face of his conviction, he could have then been impeached, based on the Maryland conviction. The Agnew case provides a useful precedent for dealing with extra-executive branch wrongdoing without need to rely on an IC. A second reform would require the IC to relinquish all other legal work while serving in this capacity, in order to avoid any conflict of interest problems and to ensure the IC's full energies and attention. A third would raise the bar or threshold for the nature of allegations that trigger an IC investigation. Allegations that are either too vague or too minor might warrant some limited form of investigation but not by the IC.[57]

Other reform ideas have been discussed but seem more problematic. For example, many observers have argued that IC prosecutions should be limited by time, or money, or both. But the obvious problem with such limitations is that they would encourage delay and discourage cooperation, tendencies that already dog such prosecutions, in the hopes of outlasting the prosecution. As Louis Fisher has properly noted, "Complaints about independent counsel expenditures are almost always partisan."[58] Some individuals have also argued that IC investigations should not be allowed to expand to other areas. But such investigations may be necessary and could also be regulated by a rule limiting investigations to official conduct, so that a new area of investigation that involved nonofficial behavior could be referred to appropriate federal or state prosecutors. Others have also proposed that IC investigations be limited to fewer officials in the executive branch. But the existing number is relatively small, and virtually all the past IC investigations have been conducted against top officials, most of whom have been top White House officials, cabinet secretaries, and assistant secretaries. This change could be made but would not seem warranted. Finally, some have argued for granting the attorney general more control over IC appointments. Though the AG could be given more control over IC appointment and jurisdiction, the greater the AG control, the closer the process comes simply to relying on the Department of Justice for all such investigations and prosecutions. It is that reliance that is both legally and politically problematic.[59]

CONCLUSION: THE INDEPENDENT COUNSEL WILL RETURN

The IC law lived a precarious political existence because of the lingering partisan animus that surrounded its genesis and implementation. Smaller-scale investigations, most of which occurred earlier in the statute's life, attracted less attention and therefore involved lower political stakes. Higher-profile investigations, however, raised the political stakes, especially for those that garnered more public attention. The Walsh investigation of Iran-Contra and the Starr investigation of Clinton both became highly public, but more important, threatened those presidents themselves. It takes no great leap of logic to conclude that the closer an investigation comes to the White House and the president, the greater the partisan fury (I do not mean to suggest this as an argument against independent counsels; quite the contrary). Just as Walsh ignited Republican fury,

Starr ignited Democratic fury. That, however, is where the similarities between these two scandals end. Unquestionably, these were very different events. As a matter of law, the sheer magnitude of Iran-Contra, encompassing as it did executive violation of specific constitutional obligations as well as federal laws across much of the Reagan presidency, lying to Congress about American foreign policy actions and policies, and covering up these illegal activities dwarfs the most apocalyptic interpretation of the Monica Lewinsky matter. Worse, Reagan and Bush White House intransigence and several pardons first delayed, and then effectively ended, the Iran-Contra investigation.[60] Whatever else can be said of the Lewinsky scandal, the pertinent facts have been fully known, even before impeachment proceedings began. As a matter of politics, the Reagan and Clinton scandals were starkly different as well. The earlier discussion of political charges leveled against Starr finds no parallel with Lawrence Walsh's background or behavior.

Despite these obvious differences, we can still say that politics played a role in the investigation of each scandal, and that each merited investigation. The political counterattack in each case—that the investigations were illegitimate political vendettas, not justifiable legal inquiries—was perfectly logical and predictable. Yet that claim gained more credibility in the Lewinsky case than for Iran-Contra because a colorable argument existed in support of it, even if we accept the justifiability of impeachment articles against Clinton. Further, the primary legacy of the Starr investigation will surely be the extent to which it has poisoned the well of support for an independent counsel law.

Charges of partisanship have been, are, and will always be a part of any IC or similar executive scandal investigation, regardless of the merits of such claims. Thus, these claims ought to hold little weight in determining the future of the IC. For the immediate future, however, they will hold considerable weight, as they will deter the reenactment of the independent counsel law for the foreseeable future. The legal questions concerning how the IC law might be amended or reformed involve relatively modest tinkering, about which lawmakers of divergent ideological stripes could well agree. The point is that no major structural, as opposed to political, impediments exist to IC resurrection.

In the light of the executive branch's susceptibility to scandal, and the attorney general's precarious politically dependent relationship to the president, post-Clinton presidents will face a public and a Congress little tolerant of misdeeds, and almost certainly suspicious of investigations of serious executive branch wrongdoing that begin and end in the Justice Department. This suggests that a time will again come when an impatient Congress and an aroused citizenry will call for some kind of revived independent counsel mechanism. When that happens, passions should have cooled sufficiently to allow a more detached and fair-minded assessment of the ICs of the 1980s and 1990s. Such an assessment will conclude, I believe, that the country, and the presidency, was better off with, than without, the office of independent counsel.

NOTES

1. See, for example, Katy J. Harriger's excellent, definitive treatment of the independent counsel in *The Special Prosecutor in American Politics* (Lawrence: University Press of Kansas, 2000), esp. chap. 5; "Symposium on Special Prosecutors and the Role of Independent Counsel," *Hofstra Law Review* 16 (fall 1987); and "The Independent Counsel Act: From Watergate to Whitewater and Beyond," Symposium, *Georgetown Law Journal* 86 (July 1998). This issue contains sixteen articles on the independent counsel (IC) law, including contributions by former prosecutors, legal commentators, and others, organized around the normative question of whether the act should be renewed.

2. One analysis discussed an interpretation of the IC statute that would have allowed an independent counsel to obtain permission to expand the jurisdiction of an investigation by going directly to the three-judge panel, simply bypassing the attorney general, since final approval rests with the panel. See Bruce D. Brown, "Independent Counsel Gain Independence," *Legal Times,* April 22, 1996, p. 1.

3. Ken Gormley, "Starr's Three Silent Chaperons," *New York Times,* March 7, 1998. p. A1.

4. Linda Greenhouse, "Ethics in Government: The Price of Good Intentions," *New York Times,* February 1, 1998, sec. 4, p. 1; Sam Dash, "Why We Have the Independent Counsel Law," *Washington Post,* January 9, 1998, p. A21; Jack Maskell, "Independent Counsel Provisions: An Overview of the Operation of the Law," *CRS Report for Congress,* Congressional Research Service, April 2, 1997.

5. Burl Noggle, *Teapot Dome: Oil and Politics in the 1920s* (Baton Rouge: Louisiana State University Press, 1962).

6. Andrew J. Dunbar, *The Truman Scandals and the Politics of Morality* (Columbia: University of Missouri Press, 1984). Independent special prosecutors have been used in particular in New York State to investigate corruption for nearly a century; see Harriger, *The Special Prosecutor,* pp. 3–4.

7. Comments of Senator William Fessenden (R-Maine), quoted by Raoul Berger, *Impeachment: The Constitutional Problems* (Cambridge: Harvard University Press, 1973), p. 300.

8. 487 U.S. 654.

9. Richard F. Fenno, *The President's Cabinet* (New York: Vintage, 1959), p. 70.

10. Michael Nelson, ed., *Guide to the Presidency,* 2 vols. (Washington, D.C.: Congressional Quarterly, 1996), p. 803.

11. Carl Bernstein and Bob Woodward, *All the President's Men* (New York: Simon and Schuster, 1974), pp. 132–133; Bob Woodward and Carl Bernstein, *The Final Days* (New York: Simon and Schuster, 1976), p. 60.

12. Jane Mayer, "Janet Reno, Alone," *New Yorker,* December 1, 1997, pp. 40–45.

13. Neil A. Lewis, "Republicans React Quickly and Angrily to Reno Move," *New York Times,* December 3, 1997, p. A31.

14. James T. Flexner, *Washington: The Indispensable Man* (New York: New American Library, 1984), pp. 328–340.

15. See, for example, Shelley Ross, *Fall from Grace* (New York: Ballantine Books, 1988), and Terry Eastland, *Ethics, Politics and the Independent Counsel* (Washington, D.C.: National Legal Center for the Public Interest, 1989), chap. 2.

16. Robert N. Roberts, *White House Ethics: The History of the Politics of Conflict of Interest Regulation* (Westport, Conn.: Greenwood Press, 1988), p. 38.

17. Ross, *Fall from Grace,* pp. 180, 182.

18. Dunbar, *The Truman Scandals,* p. 155.

19. Ross, *Fall from Grace,* p. 185.

20. Robert J. Spitzer, *President and Congress* (New York: McGraw-Hill, 1993), pp. 67, 90–91.

21. Charles W. Dunn, *The Scarlet Thread of Scandal: Morality and the American Presidency* (Lanham, Md.: Rowman and Littlefield, 2000); Dunn also notes the relative lack of attention this subject has received from the discipline (p. ix). An article published many years ago offered a theoretical formulation for the study of corruption in American politics; see John G. Peters and Susan Welch, "Political Corruption in America: A Search for Definitions and a Theory," *American Political Science Review* 72 (September 1978): 974–995. It focused no particular attention on the presidency, but it offered a conclusion that conforms with the assertion made here: "Political corruption has not yet been subjected to the sort of rigorous anaylsis received by other phenomena in American politics" (p. 982).

22. Leonard W. Levy and Louis Fisher, eds., *Encyclopedia of the American Presidency,* 4 vols. (New York: Simon and Schuster, 1994).

23. Nelson, ed., *Guide to the Presidency.*

24. Lyn Ragsdale, *Vital Statistics on the Presidency* (Washington, D.C.: Congressional Quarterly, 1996).

25. Michael A. Genovese, *The Presidential Dilemma* (New York: HarperCollins, 1995), p. 16.

26. Thomas E. Cronin, *The State of the Presidency* (Boston: Little, Brown, 1980), p. 76.

27. Harold M. Barger, "Suspending Disbelief: The President in Pre-College Textbooks," *Presidential Studies Quarterly* 20 (winter 1990): 55–70.

28. Philip B. Kunhardt Jr., Philip B. Kunhardt III, and Peter W. Kunhardt, *The American President*, with a foreword by Stephen Skowronek and an introduction by Richard E. Neustadt (New York: Riverhead Books, 1999). The Kunhardts are journalists.

29. Ibid., p. xi.

30. Thomas E. Cronin and Michael A. Genovese, *The Paradoxes of the American Presidency* (New York: Oxford University Press, 1998), p. 73.

31. Alexander Hamilton, James Madison, and John Jay, *The Federalist Papers* (New York: New American Library, 1961), p. 322.

32. See Spitzer, *President and Congress,* pp. 220–232.

33. William J. Eaton, "Senate Backs Return of Outside Counsels," *Los Angeles Times,* November 19, 1993, p. A1.

34. Holly Idelson, "House Clears Bill Reauthorizing Independent Counsel Law," *CQ Weekly Report,* June 25, 1994, p. 1718; Henry J. Reske, "The Second Act: Independent Counsel Law Signed," *American Bar Association Journal* 80 (September 1994): 32.

35. Eaton, "Senate Backs Return of Outside Counsels," p. A23.

36. Adam Clymer, "A Republican About-Face on Special Counsel Bill," *New York Times,* November 18, 1993. p. A1.

37. Philip Heyman, "Predatory Special Prosecutors," *Washington Post,* June 12,

1997, p. A1; James Bennet, "Spotlight Shifts to a Conservative Patron," *New York Times,* April 17, 1998, p. A24.

38. Mortimer Zuckerman, "A Good Idea Gone Wrong," *U.S. News and World Report,* December 16, 1996, p. 78.

39. Gormley, "Starr's Three Silent Chaperons," p. A13.

40. Ruth Marcus, "Some in the Law Uneasy with Starr's Tactics," *Washington Post,* February 13, 1998, p. A1. In June 2000, the Supreme Court ruled in the case of *U.S. v. Hubbell* that Starr abused his prosecutorial authority by forcing former assistant attorney general Webster Hubbell to produce thousands of pages of personal financial records after the sides had agreed to an immunity grant for him and then prosecuting him on a different charge from information obtained in the documents. In the eight-to-one decision, Justice John Paul Stevens quoted with approval a lower court judge who referred to Starr's action as "the quintessential fishing expedition" (Linda Greenhouse, "Justices Say Starr Broke Hubbell Immunity Deal," *New York Times,* June 6, 2000, p. A1).

41. Bob Woodward, "A Prosecutor Bound by Duty," *Washington Post,* June 15, 1999, p. A1.

42. Nancy Kassop, "The Clinton Impeachment: Untangling the Web of Conflicting Considerations," *Presidential Studies Quarterly* 30 (June 2000): 365–366. Kassop further noted Starr's "selective and untested presentation of evidence" before Congress (p. 366). Starr's ethics adviser, Watergate investigator Samuel Dash, resigned after Starr delivered his referral to the House of Representatives in September 1998, saying that Starr had improperly intruded himself into the congressional impeachment process.

43. Michael J. Gerhardt, "The Impeachment and Acquittal of President William Jefferson Clinton," in *The Clinton Scandal and the Future of American Government,* ed. Mark J. Rozell and Clyde Wilcox (Washington, D.C.: Georgetown University Press, 2000), p. 160.

44. Kirk Victor, "Not So Special," *National Journal,* February 1, 1997, p. 219.

45. Zuckerman, "A Good Idea Gone Wrong," p. 78.

46. Robert Suro, "Starr Blames His Accusers," *Washington Post*, April 15, 1999, p. A1.

47. Naftali Bendavid, "Judges, Special Prosecutors Lean to GOP," *Legal Times,* March 24, 1997, pp. 1, 20–21. IC David Barrett's selection to investigate HUD secretary Henry Cisneros was questioned because Barrett was implicated in influence peddling at HUD during the Reagan administration (see David Johnston, "Lawyer Linked to 80s HUD Scandal Is Named to Investigate Housing Chief," *New York Times,* May 25, 1995, p. A1).

48. For more on this, see Robert J. Spitzer, "The Presidency: The Clinton Crisis and Its Consequences," in Rozell, ed., *The Clinton Scandal,* pp. 1–17.

49. Louis Fisher, "The Independent Counsel Statute," in ibid., pp. 72–75.

50. Molly W. Andolina and Clyde Wilcox, "Public Opinion: The Paradoxes of Clinton's Popularity," in ibid., pp. 171–194.

51. Marcus, "Some in the Law Uneasy with Starr's Tactics," p. A1.

52. Katy J. Harriger, "Independent Justice: The Office of the Independent Counsel," in *Government Lawyers: The Federal Legal Bureaucracy and Presidential Politics,* ed. Cornell W. Clayton (Lawrence: University Press of Kansas, 1995), p. 90.

53. Jeffrey Rosen, "When Reckless Laws Team Up," *New York Times,* January 25, 1998, sec. 4, p. 15.

54. Dan Morgan, "U.S. Reverses Position on Counsel Law," *Washington Post,* March 2, 1999, p. A1.

55. For more on this, see Harriger, *The Special Prosecutor,* 121–124, and Fisher, "The Independent Counsel Statute," pp. 76–79.

56. See Harriger's good general discussion in *The Special Prosecutor*, chap. 10. The *Georgetown Law Journal* Symposium issue focused closely on the matter of reforming the independent counsel law; see "The Independent Counsel Act."

57. Reform ideas are discussed in Neil A. Lewis, "Special Prosecutors' Inquiries Have Led to Doubts About Their Usefulness,' *New York Times,* December 1, 1996, p. A38; Archibald Cox, "Curbing Special Counsels," *New York Times,* December 12, 1996, p. A37; Paul Simon, "One Attorney General for 10 Years," *New York Times,* February 1, 1998, sec. 4, p. 17; Neil A. Lewis, "Tripping over the Ghosts of Watergate," *New York Times,* May 18, 1998, sec. 4, p. 1.

58. Fisher, "The Independent Counsel Statute," p. 77.

59. Lewis, "Tripping over the Ghosts of Watergate."

60. Spitzer, *President and Congress,* pp. 227–228, and Fisher, "The Independent Counsel Statute," pp. 64–66. The main reasons for Congress's failure to adopt articles of impeachment against Reagan were not legal but political: Reagan's age, his popularity, and the impending end of his second term.

6

Executive Immunity for the Post-Clinton Presidency

Evan Gerstmann and Christopher Shortell

In 1994 Paula Corbin Jones filed suit against President William Jefferson Clinton in the U.S. District Court for the Eastern District of Arkansas, alleging that in May 1991, as governor of Arkansas, he had made unwanted sexual advances toward her. The suit made claims for sexual harassment, denial of equal protection, intentional infliction of emotional distress, and character defamation.[1] Jones claimed that while Clinton was governor, he had an Arkansas state trooper bring her to Clinton's hotel room during a conference, where he made sexual advances toward her, which she rejected. She alleged that as a result of this rejection, her superiors punished her by treating her in a "hostile and rude manner."[2] President Clinton's lawyers immediately filed a motion to dismiss the case, arguing that a sitting president cannot be sued, even for actions that occurred prior to office. The president sought immunity from the suit while he was in office, which would have allowed Jones to resume her suit after his term. At the center of national attention, the case traveled up from the district court to the Eighth Circuit Court of Appeals and finally to the Supreme Court. The Supreme Court's ultimate decision that the president enjoys no immunity, even temporary, from civil suit for unofficial acts has been seen as a key factor that led to the impeachment proceedings against Clinton.[3]

The issue of executive immunity has been brought before the highest court on only a few occasions in the history of the Union, but each case has been politically charged.[4] As we shall see, there has been a constant struggle between granting *absolute* immunity for the officeholder or *limited* immunity, which would protect the president from liability only in those cases stemming from his actions in performing official duties. This dichotomy between an absolute and a limited or functional approach is especially clear in the Clinton case. The courts, moreover, have struggled with the issue of whether the president should be granted temporary or permanent immunity. Again, this question is key to understanding the tensions the Supreme Court faced in the issues raised by President Clinton. In order to better understand how these issues developed over time, we will first explore the historical background of executive immunity. This background provides the foundation for understanding how the functional/absolute and temporary/permanent distinctions played out in the *Clinton v. Jones* case and allows us to answer the question of where the boundary of immunity now stands. We will conclude with some reflections on the implications for the institution of the presidency and a discussion of what may lie ahead.

THE HISTORY OF EXECUTIVE IMMUNITY

Maclay's Diary

The issue of executive immunity was not explicitly addressed by the Framers during the Constitutional Convention. The first recorded discussion of immunity arose from a conversation during the First Congress between then vice president John Adams and Senator Oliver Ellsworth that William Maclay, a senator from Pennsylvania, recorded in his diary.[5] According to Maclay, both Adams and Ellsworth were of the opinion that the "president, personally, was not subject to any process whatever."[6] Although Maclay expressed his surprise at this conjecture, the stature of Adams and Ellsworth as leaders in the early Republic requires some consideration of the passage. In the majority opinion in *Clinton v. Jones,* however, Justice John Paul Stevens dismisses this reference as irrelevant since it is "hardly proof of the unequivocal common understanding at the time of the founding."[7] Given the lack of contextual information and the absence of any other similar references at the time, it is difficult to evaluate the comment's reflection of original intent. Indeed, in the trial of Aaron Burr, the first court case featuring the issue of executive immunity, the great Chief Justice John Marshall rejected this extreme view.

United States v. Burr

The opinions in *Clinton v. Jones,* as well as in most other executive immunity cases, refer frequently to the first case to consider the issue, *United States v. Burr.*[8] This case was critical as a first step in answering the question of whether the president was answerable to the judicial branch or if the separation of powers between branches required that he be outside the reach of the judiciary. Further, it involved President Thomas Jefferson and Chief Justice John Marshall, two political rivals, providing some insight into the intentions of the founders and their contemporaries. Given that the decision and resulting communications from Jefferson in reference to this case have significantly influenced the Court's shaping of executive immunity, it is necessary to take a closer look at the admittedly complicated circumstances.[9]

In 1807 the country was gripped by a scandal that reached to the highest levels of government. Aaron Burr, who had recently lost the presidential election by only one vote in Congress, was on trial for treason. He was accused of attempting to raise an army against Spain in a quest to divide the nation.[10] During the course of the trial, it came to Burr's attention that President Thomas Jefferson, who was an outspoken opponent of Burr and had ordered his arrest and trial, was in possession of a letter from General John Wilkinson, the government's star witness, that detailed Burr's alleged treason. Burr asked the court to issue a subpoena *duces tecum* (a legal demand for a document or a piece of physical evidence)[11] for the letter so that he could effectively prepare his defense. This was the first attempt to subpoena a sitting president.[12] Not surprisingly, Jefferson, through Attorney General George Hay, objected strenuously, claiming that the court should not issue the subpoena in the first place.[13] Hay argued that the president should not have to disclose confidential communications, especially when that disclosure might produce some threat to U.S. national security interests. Burr's defense team responded heatedly, inspiring some of the strongest rhetoric in what was an already tense trial. They accepted that there might be some threat to national security by the release of the letter, but they argued that the president could make that claim in response to the subpoena, not use it to prevent the subpoena from being issued. One of Burr's lawyers, John Wickham, argued that "the writ of subpoena *duces tecum* ought to be issued, and if there be any state secrets to prevent the production of the letter, the president should allege it in his return."[14]

The Opinions

In his much-cited opinion, Marshall addressed the question of the subpoena, basing his analysis on the Sixth Amendment's protection of the right to a compulsory process for obtaining witnesses.[15] Although the government had accepted the court's ability to issue a subpoena *ad testificandum* (which demands only oral testimony),[16] Marshall included consideration of the point in his opinion. Since the language of the Sixth Amendment contains "no exceptions," he concluded that the president was not beyond its reach.[17] He launched into an extended discussion of the distinction between the American president and the British monarch. In England, the prevailing doctrine at the time was that the "king could do no wrong" and "can never be a subject." Marshall contrasted this with the role of the president, citing impeachment and term elections as proof that the president is not and should not be above the law. He did recognize, however, that the president plays a special role in society and could be treated somewhat differently (a key to the Clinton case). In an earlier case, *Marbury v. Madison,* Marshall had considered whether a court could issue a writ of mandamus to the president. Such a writ would be a judicial order to the president to take certain specific actions. In *Marbury,* Marshall acknowledged that the Court could issue a writ of mandamus to the president only if it was ordering the president to carry out a specific legal obligation. He acknowledged that the Court could not issue such a writ with regard to what Marshall called the president's "high functions"—those duties that are political and discretionary in nature: "I declare it to be my opinion, grounded on a comprehensive view of the subject, that the president is not amenable to any court of judicature for the exercise of his high functions, but is responsible only in the mode pointed out in the constitution."[18] Responding to a subpoena is obviously a specific legal obligation rather than a political or discretionary matter, so pursuant to *Marbury,* the Court can order the president to comply with such a subpoena. But even on this issue, Marshall was cautious. In *Burr,* he showed a deference to the chief executive, admitting to "some doubt concerning the propriety" of issuing a subpoena to the president. Yet he concluded that he could find "no legal objection to issuing a subpoena *duces tecum* to any person whatever, provided the case be such as to justify the process."[19] Though this established the president's amenability to process, Marshall was careful to spell out certain protections and exemptions. Foreshadowing the issues in *Clinton v. Jones,* he recognized that being subpoenaed might be unduly burdensome for the president, given the demands of national duty. For Marshall, though, this complaint was to be addressed after the issuance of the subpoena, not as a reason to prevent it from being issued in the first place. The second qualification that he noted is that material that could "endanger the public safety" would be suppressed unless it was "immediately and essentially applicable to the point."

After Marshall issued his opinion, an outraged Jefferson sent the letter to Attorney General Hay, instructing him to use his discretion in its release. When Burr's lawyers sought to enter the letter into evidence, they had to appeal to Marshall once again to get the entire letter from Hay rather than the sections he was willing to release. In his opinion on this matter, Marshall further clarified the protections for the president. In addition to broadening the protections of executive privilege from the first opinion, Marshall recognized that "in no case of this kind would a court be required to proceed against the president as against an ordinary individual."[20] Jefferson, still unhappy with the decision, sent letters to Hay wondering "would the executive be independent of the judiciary . . . if the several courts could bandy him from pillar to post, keep him constantly trudging from north to south & east to west, and withdraw him entirely from his constitutional duties?"[21] However, before the issue could be pressed any further, a separate ruling regarding admissibility of government evidence forced the government to drop the entire case, effectively putting an end to the dispute. This resolution of the conflict between Jefferson and Marshall thus did not provide clearer answers to the question of executive immunity. Marshall did establish that the president was not entirely beyond the reach of the judiciary, rejecting the arguments of Adams and Ellsworth. Marshall did concede, though, that his authority was circumscribed in a number of ways, such as the need to recognize the burden that testifying may put on the president and allowing the president to keep certain materials out of the trial. These concessions implied a certain amount of deference to the president. To confuse matters further, Jefferson never actually complied with the subpoena, sending the letter instead to his attorney general. In later cases, this fact has been used to call into question whether the Court had the authority to issue the subpoena in the first place.

Given this mix of details, it is clear that the issue was far from resolved. Marshall's opinions, though, did establish several important principles that would feature prominently in later cases. Immunity, for Marshall, was a question of *balancing* the principle that the president is not above the law with the need to defer to the president on the basis of separation of powers, national security, and the necessity that the president be able to carry out his duties without undue distraction and interference.

Story's Commentaries

Following the Burr case, the issue of executive immunity lay dormant for over fifty years and raised its head only rarely after that. The only important statement about immunity during this period did not come in the context of a legal case. Justice Joseph Story published his *Commentaries on the Constitution of the United States* in 1833, and its impact on constitutional thought was substantial. The work is particularly relevant to the question of immunity because of a passage cited in several executive immunity cases to support immunity for presidents in civil litigation. Story wrote, "There are . . . incidental powers, belonging to the executive department, which are necessarily implied from the nature of the function, which are confided to it. Among those, must necessarily be included the power to perform them, without any obstruction or impediment whatsoever. The president cannot, therefore, be liable to arrest, imprisonment, or detention, while he is in the discharge of the duties of his office; and for this purpose his person must be deemed, in civil cases at least, to possess an official inviolability."[22] This passage seems to imply not only that the president should be free from imprisonment and arrest but also from any kind of substantial intrusion upon the discharge of his duties from the courts. For Story, civil cases would present a substantial intrusion and should not be permitted. This section thus had a significant impact on cases to follow.

BETWEEN BURR AND CLINTON

Mississippi v. Johnson

There are four notable cases prior to *Clinton* that bear directly on our understanding of executive immunity today. The first of these, *Mississippi v. Johnson*,[23] arose immediately following the Civil War. The South, outraged by the process of Reconstruction, attempted to block the actions of the Radical Republicans by asking the Court to issue an injunction against President Andrew Johnson. In response to the First and Second Reconstruction Acts of 1867, which divided the Southern states into military districts, Mississippi asked the Supreme Court to declare that these laws were unconstitutional and to prevent the president from enforcing them.[24] The question at hand was whether the Court "could properly entertain a bill to restrain the president from carrying into effect an Act of Congress, alleged to be unconstitutional."[25] The case, which was decided in favor of Johnson, reinforced important protections for the president. Expanding on Marshall's distinction in *Marbury,* as a practical matter the Court granted broad immunity in substance to the president when carrying out *discretionary* actions, such as how to implement legislation, but did not extend immunity to the performance of *ministerial* actions, defined as "a simple, definite duty, arising under conditions admitted or proved to exist, and imposed by law."[26] An example of a ministerial duty would be the president's duty, absent a claim of executive privilege, to produce documents subpoenaed by Congress. Violation of that clearly imposed duty would most likely not fall under the protections afforded by *Johnson.* An example of a discretionary action, on the other hand, would be a presidential veto—neither the Court nor Congress would ever order the president to veto or not to veto a piece of legislation.

The Court additionally emphasized the dangers of entangling the various branches of government. In his opinion for the Court, Chief Justice Salmon Chase made it clear that the Court is not able to stop the president from carrying out discretionary duties, since that would necessarily interfere with the separation of powers. If the Court prevented Johnson from carrying out the law, Congress could impeach him. Could the Court then restrain the Senate from trying the president since he was only following a judicial order? Chase's concern was with the "strange spectacle" of the judiciary getting tangled up in the proceedings of impeachment, thus leading to a dangerous clash among the branches of government. The Court's reasoning in this case severely limited the president's amenability to suit. By granting broad discretion to the president in cases involving execution of legislation, the Court established separation of powers as a potent argument against judicial interference. Lower courts regularly used the ministerial/discretionary distinction to dismiss suits against executive officials, and the reasoning has remained an influential factor in cases dealing with immunity.[27] *Mississippi v. Johnson* also firmly established the tradition of viewing the president's immunity as *functional*—relating to the duties of the office rather than generally to the officeholder himself. Functionally determined immunity has been and remains the dominant approach for all other executive and judicial officials. The functionalism approach has also dominated questions of presidential immunity, albeit with some exceptions. Functionalism, however, was key in the *Clinton* decision.

Youngstown Sheet & Tube Co. v. Sawyer

The impact of *Johnson*'s definition of the proper relationship between the judiciary and executive was clear in the Korean War case, *Youngstown Sheet & Tube Co. v. Sawyer.*[28] The suit was brought in response to President Harry Truman's seizure of the nation's steel mills to guarantee their continued wartime production. Truman issued an executive order to Secretary of Commerce Charles Sawyer, who carried out the action. The Court held that the president had no power to seize the mills because the claimed power relied on lawmaking authority that was exclusively vested in Congress. In *Clinton,* Justice John Paul Stevens refers to *Youngstown* as a "dramatic" example of judicial determination of "whether [the president] has acted within the law."[29] But though the case firmly established that the president is not above the law and did attempt to set the limits of executive power, it in fact did not determine whether the president himself could be held accountable in court.[30] Neither the majority opinion nor any of the other opinions filed in the case mentioned whether it would have been appropriate to name President Truman as the defendant instead of secretary Sawyer.

United States v. Nixon

United States v. Nixon[31] is one of the best-known recent Supreme Court cases and certainly one of the most prominent involving a president. President Richard Nixon, under investigation for his role in the Watergate break-in and subsequent cover-up, had been subpoenaed by a grand jury to turn over copies of audiotapes that had been made in his offices.[32] Nixon claimed that he would "follow the example of a long line of my predecessors as President of the United States who have consistently adhered to the position that the president is not subject to compulsory process from the courts."[33] Both the district court and the appeals court ruled against him, relying heavily on *Burr* as proof of the president's responsibility to the judiciary. Nixon decided not to appeal the decision but once again challenged the special prosecutor, Leon Jaworski, when he requested more tapes. Jaworski appealed directly to the Supreme Court before the district court decided. Both the special prosecutor and the president's attorneys raised the immunity issue in their briefs, each side using historical precedents.

Despite mention of the issue in the briefs, it was barely mentioned during oral arguments and the Court showed little interest in the question. As a result, the opinion in this case provides only limited guidance for the question of executive immunity even though the Court ordered Nixon to comply with the subpoenas. The president's argument rested on two separate claims. The first involved *immunity* and claimed that the president should not have to respond to the Court at all. The second involved the related but distinct concept of executive *privilege,* which is the idea that the president has the authority to keep certain information confidential. Nixon argued that the president should not have to turn over materials that he deems confidential. Certainly, the fact that the Court was able to compel the president to obey the subpoena implies that the president is subject to judicial power, but the Court's opinion blurs these issues of immunity and privilege.[34] After rejecting arguments of separation of powers and confidentiality as a basis for "an absolute, unqualified presidential privilege of immunity from judicial process under all circumstances," the Court immediately shifted away from the question.[35] However, the Court did establish a balancing test that weighs the president's need for confidentiality against the legal system's need for relevant evidence in criminal prosecutions. This balance builds on the one established in *Burr* between the president's accountability under the law and deference to the separation of powers and national security concerns. The *Nixon* balance, however, is noticeably narrower, limiting the consideration to specific aspects of each side of the issue. According to Chief Justice Warren Burger's majority opinion, this test is construed narrowly because it deals only with the issue of criminal prosecutions, leaving the questions of civil litigation and congressional inquiries untouched.[36] Thus, despite being well known and influential in regard to the judiciary-executive relationship on the question of immunity *United States v. Nixon* largely affirms *Burr* and actually sheds little further light on the issue at hand. The case may be most significant for the fact that Nixon, unlike Jefferson, did hand the information over. As a result, the judiciary's power over the president was probably strengthened in fact if not in law.

Nixon v. Fitzgerald

This review brings us to the most explicit and deferential case involving immunity, *Nixon v. Fitzgerald,* decided in 1982.[37] Nixon had left office in 1974, but his presidency was still causing reverberations in the courts. A. Ernest Fitzgerald was a management analyst with the Department of the Air Force who was dismissed in January 1970. His dismissal was officially the result of a departmental reorganization to promote economy and efficiency. However, Fitzgerald had previously testified before a congressional subcommittee about substantial cost overruns and technical deficiencies on the C-5A military transport plane.[38] The dismissal drew a fair amount of public and congressional criticism, which encouraged the Nixon administration to reassign him to a different department. This pressure, however, led to some revealing memorandums that established the involvement of the White House in Fitzgerald's dismissal.[39] Even after the Civil Service Commission ordered him reinstated, the White House and the Defense Department refused. Fitzgerald then filed a civil suit against officials of the Defense Department and the White House in the District Court for the District of Columbia. By 1980 the suit focused on Nixon and two aides, Alexander Butterfield and Bryce Harlow, charging them with wrongful termination of employment.

Nixon claimed absolute immunity from all civil claims arising from his time as president and asked that the suit be dismissed. Both the district court and the appeals court rejected this claim, relying on cases that provided only limited immunity to executive officials.[40] The Supreme Court granted certiorari in the case,[41] claiming that the issue of presidential immunity had not been settled. Justice Lewis Powell delivered the opinion of the Court in this case, speaking for a slim five-justice majority. In addressing Nixon's claim of absolute immunity, the Court agreed that the president has absolute immunity from civil suit for all official actions within the "outer perimeter" of his official responsibility.[42] Although the Court did not define where the outer perimeter lies, it seemed to imply that the courts were willing to accept very broad constructions of what falls within the boundaries of an official duty. Powell argued that the unique nature of the presidency required that the Court show the utmost deference toward its officeholders.[43] To this end, Powell turned to the balancing test in *United States v. Nixon* to use in determining the president's amenability to suit. The test balances "the constitutional weight of the interest to be served against the dangers of intrusion on the authority and functions of the executive branch."[44] The Court determined that since the interest in the case was "merely" a "private suit for damages," the interests of the executive branch are weightier.[45] Fear of suit should not alter the president's decisions when he is within the realm of his duties. As a historical matter, Powell relied on Jefferson's resistance to the *Burr* subpoena as well as on the silence of the Framers on the issue of immunity during the Constitutional Convention, concluding from this admittedly fragmentary review of history that there is a long-standing tradition of deference to the president. Powell also cited the opinion in *Mississippi v. Johnson* as an example of the Court's deference to the executive.

Chief Justice Warren Burger wrote a concurring opinion that further emphasized the historical tradition of deference and pointed to the separation of powers as mandating judicial noninterference.[46] He limited the reach of *United States v. Nixon* to apply only to those cases with "imperative constitutional necessity."[47] Burger did identify two limitations on the absolute immunity that was granted. He noted that the decision in *Fitzgerald* was limited to cases of civil liability and that the question of whether a president's actions fall under the office's official duties is relevant to ask before dismissing a case.[48] At the same time, Burger, in disagreement with the majority opinion, would prevent Congress from passing any statutes that would make the president liable.[49] Burger was attempting to establish the president's immunity as a constitutional rule, which would prevent Congress's interference. This issue was reversed in *Clinton* when Justice Stevens explicitly denied that the issue was a constitutional rule and invited Congress to increase protection for the president if it so desired.

THE STATE OF EXECUTIVE IMMUNITY BEFORE CLINTON

Where exactly did executive immunity stand following *Fitzgerald*? And what has changed since *Clinton v. Jones*? The first of these questions we can address now;

the second will be the focus of the remainder of the chapter. The functional approach appears to be the clear winner over any grant of absolute immunity, even in *Fitzgerald*. While the Court granted permanent absolute immunity to presidents for duties arising out of their office, the immunity is crucially linked to the official nature of the actions in question. Two foundations for immunity emerge from the preceding cases and were clarified in the *Fitzgerald* opinion. The president requires immunity because he should not fear any reprisals from official actions since that could affect his ability to make decisions in the best interest of the country. This reasoning began with Marshall's deference to Jefferson in *Burr* and is strengthened by the existence of executive privilege. At the same time the Court offered a second rationale. Separation of powers and concern regarding demands on the president's time point to the significant dangers of dragging a president through a lengthy and time-consuming judicial process. *Johnson* is particularly relevant as support for this rationale, given the Court's concern about unseemly tangling of the branches. As will become evident, the Court in *Clinton* relied heavily on the first rationale for its decision while Clinton's lawyers pushed for protection under the second reason.

There are, however, several issues that had been clarified. After *Fitzgerald*, the question of whether the president is covered by executive immunity depends in part on whether the case is criminal or civil. If a case is merely a "private suit for damages," then the Court has less need to risk interfering with the president's time and duties. But, overall, precedent has been clear that the president is not entirely beyond the reach of the judiciary. The president can be subpoenaed to testify in criminal proceedings, although the Court must defer to the president's schedule, usually allowing taped or written testimony.[50] The president can be compelled to produce documents in criminal cases as long as they do not interfere with executive privilege.[51] The president is immune from all civil suits that are within the outer perimeter of his official duties, either brought by the state or individuals. Further, this latter immunity is permanent—the president cannot be sued even after he has left office. However, the Court does have the ability to evaluate executive conduct when the case involves delegation to another executive official.

These issues have been resolved over the course of 200 years of jurisprudence, but there are still gray areas. For example, what immunity, if any, does a sitting president have for actions that were not undertaken in the fulfillment of his official duties? It is to this question and the *Clinton* case that we now turn.

PRESIDENT CLINTON ON TRIAL

The District Court

When Paula Jones filed her lawsuit in federal district court on May 6, 1994, the president's lawyers immediately filed a motion to have the court consider the immunity question prior to dealing with any other issues. In an opinion issued in July of that year, Judge Susan Webber Wright agreed that the immunity issue should be dealt with before allowing any further motions or pleadings.[52] Citing *Nixon v. Fitzgerald,* she argued that "because of the 'singular importance of the president's duties,' and because suits for civil damages 'frequently could distract a president from his public duties, to the detriment of not only the president and his office but also the nation that the Presidency was designed to serve'" the issue of presidential immunity needed to be decided before allowing the suit to continue any further.[53] The president's lawyers then filed their motion to have the complaint dismissed "without prejudice," which means that Jones could revive her suit as soon as Clinton left office.[54] Failing that, the Department of Justice asked that the court stay the case until the end of Clinton's presidency.[55] In other words, Clinton sought temporary immunity from the lawsuit.

The Opinion

Judge Wright handed down her opinion on the question of executive immunity in December 1994.[56] She carefully traced the history of executive immunity in British law from the Magna Carta to the adoption of British common law by the individual states, concluding that when the states adopted British common law in the seventeenth and eighteenth centuries the king's prerogative was unquestionably limited.[57] She argued that this translated into the American context as a limitation on the powers of the president. Following the history of the Constitutional Convention as well as *Burr,* Judge Wright determined that the president was responsible to the judiciary. She cited *Johnson* as an example of how the president could be granted absolute immunity but distinguished the *official* actions of Johnson from the unofficial actions of Clinton.[58] She also noted the three previous sitting presidents who had been sued in civil litigation. Complaints against Theodore Roosevelt and Harry Truman were dismissed prior to their taking office, and the dismissals were affirmed after their inaugurations. John F. Kennedy was also sued for an incident arising from an automobile accident during his presidential campaign. Kennedy argued that his status as commander in chief gave him a right to a stay in accordance with the Soldiers' and Sailors' Civil Relief Act of 1940. The motion was denied by the district court and Kennedy settled the suit out of court.

None of these cases provided the court with guidance or direction. Following this review, she agreed with Clinton that the most relevant case to look at was *Fitzgerald.* The facts between the cases, however, were substantially different. Key for Judge Wright was the fact that Clinton was not president or even president-elect at the time of the alleged violation. Recognizing that this was a situation where neither the Constitution nor precedent spoke directly to the issue at hand, Judge Wright concluded that the protections of *Fitzgerald* were not meant to extend absolute immunity to the actions of a president "prior to assuming the office."[59] As a result, she denied President Clinton's motion to dismiss the case.

The question did not end there, however. In the next section of the opinion, Judge Wright addressed the question of temporary or limited immunity for the president. She claimed that the opinion in *Fitzgerald* used broad and "quite firm" language to establish that "to disturb the president with defending civil litigation that does not demand immediate attention under the circumstances would be to interfere with the conduct of the duties of the office."[60] Regardless of whether the offending actions took place before his tenure as president, defending against a civil lawsuit while in office could have a detrimental effect on the president's ability to lead the country. She therefore decided to stay the trial until after Clinton left office, although she noted that there could be cases against presidents where trials would go forward if the need for relief was immediate. She based this conclusion not only on her reading of *Fitzgerald* but also on Rule 40 of the Federal Rules of Civil Procedure allowing district courts to place matters upon the trial calendar "as the courts deem expedient."[61] Finally, Judge Wright decided to proceed with discovery and depositions immediately in order to minimize the risk of witnesses dying or evidence being lost in the interim. Thus, President Clinton would not have to devote the resources actually to defend himself in a trial but would be required to produce evidence for the lawyers and the court. In her opinion, Judge Wright attempted to balance the dictate of *Fitzgerald* against Paula Jones's right to seek relief from the courts.

It is also worth noting the highly politicized and charged atmosphere surrounding this case. Paula Jones filed her lawsuit merely three days before the statute of limitations would have expired, leading many observers to question her motives and those of her supporters and financial backers. President Clinton went on the offensive against his accusers, attempting to portray them as right-wing extremists, prosecutorial zealots, and moral busybodies.[62] All of this heightened the drama surrounding the case and fractured sides based on ideological leanings. The courts had to move carefully to avoid being perceived as too partisan one way or the other.

THE COURT OF APPEALS

The Majority Opinion

Not surprisingly, both President Clinton and Paula Jones appealed the decision to the Eighth Circuit Court of Appeals.[63] Clinton challenged both the decision not to terminate the case and the requirement that discovery proceed. Jones requested that the stay on the trial be lifted so that it could move forward. A three-judge panel from the Eighth Circuit heard the case and decided both appeals at the same time.[64] The question before them, as the circuit court construed it, was whether "the person currently serving as president of the United States is entitled to immunity from civil liability for his unofficial acts, i.e., for acts committed by him in his personal capacity rather than in his capacity as president."[65] Judge Pasco M. Bowman wrote the opinion of the divided court (the vote was two to one) and addressed each point of contention raised by President Clinton. He accepted Judge Wright's conclusion that the president does not have absolute immunity in civil cases arising from actions that are not related to official duties. Judge Bowman argued that immunity is "not the product of a prudential doctrine created by the courts and is not to be granted as a matter of judicial largesse."[66] The decision to grant immunity instead arises from the "Constitution, federal statutes, and history."[67] The opinion concluded that presidential immunity arises from considerations of the separation of powers and that the separation of powers doctrine does not require extending immunity to actions outside the scope of official duties. Judge Bowman's opinion relies on Burger's concurrence in *Fitzgerald* to make this point: "A president, like Members of Congress, judges, prosecutors, or congressional aides—all having absolute immunity—[is] not immune for acts outside official duties."[68]

Judge Bowman also rejected Clinton's claim that the court should balance the importance of the lawsuit against the president's immunity. Clinton and his lawyers argued that Jones's suit was "neither important nor urgent, and certainly not consequential enough to trump Mr. Clinton's claim to temporal immunity from suit."[69] This argument hearkens back to the balancing test used in *Fitzgerald* for official acts that required the Court to "balance the constitutional weight of the interest to be served against the dangers of intrusion on the authority and functions of the Executive Branch."[70] Judge Bowman stated that Jones, as with any other citizen, had the right to claim protection of the laws and that her motives for filing suit were irrelevant to determining the question of immunity. He also denied Clinton's claim that a civil lawsuit filed against the president would interfere with the performance of his duties. The majority in *Fitzgerald* was concerned not with the use of the president's time but with the impact on future policy decisions that fear of civil lawsuits may cause. Judge Bowman argued that judicial management of scheduling and timing could accommodate any concerns that the president might have and would be sensitive to the needs of the country. On a related issue, he dismissed the president's concerns that this would lead to a glut of civil suits. The distinction between official and unofficial conduct was critical for this, as Judge Bowman argued that unofficial conduct will affect only those who traffic with the president in his personal capacity. Thus the universe of potential plaintiffs who might seek to hold the president accountable for his alleged private wrongs through a civil lawsuit is considerably smaller than the universe of potential plaintiffs who might seek to hold the president accountable for his official conduct.[71]

Significantly, the Eighth Circuit also struck down Judge Wright's claim that Rule 40 of the Federal Rules of Civil Procedure granted her authority to stay the trial until after Clinton's presidency. According to Judge Bowman, this constituted an "abuse of discretion" and was "the functional equivalent of a grant of temporary immunity to which, as we hold today, Mr. Clinton is not constitutionally entitled."[72] As a result, the Eighth Circuit ordered the district court to remove the stay immediately and to allow the trial to proceed.

The Dissenting Opinion

Judge Donald R. Ross wrote a dissent in which he argued that the true concern of *Fitzgerald* involved the impairment of presidential duties if the president were subject to any and all lawsuits. He claimed that "unless exigent circumstances can be shown," all civil suits against a sitting president must be stayed until the end of their term.[73] Judge Ross saw no reason why Paula Jones could not obtain equal justice after President Clinton left office. Judge C. Arlen Beam, in a concurrence, responded to this by detailing potential problems that could develop for Paula Jones if the case was stayed, including loss of evidence and death of witnesses. He concluded that each citizen has the right to timely disposition of claims of alleged abuse by government officials.[74]

THE SUPREME COURT

The Majority Opinion

The Eighth Circuit denied a request for rehearing the case as a full panel, and President Clinton filed a petition for certiorari from the Supreme Court. In recognition of the importance and scope of the case, the Supreme Court granted the motion.[75] Justice John Paul Stevens wrote the opinion for a unanimous Court and unequivocally determined that the claim that "the Constitution affords the president temporary immunity from civil damages litigation arising out of events that occurred before he took office—cannot be sustained on the basis of precedent."[76] Stevens supported Judge Bowman's interpretation of *Fitzgerald,* contending that immunity for the president in civil cases arises as a result of concern about the impact that civil litigation may have on future policy decisions. Unofficial actions do not fall within that framework since, by definition, they are outside the scope of the president's duties. Stevens emphasized this point by clarifying that the "dominant concern [in *Fitzgerald*] was with the diversion of the president's attention during the decision making process caused by needless worry as to the possibility of damages actions stemming from any particular official decision."[77] This approach to immunity reflects the functional approach that the Court has used since *Johnson.* Stevens pointed this out, stating, "when defining the scope of an immunity for acts clearly taken within an official capacity, we have applied a functional approach."[78] Immunities are grounded in "the nature of the functions performed, not the identity of the actor who performed it."[79]

Stevens reviewed the historical support, outside of case law, for immunity, citing Jefferson's response to *Burr,* the Maclay diary, and Justice Story's *Commentaries,* dismissing each one. He concluded that Justice Jackson's observation regarding the historical record of the Founding in *Youngstown Sheet & Tube Co. v. Sawyer*[80] applied to this case as well. "A century and a half of partisan debate and scholarly speculation yields no net result but only supplies more or less apt quotations from respected sources on each side. . . . They largely cancel each other."[81]

The bulk of the opinion is spent discussing the most difficult point of contention—the scope of protection provided by the separation of powers. The Court accepted the basic premise of the argument, that the office of the president is unique and requires undivided time from its occupant.[82] However, the Court argued that the doctrine of separation of powers is "concerned with the allocation of official power among the three co-equal branches of our Government."[83] Since there is no suggestion that the judiciary would perform a function that might be described as executive, there seems to be little conflict between the branches. Stevens concluded that the courts were merely being asked to exercise their core jurisdiction under Article 3 of the Constitution to decide cases. However, the Court in the past has held that "the separation of powers doctrine requires that a branch not impair another in the performance of its constitutional duties."[84] The Court needed to confirm that its decision would not unconstitutionally prevent the effective performance of the president's duties. The contention that a lack of immunity would significantly impair the president's ability to carry out his responsibilities was at the heart of President Clinton's argument, requiring the Court to address it in some way. In response to this claim, Stevens wrote that separation is not absolute and that the judiciary's actions could significantly burden the time and energy of the president without rising to the level of a constitutional violation. As support for this, Stevens relied on both *Youngstown* and *Burr* as cases that established judicial authority, even when it constrained the actions of the president. Further, Stevens concluded that "the burden on the president's time and energy that is a mere by-product of such review surely cannot be considered as onerous as the direct burden imposed by judicial review and the occasional invalidation of his official actions."[85] Justice Antonin Scalia made a telling and instructive comment on this issue during oral arguments for the case. In responding to Solicitor General Walter Dellinger's claims regarding the impact on the president's time, Justice Scalia stated, "But we see presidents riding horseback, chopping firewood, fishing [laughter in the courtroom], playing golf and so forth and so on. Why can't we leave it to the point where, if, and when a court tells a president to be there or he's going to lose his case, and if and when a president has the intestinal fortitude to say, 'I am absolutely too busy'—so that he'll never be seen playing golf for the rest of his Administration [laughter]—if and when that happens, we can resolve the problem. But really, the notion that he doesn't have a minute to spare is just not credible."[86] This dismissal of the president's claim regarding time is particularly important, since it significantly undercuts his claim to any sort of immunity for unofficial actions.

The Court then turned to the court of appeals' decision regarding the temporary stay of the trial until the end of Clinton's presidency. The Supreme Court agreed that the stay should not have been granted but differed in the reasoning. The Court felt that the question of issuing a stay was far more complex than the court of appeals recognized. The district court retains broad discretion and authority in its scheduling, and a stay may result from considerations that do not involve questions of constitutional immunity. Given the unique nature of the office of the presidency, respect for the burdens that are imposed should "inform the conduct of the entire proceeding, including the timing and scope of discovery."[87] The Court, however, did reject the categorical stay until the end of Clinton's term, since it took no account of Paula Jones's interest in bringing the case to trial. Further, Stevens argued that the district court did not have sufficient evidence to establish the need for a stay of that length. Absent any clear evidence of infringement on the president's duties, the Court held that the temporary stay was an abuse of discretion.

Overall, the Court dismissed concerns about a flood of frivolous civil litigation against the president, stating that the "availability of sanctions provides a significant deterrent to litigation directed at the president in his unofficial capacity for purposes of political gain or harassment.'[88] The Court also accepted the court of appeals' reasoning that the president has only a small circle of people who could bring private civil actions. In matters of frivolous lawsuits as well as questions of national security, the Court expressed its certainty that the district courts could handle those concerns through appropriate scheduling and sealing of records. Finally, Stevens addressed the question of whether Congress could extend stronger protection against civil suits. He concluded that Congress could provide for the deferral of civil litigation, in keeping with acts such as the Soldiers' and Sailors' Civil Relief Act of 1940. This is an important issue and one that we will revisit.

The Concurring Opinion

Although the Court's opinion in *Clinton v. Jones* was unanimous, Justice Stephen Breyer did file a concurring opinion that provided the potential groundwork for a later narrowing of the decision. As he explained, he agreed with the Court's reasoning that the president does not have categorical immunity from civil lawsuits based upon his private conduct. Breyer was particularly concerned with providing immunity without requiring any demonstration of need from the president. However, once the president does "set forth and explain a conflict between judicial proceeding and public duties, the matter changes."[89] For Breyer, that demonstration of a conflict would prevent the courts from scheduling a trial in cases where postponement is possible without overwhelming damage to the plaintiff.

He was also concerned that the Court may have been wrong, and a flood of civil lawsuits could appear. In that case, the Court would need to provide some type of institutional safeguard. As a result, Breyer reviewed the case law and historical support for a much stronger reading of presidential immunity. Responding to the historical review in the majority opinion, he explored the Maclay diary, Story's *Commentaries,* and Jefferson's response to *Burr* in more detail, providing a stronger case for immunity. He also provided a much stronger interpretation of *Fitzgerald,* arguing that it did in fact rest "upon the assessment of the threat that a civil damage lawsuit poses to a public official's ability to perform his job properly."[90] Since *Fitzgerald* applied to both sitting and former presidents (the case involved Nixon long after he left office), Breyer argued that concern solely with impact on policy decisions does not explain the breadth of the decision. Only concern with the ability to carry out a president's duties effectively could explain it. Breyer's critique is a powerful one, and it could limit significantly future civil litigation against presidents.

Resolution of the Case

After the Supreme Court remanded the case to the district court, it was dismissed on April 1, 1998. The judge determined that Jones had failed to establish her claims of sexual harassment.[91] Jones appealed this dismissal to the Eighth Circuit, but on November 13, 1998, agreed to settle the case out of court for $850,000. We turn now to how this case has changed executive immunity and what recommendations for changes, if any, may be appropriate.

MOVING FORWARD AFTER CLINTON

Clinton v. Jones: Some Problems

In light of the decision in *Clinton v. Jones,* where does executive immunity stand today? The Court reaffirmed the functional approach to immunity that has been the hallmark of that line of cases since *Mississippi v. Johnson.* The president is immune from civil litigation only when official functions of the office are related. Though *Clinton* did clarify a number of gray areas in executive immunity law, there remains a number of outstanding issues. In the majority opinion in *Clinton,* Stevens was explicit as to what the Court did not touch upon. The decision did not deal with the question of whether a president could be sued in a state court for private actions, since that might introduce federalism concerns.[92] The decision also did not deal with whether the president could be compelled to attend court at any specific time or place. Stevens wrote, "We assume that the testimony of the president, both for discovery and for use at trial, may be taken at the White House at a time that will accommodate his busy schedule, and that, if a trial is held, there would be no necessity for the president to attend in person, though he could elect to do so."[93] Moreover, the scope of criminal immunity is still unclear. Could a sitting president be indicted or even tried before being impeached? For instance, could Kenneth Starr have decided to pursue a grand jury indictment against President Clinton before the impeachment hearings? The limited precedent that exists seems to indicate that impeachment is likely to precede criminal indictment, but the Court has never ruled on the issue. Prosecutors in both the Nixon and Clinton impeachments decided to send the impeachment referral to Congress rather than attempt to get an indictment. In fact, Nixon was named as an unindicted coconspirator in the Watergate investigation only because the special prosecutor did not think that he could be indicted. However, it seems highly unlikely that President Clinton could have made any claim of immunity from criminal charges of perjury after he left office.[94]

Criticisms and Controversies in the Wake of *Clinton v. Jones*

The decision in the *Clinton* case sparked an enormous amount of controversy, not the least because of its relationship to the subsequent impeachment hearings. To be fair, the decision regarding immunity was hardly the sole factor leading to the impeachment. Countless other factors, including President Clinton's own behavior as well as an intensely partisan and aggressive political climate abroad in the land, led to the impeachment.[95] However, serious doubt remains about the majority's optimistic view that the president need not fear a host of politically motivated lawsuits. Though there were not subsequent lawsuits against President Clinton, it is not clear that the political environment would have tolerated any more at the time. There was no need for Clinton's political foes to initiate any further lawsuits because the one that did go through substantively changed the political situation. Future presidents who are able to avoid accusations of perjury in one case may very well face subsequent lawsuits.

Further, the *Clinton* Court, taking its cue from the Court in *Fitzgerald,* focused its attention on the danger that without sufficient immunity the president might have to fear future lawsuits that could arise from his official decisions as president. But the Court did not seem to focus on the question of just how time-consuming and distracting even a single present lawsuit could be, particularly one involving allegations of sexual misconduct where the Federal Rules of Discovery are quite broad.

Constitutional scholar Randall K. Miller, among others, has argued that the Court failed sufficiently to consider the impact that civil litigation has upon the time and duties of the president.[96] The majority opinion is noticeably lacking any careful consideration of the president's valid concerns. The Court seems to dismiss these concerns in statements such as "[The president's] predictive judgment finds little support in either history or the relatively narrow compass of the issues raised in this particular case. . . . If the past is any indicator, it seems unlikely that a deluge of such litigation will ever engulf the Presidency. As for the case at hand, if properly managed by the District Court, it appears to us highly unlikely to occupy any substantial amount of [the president's] time."[97] Given the president's unique role in the constitutional structure of government, it is problematic that his ability to be available twenty-four hours a day should be compromised without at least a consideration of what that would mean. As Justice Breyer established in his concurrence, the executive power of the government is vested entirely in one person, and interference with his performance necessarily impacts the entire executive branch.[98]

The Unique Nature of the Office of the Presidency

Another problematic area in the *Clinton* opinion is the Court's use of analogies to the situation in question. Stevens drew a comparison between immunity for federal judges and immunity for the president to show that immunity for other federal officials is limited strictly to official acts, excluding even administrative duties.[99] But the positions of judge and president are quite different and make different demands upon these officeholders. Thus, it may be misguided to equate judges with presidents.[100] Perhaps the vastly more encompassing duties and responsibilities of the president should result in a broader grant of immunity, and indeed they usually have. By relying on the substantially narrower protections afforded to judges, the Court sidestepped the issue of how civil lawsuits will affect the uniquely demanding office of the presidency. The Court also drew analogies to cases where former presidents have acted as witnesses in civil and criminal trials. Again, the Court avoided directly facing the question of distraction for the president by relying on a very different situation from the one Clinton was in. There is a major difference between serving as a witness and serving as a defendant in a civil case. The requirements that a defendant faces are much more strenuous, time-consuming, and costly (both financially and emotionally) than those of a witness. By failing to recognize that, the Court ignored the question of just how being a defendant would affect a president.

Broad Rules of Discovery

Perhaps the biggest threat facing the presidency as a result of the *Clinton* decision is the opportunity for opposing counsel in a civil trial to depose the president on matters that would not even be admissible in the trial.[101] This was the case in regard to the information on Monica Lewinsky in President Clinton's deposition. Just two weeks after the deposition, Judge Wright ruled that the testimony relating to Lewinsky was "not essential to the core issues in this case" and "might be inadmissible as extrinsic evidence."[102] But by then, the damage was beyond control. Such information could then be used to trigger a congressional investigation, a Justice Department inquiry, or even the appointment of an independent counsel.

The rules of discovery in federal civil cases are especially broad when it comes to an allegation of sexual misconduct. Ironically, President Clinton himself signed into law changes in the Federal Rules of Evidence allowing broad questioning of a defendant's sexual history. The combination of broad discretion in discovery regarding sexual activity and a lack of protection for sitting presidents from such lawsuits is a volatile combination. Again, the justices seemed woefully to underestimate the scope and reach of civil litigation into the matters and affairs of both parties at the trial. This is particularly critical when one of those parties is the president and is the focus of unparalleled scrutiny as well as unparalleled responsibilities.

WHERE DO WE GO FROM HERE?

Reconsideration by the Supreme Court

Regardless of its problematic implications, *Clinton v. Jones* is now controlling precedent for presidential immunity. Analysts and politicians concerned about the result of the *Clinton* case face three primary options for limiting or reworking the Supreme Court's decision. The first option involves just the Supreme Court. As events unfolded in the Clinton impeachment, it became clear that the Court had significantly underestimated the demand and the toll of a civil suit on the president. Were the Court to reconsider this issue it might very well reverse or seriously limit the reach of the decision. Monetary costs alone have been a controversial issue. The costs of mounting a defense can be prohibitive, the Clintons having incurred approximately $10 million in legal fees. The first presidential Legal Expense Trust Fund raised $1.3 million but had to return almost half of that amount when it was determined that those contributions were illegal. The second fund, however, went on to raise $4.6 million. These legal expenses can leave presidents open to accusations of conflicts of interest and influence peddling.[103] Moreover, the facts of the Clinton case were quite unfavorable for granting protection to the president. The actions had been taken before he was president or even president-elect. The case was largely seen as insignificant by the media and observers. Finally, the president's claim of limited time was undermined by the prominent news stories about the amount of time he spent hosting coffees for Democratic donors. Thus, it is possible that in a subsequent case, with different facts and with a greater appreciation for the problems that civil suits can cause the president, the Supreme Court may alter course and offer greater protection to future presidents.

District Court Discretion

Another potential solution presents itself at the district court level. A group of scholars has focused on the district court's continuing discretion to schedule cases.[104] As noted in the majority opinion, the district courts retain broad powers to handle scheduling and timing issues for the cases in their dockets. Relying on both the majority opinion and Justice Breyer's concurrence, it would seem likely that a district court could issue a stay much like that granted in *Jones* as long as the reasoning avoided the issue of immunity. If the president could establish that the demands of the office would be substantively impeded, district court judges could be sympathetic to issuing extensive stays. As Miller argues, the *Clinton* case "ultimately may stand for the limited proposition that, although separation of powers does not require categorical immunity, a functional analysis of the needs of the executive branch in a particular case and a consideration of the development of history and practical realities since the [*Clinton*] decision could result in a stay of proceedings."[105] District court judges wishing to avoid an onslaught of civil litigation against presidents may very well construe the president's liability narrowly. Such an approach would appear to fall within the scope of the *Clinton* decision (certainly at least within Breyer's concurrence) and would maintain de facto protections for the president. However, the Supreme Court may be leery of granting such power to the district courts since to do so could implicate a serious question of separation of powers. By leaving to the judiciary the determination of what constitutes an impermissible interference, the balance of power among the three branches could be impacted. Justice Scalia has expressed concern about this issue in the past, saying, "frequently an issue of [allocation of power among the three branches] will come before the Court clad . . . in sheep's clothing: the potential of the asserted principle to effect important change in the equilibrium of power is not immediately evident, and must be discerned by a careful and perceptive analysis."[106] Whether this concern would be sufficient to limit the discretion of the district courts remains to be seen.

Congressional Involvement

The final option was mentioned by Justice Stevens in his opinion. Congress always retains the power and authority to statutorily increase the temporary protection that is available for a president to accommodate important public interests.[107] Examples of past actions of Congress in this vein include protection for debtors against litigation after filing bankruptcy[108] and a stay of civil claims against military personnel during the course of active duty.[109] Stevens makes it clear that congressional action in this case would not run afoul of the Constitution in the Court's mind since the protection the president seeks is not embodied in the Constitution. The Court confirmed that "our holding today raises no barrier to a statutory response to these concerns."[110] Several scholars have picked up on this approach and have offered potential legislation for consideration.[111] Jennifer L. Long was one of the first to propose such legislation prior to the Supreme Court decision.[112] Containing several parts, her proposed legislation would codify the immunity established in *Fitzgerald,* suspend the enforcement of civil liabilities for unofficial actions until three months after the president leaves office unless the litigation would not materially affect the president's duties, and place the burden of proof on the plaintiff to show that such litigation should go forward. Further, it would reduce the statute of limitations to two and a half years, allow discovery to proceed under seal of the court, allow transfer of the venue to the District of Columbia, offer additional damages in the form of prejudgment interest to compensate for the delay, and finally, apply these protections equally to the vice president. Alternatively, the political scientist Richard Pious has pointed out that Congress could revise the Federal Rules of Civil Procedure to permit a simple showing that litigation has political origins in order to have it dismissed.[113] Congressional legislation to increase the protection of the president is certainly a possible response to the *Clinton* decision in the future. But as of now, with intense partisanship between the major parties, it seems unlikely that either party would be interested in passing protective legislation for the president.

The history of executive immunity in the United States has represented a continuing struggle between executive prerogative and judicial authority. Beginning with *Burr* and carrying all the way through to *Clinton,* the issue is one that has long troubled the judiciary. The separation of powers established by the Constitution offers a general approach, but many difficult questions exist at the intersection of the branches. Through time, a number of these difficult questions have been answered one way or the other, often granting extensive deference to the president. However, *Clinton v. Jones* established the outer limits of discretion for the president and reaffirmed Chief Justice Marshall's long-standing opinion in *Burr* that the executive is responsible to the judiciary. Presidents following Clinton will face the reality of an increasingly narrowed area of ambiguity within which to exercise discretion when it comes to executive protections. In some cases, such as *United States v. Nixon,* this narrowing can be regarded as a positive step. In *Clinton v. Jones,* however, the waters are much muddier. Although many of Clinton's constitutional claims during his presidency pushed the envelope and have been considered invalid, his argument for temporary immunity does seem to have historical, legal, and political support.[114]

The controversial 2000 election is likely to impact significantly how the Court's decision plays out. Continued divided government and partisan hostility could very well mean increased civil litigation against the president, with little or no response from Congress. Questions about the legitimacy of the Bush victory might make Congress even less likely to grant the president new protections. In that case, it would not be surprising to see the district courts exercising greater discretion in preventing litigation from proceeding. With unified government, the issue could return to the back burner, and the Court's prediction of only a minimal number of civil cases might be vindicated. However, politics is a rough-and-tumble arena. Any tactic or method that can be used against a president usually is. There is little doubt that this issue will raise its head again in the future. The law has been clarified a bit, but the direction of future immunity claims, like so many interbranch conflicts, will be set by politics as much as by law.

NOTES

1. *Clinton* v. *Jones,* 520 U.S. 681 (1997).

2. Ibid., at 685.

3. A number of articles cited the decision in *Clinton v. Jones* to allow the case to go forward as a key event in the Lewinsky scandal. For example, see Jonathan Rauch, "The People Are Right: Keep Him," *National Journal,* September 26, 1998 ("The law has behaved rashly and boorishly from the day the Supreme Court allowed Paula Corbin Jones to proceed with her sexual harassment suit against a sitting president") p. 2212; and Robert Scheer, "Scandal Is Not His Only Legacy," *Los Angeles Times,* August 18, 1998 ("The ruling of the U.S. Supreme Court to permit the Paula Jones case to go forward on the grounds that it would not intrude on the work of the presidency will go down as the stupidest decision in the court's history"), p. B7.

4. Executive immunity as it is used here refers only to exemption from the legal process for the president. For a discussion on immunity of executive branch employees and appointees, see generally, Mark J. Rozell, *Executive Privilege* (Baltimore: Johns Hopkins University Press, 1994); Adam C. Breckenridge, *The Executive Privilege* (Lincoln: University of Nebraska Press, 1974); and Louis Fisher, *Constitutional Conflicts Between Congress and the President,* 4th ed., rev. (Lawrence: University Press of Kansas, 1997).

5. William Maclay, *Journal of William Maclay, United States Senator from Pennsylvania, 1789–1791,* ed. Edgar S. Maclay (New York: D. A. Appleton, 1890), September 26, 1789, journal entry, p. 167.

6. Ibid., as quoted in *Clinton v. Jones,* at 716.

7. Ibid., at 695.

8. *United States v. Burr,* 25 F. Cas. 30 (C.C.D. Va. 1807) (No. 14,692d).

9. In *Clinton,* though the case is cited on a number of occasions, most of the attention is focused on Jefferson's letters to George Hay rather than on Marshall's opinion. This is a common feature of the fragmented historical review that usually accompanies presidential immunity cases. We hope here to provide a fuller picture of the issues in play.

10. For detailed accounts of Burr's alleged treason and the circumstances leading up to it, see Albert J. Beveridge, *The Life of John Marshall,* 4 vols. (Boston: Houghton Mifflin, 1919), vol. 3, and David Robertson, 2 vols. *Reports of the Trials of Colonel Aaron Burr* (New York: Da Capo Press, 1808), vol. 1.

11. A subpoena *duces tecum* is "an order compelling a person to produce a document or other piece of physical evidence that is relevant to issues pending before a court, legislative hearing, or grand jury" (from Lee Epstein and Thomas G. Walker, *Constitutional Law for a Changing America* [Washington D.C.: CQ Press, 1998], p. 843).

12. George Washington had made some claims of executive privilege regarding letters in his possession, but that was an issue between Congress and the presidency, which never made it to court. Further, Jefferson had shielded some cabinet members from testifying and turning over evidence earlier in his presidency, but again the court did not rule

on the president's authority to do so. See Mark Rozell's chapter 3 in this book for further details.

13. In Jefferson's claim, we see reflections of Adams and Ellsworth's earlier opinion.

14. Robertson, *Reports of the Trials of Colonel Aaron Burr,* 1: 146.

15. The Sixth Amendment of the U.S. Constitution reads: "In all criminal prosecutions, the accused shall enjoy the right to a speedy and public trial, by an impartial jury of the State and district wherein the crime shall have been committed, which district shall have been previously ascertained by law, and to be informed of the nature and cause of the accusation; to be confronted with the witnesses against him; to have compulsory process for obtaining witnesses in his favor, and to have the Assistance of Counsel for his defense."

16. A subpoena *ad testificandum* is "an order compelling a person to testify before a court, legislative hearing, or grand jury" (from Epstein and Walker, *Constitutional Law,* p. 843).

17. Robertson, *Reports of the Trials of Colonel Aaron Burr,* 1: 180–181.

18. *Marbury v. Madison,* 5 U.S. (1 Cranch) 137 (1803).

19. Robertson, *Reports of the Trials of Colonel Aaron Burr,* 1: 35.

20. Ibid.

21. Thomas Jefferson, *Works of Thomas Jefferson,* ed. Paul L. Ford, 10 vols. (New York: G. P. Putnam's Sons, 1892–1905), letter of June 17, 1807, from Thomas Jefferson to George Hay, 1: 404.

22. Joseph Story, *Commentaries on the Constitution of the United States* (Boston: Hillard, Gray, 1833), pp. 418–419.

23. *Mississippi v. Johnson,* 71 U.S. 475 (1867).

24. The case came before the Court as a motion to file a bill, which was typically approved without review. However, the president and his cabinet had been notified in advance and decided to contest the motion. The rules of the Court have since been revised to ensure that "the initial pleading in any original action shall be prefaced by a motion for leave to file such pleading" (*Revised Rules of the Supreme Court* [1970], Rule 9, 398 U.S., 1011, 1019).

25. Charles Fairman, *Reconstruction and Reunion, 1864–1888* (New York: Macmillan, 1971), p. 380.

26. 71 U.S., at 498. The immunity in this case can be described only as a practical matter rather than clearly as law because the Court was unclear whether it was relying exclusively on executive immunity or on separation of powers. The Court's stated reason for dismissing the case was that if the president refused to obey the injunction, the Court would be powerless to enforce it. Either way, the end result is that the president effectively has immunity since he cannot be held responsible in a court for discretionary duties.

27. See, for example, *Winsor v. Hunt,* 243 P. 407, 411 (Ariz. 1926); *State v. Staub,* 23 A. 924, 927 (Conn. 1892); *Dunagan v. Stadler,* 29 S.E. 440, 440 (Ga. 1897); *Nagle v. Wakey,* 43 N.E. 1079, 1082 (Ill. 1896) (Phillips, J., dissenting). The Supreme Court has also relied on this reasoning in cases such as *Gaines v. Thompson,* 74 U.S. 347, 353 (1869), and *Colegrove v. Green,* 328 U.S. 549, 556 (1946) ("The duty to see to it that the laws are faithfully executed cannot be brought under legal compulsion").

28. 343 U.S. 579 (1952).

29. 520 U.S., at 703.

30. For a further discussion of *Youngstown*'s impact on executive immunity, see Laura Krugman Ray, "From Prerogative to Accountability: The Amenability of the President to Suit," *Kentucky Law Journal* 80 (1992): 739.

31. 418 U.S. 683 (1974).

32. For more details on the Watergate scandal, see Michael Genovese, *The Watergate Crisis* (Westport, Conn.: Greenwood Press, 1999).

33. *In re Subpoena to Nixon,* 360 F. Supp. 1, 3 (D.D.C. 1973).

34. For further discussion, see Gerald Gunther, "Judicial Hegemony and Legislative Autonomy: The Nixon Case and the Impeachment Process," *UCLA Law Review* 22 (1974): 30.

35. 48 U.S., at 706.

36. Ibid., at 712 n.19.

37. 457 U.S. 731 (1982).

38. Ibid., at 731–740.

39. Arthur Galub, *The Burger Court, 1968–1984* (Millwood, N.Y.: Associated Faculty Press, 1986), p. 240.

40. The court of appeals dismissed the case based on its "collateral order" doctrine, which precludes review of an interlocutory order unless it involves an unresolved question of law. The appellate court relied on its decision in *Halperin v. Kissinger,* 606 F. 2d 1192 (D.C. Cir. 1979), which the Supreme Court had affirmed in part.

41. When the Supreme Court grants certiorari, it agrees to review the case.

42. 457 U.S., at 765.

43. The word "unique" was used four times in three pages in the majority opinion, distinguishing the president from other executive officials who receive only qualified immunity.

44. 457 U.S., at 754.

45. Ibid.

46. Ibid., at 758–761.

47. Ibid., at 761.

48. 457 U.S., at 759, 761 n.4.

49. Ibid., at 763.

50. There are a number of historical cases where presidents provided testimony. Ulysses Grant gave a deposition in a criminal trial, James Monroe responded to written interrogatories, Gerald Ford gave a deposition in a criminal trial, Jimmy Carter provided videotaped testimony for a criminal trial, and Clinton gave videotaped testimony in two criminal trials (see *Clinton v. Jones,* 520 U.S., at 705).

51. Note that there have been no decisions on whether the president is required to turn over materials in a civil case, although it is likely that he would.

52. *Jones v. Clinton,* 858 F. Supp. 902 (E.D. Ark. 1994).

53. Ibid., at 904–905.

54. In order to allow Jones to renew the suit after Clinton left office, Judge Wright would have had to "toll" the statute of limitations. Since the lawsuit was filed only three days before the statute of limitations would have run out, the court would need to grant an extension on that limit until the end of Clinton's presidency.

55. This option would have kept the case alive during that time but no action, including discovery of evidence, could have taken place until the stay was removed.

56. *Jones v. Clinton,* 869 F. Supp. 690 (E.D. Ark. 1994).

57. Ibid., at 693. It is interesting to contrast this conclusion with Marshall's charac-

terization of the British system in Robertson, *Reports of the Trials of Colonel Aaron Burr,* where he concludes that the United States is not like England *because* the president is not above the law.

58. *Jones v. Clinton,* at 697.

59. Ibid., at 698.

60. Ibid.

61. Ibid., at 699.

62. See Richard M. Pious, "The Paradox of Clinton Winning and the Presidency Losing," *Political Science Quarterly* 14 (1999): 591.

63. *Jones v. Clinton,* 72 F. 3d 1354 (8th Cir. 1996), hereafter referred to as *Jones II.*

64. The three-judge panel consisted of circuit judges Bowman, Ross, and Beam.

65. 72 F. 3d, at 1356.

66. Ibid., at 1358.

67. Ibid., citing *Fitzgerald,* 457 U.S. at 747.

68. Ibid., at 759.

69. 72 F. 3d, at 1360.

70. 457 U.S., at 754.

71. 72 F. 3d, at 1362.

72. Ibid., at 1361.

73. Ibid., at 1367.

74. Ibid., at 1363–1366.

75. *Clinton v. Jones,* 520 U.S. 681 (1997).

76. Ibid., at 692.

77. Ibid., at 694 n. 19.

78. Ibid., at 694.

79. Ibid., citing *Forrester v. White,* 484 U.S. at 219, 229–230 (1988).

80. 343 U.S. 579 (1952).

81. 520 U.S., at 634–635.

82. At the same time, Stevens referred back to Chief Justice Marshall's opinion that the duties of the president are not entirely "unremitting" when it comes to facing the courts (ibid., at 699).

83. Ibid.

84. *Loving v. United States,* 517 U.S. 757 (1996).

85. 520 U.S., at 705.

86. Linda Greenhouse, "The Justices and Paula Jones: The Ruling that Entangled the President," *New York Times,* March 15, 1998, p. A1, and sec. 4, p. 1.

87. 520 U.S., at 707.

88. Ibid., at 708–709.

89. Ibid., at 710.

90. Ibid., at 721.

91. *Jones v. Clinton,* 990 F. Supp. 657 (1998).

92. Ibid., at 691.

93. Ibid., at 691–692.

94. For a more extended discussion of the question of criminal immunity, see Pious, "The Paradox of Clinton Winning and the Presidency Losing," pp. 574–577.

95. Though it was Clinton's perjury that led to impeachment, we cannot forget that the perjury itself took place during the depositions for the lawsuit. Although it might not have resulted in impeachment, had President Clinton told the truth about his relationship

with Monica Lewinsky during the deposition, it is difficult to imagine that there would not have been a number of negative consequences as well.

96. Randall Miller, "Presidential Sanctuaries After the Clinton Sex Scandals," *Harvard Journal of Law and Public Policy* 22 (1999): 647.

97. 520 U.S., at 702.

98. Ibid., at 711–721.

99. Ibid., at. 693–695.

100. This was a hotly debated topic during the impeachment hearings, since there was serious question about using the standards for impeaching judges to impeach the president. See Miller, "Presidential Sanctuaries," 259 n, and Charles J. Cooper, "A Perjurer in the White House? The Constitutional Case for Perjury and Obstruction of Justice as High Crimes and Misdemeanors," *Harvard Journal of Law and Public Policy* 22 (1999): 615.

101. The discovery rules are broad and liberally construed. See Federal Rules for Civil Procedure 26(b)(1): "The information sought [in discovery] need not be admissible at the trial if the information sought appears reasonably calculated to lead to the discovery of admissible evidence").

102. *Jones v. Clinton,* No. LR-C-94-290, 1998 U.S. Dist. LEXIS 696, at 3 (E.D. Ark. January 29, 1998).

103. Pious, "The Paradox of Clinton Winning and the Presidency Losing," pp. 592–593.

104. See, generally, Jennifer Motos, "Failing to Score: *Clinton v. Jones* and Claims of Presidential Immunity," *Mercer Law Review* 49 (1998): 583, and L. Darnell Weeden, "The President and Mrs. Jones Were in Federal Court: The Litigation Established No Constitutional Immunity for President Clinton," *George Mason Law Review* 7 (1999): 361.

105. Miller, "Presidential Sanctuaries," p. 647.

106. *Morrison v. Olson,* 487 U.S. 654, 699 (1988) (Scalia, J., dissenting).

107. This seems to be a one-way street. See Burger's concurrence in *Fitzgerald,* arguing that Congress should not be permitted to increase the president's liability.

108. 11 U.S.C. 362.

109. Soldiers' and Sailors' Civil Relief Act of 1940, 50 U.S.C. App. 501–525.

110. 520 U.S., at 710.

111. See, generally, Pious, "The Paradox of Clinton Winning and the Presidency Losing," p. 574; Diann D. Alexander, "In the Aftermath of *Clinton v. Jones:* An Argument in Favor of Legislation Permitting a Sitting President to Defer Litigation," *Southwestern University Law Review* 28 (1998): 71.

112. Jennifer Long, "How to Sue the President: A Proposal for Legislation Establishing the Extent of Presidential Immunity," *Valparaiso University Law Review* 30 (1995): 283.

113. Pious, "The Paradox of Clinton Winning and the Presidency Losing," p. 574.

114. See, especially, David Gray Adler's "Clinton, the Constitution, and the War Power," chapter 2 of this book.

7

In the Wake of 1996: Clinton's Legacy for Presidential Campaign Finance

Victoria A. Farrar-Myers

The landscape of campaign financing in modern presidential elections reveals the indelible effect left behind by political reforms in the 1960s and 1970s and by their subsequent implementation. The major political parties, for example, altered the process by which they selected their presidential candidates. Reforms initially developed at the Democratic National Convention in 1968 and further refined by the McGovern-Fraser Commission led to greater reliance on primaries as the means to choose a party's nominee. Congress, by passing the 1971 Federal Election Campaign Act (FECA) and subsequent amendments in 1974 in the wake of Watergate, restructured the way candidates raised and spent money in presidential elections. The system that Congress created, however, changed, following the Supreme Court's decision in *Buckley v. Valeo,* which gutted important provisions in FECA related to spending limits. Subsequent judicial decisions also shaped the legal rules guiding campaign finance. Furthermore, as Congress continued to adjust the nation's campaign finance laws, the Federal Election Commission (FEC) needed to interpret the changes. This led to the advent of soft money, originally designed to help the major parties but which has become an important component of recent presidential elections. Thus, the landscape of contemporary presidential campaign finance is dotted with a series of party rules, legislation, court decisions, and administrative rulings.

Today's postreform era is one where most delegates to the national conventions are chosen by the public, where the selection process is relatively open, and where favorite sons are supposed no longer to exist. The presidential nomination system also has become one where an invisible primary process has developed more than a year in advance, where the process is so front-loaded and the pace so furious that candidates drop out right and left once the process begins, and finally where the cost of seeking the office has become prohibitive. These changes call into question the legitimacy and openness of the presidential selection process.

They also have placed an increased burden on presidential candidates to raise funds early and often in the nomination process.

Facing this landscape in 1996, President Bill Clinton attacked fund-raising with an aggressiveness heretofore not seen, especially from a sitting president. Clinton took existing loopholes and opened them even further; and where none had existed before, he established new means for raising funds to aid in his re-election. Without assessing the possible legality or illegality of his actions here, one sees that Clinton clearly did one thing—he left his own indelible imprint on the landscape of the presidential campaign finance system.

THE EFFECT OF UNINTENDED CONSEQUENCES

Although the reforms of the 1970s were well meaning, they brought unintended consequences along with their implementation. On the surface some appear to make the process more democratic and open to the public, but many reforms have led to the lengthening of the nomination process and a greater emphasis on campaign funding. For example, the rules that allow candidates to receive matching contributions from the federal government encourage candidates to raise as much money as possible in the year before an election.[1] Moreover, the increased use of Leadership Political Action Committees (PACs) stretch out the fund-raising process. Potential presidential candidates often will form PACs to raise funds to cover organizational costs as well as travel and other expenses associated with building support in the years before an election. Because donors can contribute to Leadership PACs each year they exist, potential presidential candidates can form a PAC to raise funds two or three years before they formally announce their candidacy.[2] One effect of extending the fund-raising period, for example, is the advantage it provides to senators, whose six-year terms allow them more flexibility in planning and conducting a campaign, when compared to governors, who generally have two- or four-year terms, or House members, who serve two-year terms.[3] Thus, although these reforms were designed to make it easier to pursue the highest office, they have to some degree actually made running for president more difficult because candidates must establish themselves financially long before the first votes in the Iowa caucuses are cast.

Further, as recent elections have demonstrated, candidates need to place even more emphasis on campaigning and the raising of funds, both for their own campaign and for their party, once they officially enter the race. As a result, candidates have sought to develop new and more effective ways to raise funds as well as to spend more time fund-raising than ever before. For example, candidates often will "go where the money is"—that is, to certain areas in the nation where wealthy contributors can be easily aggregated for fund-raising events. Nelson Polsby and Aaron Wildavsky term this phenomenon "The Beverly Hills Primary" after the tendency of Democratic candidates to seek contributions and support from Hollywood celebrities. Candidates also have used direct-mail solic-itation as another fund-raising tool in recent elections.[4] Pat Buchanan ran one of the more successful recent direct-mail efforts by raising over $4 million in 1992, with 85 percent being eligible for matching funds.[5] Furthermore, candidates have explored other ways to seek funds, including running full-page newspaper ads, offering toll-free telephone numbers, and making highly publicized appearances in certain media outlets.[6] More recently, the Internet has become an effective means to raise funds, particularly from people who may not have otherwise con-tributed to a campaign. One recent study has concluded, "Online contributors are newer, younger and give smaller contributions."[7]

In addition to these more straightforward but time-consuming fund-raising techniques, the same exploitation of the campaign finance rules that has plagued the congressional electoral process has begun to be just as pervasive in the presidential arena. Most notably, soft money has come to dominate much attention in presiden-tial fund-raising. Stemming from the 1979 amendments to FECA, the advent of soft money was designed to promote party-building activities, such as voter registration and get-out-the-vote drives. Instead, such money has been used to promote the par-ties' message, which in a presidential election year is nearly synonymous with their presidential candidate's message, even though the candidates are not supposed to coordinate spending of the party's soft money. At times, however, presidential can-didates come close to crossing over the line and may in fact do so—certainly, this was one of the many charges of campaign finance abuses levied against President Clinton following the 1996 election.[8] These practices highlight one key point to remember: because presidential candidates often are their party's best soft-money fund-raisers, presidential campaigning and soft money have become linked.[9]

These issues raise questions about the integrity of the process. The public financing scheme that was supposed to protect the presidential election process from special interests and corruption is now being manipulated by presidential candidates seeking to create an advantage. Bill Clinton in 1996 demonstrated how soft money and perpetual campaigning can place this system in jeopardy. Clinton worked the rules of the presidential campaign finance system to his advantage, showing just how malleable the rules designed to put candidates on an equal footing could be. In doing so, he perhaps eradicated the line separating the roles a sitting president plays as a candidate seeking election and the elected leader of the nation. Further, his activities laid bare the inadequacies of the pub-lic financing program, and the fissures in the system were blasted wide open in the 2000 run for the presidency.

HISTORICAL OVERVIEW

Understanding the current presidential campaign financing problems requires one to consider how and why they developed. The place to start is the 1970s campaign financing reforms to see what issues Congress intended and did not intend to address. Further, one should assess how the reformers and political analysts of the 1970s viewed the newly implemented system to gain insight into how the current problems have evolved.

The Tax Checkoff System: The Foundation of Public Financing

Public financing of presidential elections is not a recent policy initiative.[10] As early as 1904 the idea of public financing of presidential campaigns was introduced as a means to protect the electoral process from the corrupting force of private money.[11] The idea again gained momentum in the mid-1950s, and in 1966 Congress passed a presidential campaign public financing plan. Under this plan, a fund would be established through a voluntary $1.00 tax checkoff, with the money distributed to the political parties. Congress, however, rescinded this plan before it took effect.

In 1971, Senator John Pastore (D-R.I.) offered an amendment to that year's revenue act to establish public financing of presidential elections. After a great deal of political wrangling, including a veto threat from President Nixon and an agreement that would delay implementation until the 1976 election, the amendment passed. Beginning in 1972, federal tax returns featured a box by which taxpayers could choose to allocate $1.00 ($2.00 on a joint return) of their taxes to go automatically into a fund for presidential candidates. This scheme, working in conjunction with the voluntary spending limits imposed by the 1974 FECA amendments and that survived challenge in *Buckley v. Valeo,*[12] has doled out $890.9 million to presidential candidates and parties between 1976 and 1996: to seventy-four primary candidates, $256.6 million; to two major parties for twelve nominating conventions, $92.7 million; and to twelve major party nominees and two independents in the general election, $541.6 million.[13]

Although the tax checkoff system has generated a significant pool of funds for presidential candidates to draw on if they choose[14] and if they qualify to do so, it has not proved to be the panacea that proponents had hoped it would be. First, an ever-dwindling minority of taxpayers checks off the box to direct funds for use in presidential campaigns (see Table 7.1). Even with an adjustment for inflation in 1993, when Congress increased the $1.00 checkoff to $3.00 to combat a projected shortfall of funds for the 1996 presidential election, the checkoff system is becoming increasingly irrelevant to presidential campaign politics. Not only are fewer people contributing to presidential campaigns with the $3.00 checkoff, but the money that is raised has not kept pace with inflation.

Herein lies the second problem with the checkoff system as it currently operates. The funds that are raised and distributed to candidates have not kept pace with the ever-increasing costs of campaigning (hiring staff and consultants, travel expenses, television and radio advertisements) at any stage of the election

Table 7.1. Federal Income Tax Presidential Checkoff, 1976–1997

Year	Percentage Checked Off	Amount Checked Off (in dollars)	Adjusted Checked Off (in dollars)
1976	25.5	33,731,945	59,267,027
1977	27.5	36,606,008	60,363,307
1978	28.6	39,245,639	60,125,928
1979	25.4	35,941,347	49,599,059
1980	27.4	38,838,417	47,188,677
1981	28.7	41,049,052	45,071,859
1982	27.0	39,023,882	40,389,718
1983	24.2	35,631,068	35,737,961
1984	23.7	35,036,761	33,670,327
1985	23.0	34,712,761	32,213,442
1986	23.0	35,753,837	32,643,253
1987	21.7	33,651,947	29,613,713
1988	21.0	33,013,987	27,929,833
1989	20.1	32,285,646	26,054,516
1990	19.8	32,462,979	24,866,642
1991	19.5	32,322,336	23,724,595
1992	17.7	29,592,735	21,099,620
1993	18.9	27,636,982	19,124,792
1994a	14.5	71,316,995	48,138,972
1995	13.0	67,350,127	44,516,243
1996	12.9	66,903,788	42,684,617
1997	12.4	66,347,632	41,334,575

Source: Compiled from the Center for Responsive Politics from Federal Election Commission data and 1997 IRS Taxpayer Usage Study. Adjusted checkoff values calculated using the 1999 Statistical Abstract, Table no. 775, Purchasing Power of the Dollar: 1950–1998.
aTax checkoff amount was increased from $1.00 to $3.00 in 1994.

process.[15] This, in turn, has put pressure on candidates to allocate their resources more effectively and quite possibly to look elsewhere, including outside the system if need be, for funding opportunities.[16]

The 1976 Election: The Lessons That Hindsight Provides

The first presidential election cycle that took place under the public financing rules occurred in 1976. The media and the public, wary of campaign finance corruption on the heels of the Watergate scandal, closely watched the election and the candidates, Gerald Ford and Jimmy Carter. Also under scrutiny, however, was the new presidential campaign finance system that Congress established. A number of commentators at that time regarded the new system as effective in fulfilling its stated goals. The new rules were successful in constraining the impact of individual contributors and the cost of campaigns at that time. But the system did have its limitations: the real problems would arise outside the public financing scheme. With almost a quarter-century of hindsight, these commentators' evaluations almost seem prophetic.

In enacting the 1974 FECA amendments, Congress sought to minimize the relative importance of contributions from wealthy donors and special interests so that they would not be able to "buy a piece of the candidate."[17] Thus, for example, one *New York Times* columnist noted that one Democratic supporter who gave $320,000—equal to approximately $1.3 million today—could give only $1,000 in 1976. Moreover, this amount was "infinitesimal" compared to the estimated $6.5 million Jimmy Carter was expected to spend to win the Democratic nomination.[18] Thus, the $1,000 contribution limit seemingly achieved its goal of making elections more democratic by restricting the influence that wealthy individuals could have.

Similarly, the 1976 election also highlighted FECA's success in constraining the cost of presidential campaigns, at least when compared to the 1972 election. With history on our side now, one may not think that it is appropriate to use 1972, with its well-documented campaign finance abuses, as a benchmark with which to compare the public financing system's impact on the 1976 election. But in 1976, that was the comparison that commentators made. In doing so, they pointed out that in 1972, candidates Nixon ($30 million) and McGovern ($61.4 million) combined to spend over $90 million. By contrast, the spending limits imposed by FECA for candidates accepting public funds meant that no more than $70 million would be spent in 1976.[19]

But for all the successes that the public financing system achieved in 1976, many commentators saw that the real problems stemmed from contributions that occurred outside FECA's rules and from the public financing system's inability to satisfy the escalating financial demands of conducting a presidential campaign. These analysts also pointed out nearly twenty-five years ago the loopholes in the contribution/financing system that are being exploited today:

- private individuals could still contribute funds to party committees (today's soft money problem);
- candidates could contribute large sums of their own money to their campaigns (the wealthy candidate problem);
- private interests, including corporate and union political action committees, could make independent expenditures to support candidates (the sham issue ad problem); and
- potentially, incumbent presidents could "blatantly [exploit] their office" for reelection fund-raising purposes (the Clinton fund-raising scandals).[20]

One commentator also noted that the amount of public funds allotted to the candidates in 1976 "was not nearly enough to finance some traditional forms of campaigning."[21] The fact that funds were limited forced candidates to spend their money more judiciously and effectively so that each dollar spent would reach the widest possible audience. Thus, campaign buttons and bumper stickers gave way to increased reliance on television ads. Even within this first election, the public finance system showed signs of beginning to bulge at the seams.

FACING THE CONSEQUENCES: THE NEED FOR FUNDS
IN A CHANGING POLITICAL CONTEXT

The nomination process reforms have led to some unintended consequences. The primary and caucus season is crowded, especially when a party does not have an incumbent president seeking nomination. Then, candidates are likely to come out of the woodwork seeking the party's nomination. With the prospect of being able to obtain at least some matching funds from the federal government, lesser-known or poorly financed candidates have been able to hang on perhaps longer than they should have with the hope of eventually generating some excitement to help fill their war chests. Even incumbent presidents are not immune from primary challenges, though, as evidenced by Reagan's challenge of Ford in 1976, Kennedy against Carter in 1980, and Buchanan against Bush in 1992. As the history since 1976 has shown, the nomination process is like running a gauntlet, making it hard for candidates to survive, let alone muster enough support and finances to win.

A second consequence of the political parties' reforms of the nomination process is that states have started to compete among themselves to be the one that puts the candidate over the top in securing the nomination. This has led to frontloading, where states have placed their primary dates earlier in the year so that they can have a say in who gets the nomination. In the past, several large states like California would hold their primaries in June. Now, the process begins in early January and has the potential to be over by early spring. Further, several key dates, known as super days, where many states or a number of states in a certain region hold their primaries on the same day, have become vital testing grounds for any potential nominee. These changes in primary dates have forced candidates to modify how they campaign to take into account the altered primary schedule. These changes also have placed additional stress on the candidates' time, money, and resources. In the past, candidates could spread their campaign expenses over a period of time and hope that a few early successes could raise money to fund later primaries; now, candidates do not have time on their side. Instead, they must have their finances in order before the first vote or risk an early departure.

Because of these changes to the nomination system, candidates are forced to make the decision to run much sooner, creating in the media and public forum an almost "invisible primary" process. This process occurs sometimes years in advance of the actual election year; indeed, candidates often employ fund-raising mechanisms that allow them to participate in the invisible primary while they decide whether in fact to run. In this process, until the first votes are cast, a candidate's ability to raise money is often used by the media, the public, and candidates themselves as a surrogate for a candidate's viability. As a result, underfunded candidates may drop out of the race before the Iowa caucus and the New Hampshire primary. Similarly, potential candidates during the invisible primaries can generate headlines for publicly weighing the decision to run, only later choosing not to do so.

Table 7.2. Costs of Presidential Nominations, 1976–1996 (in Millions of Dollars)

Year	Democrats	Republicans
1976	40.7	26.1
1980	41.7	86.1
1984	107.7	28.0
1988	94.0	114.6
1992	66.0	51.0
1996	46.1	187.0

Source: Compiled in Stephen J. Wayne, *The Road to the White House, 2000: The Politics of Presidential Elections* (Boston: Bedford/St. Martin's, 2000), Table 2.3, p. 29. Data originally drawn from 1976–1984, Federal Election Commission, "Reports on Financial Activity, 1987–1988," *Presidential Pre-Nomination Campaigns* (August 1989), Table A-7, p. 10; Herbert E. Alexander, "Financing the Presidential Elections," paper presented at the Institute for Political Studies in Japan, Tokyo, September 8–10, 1989, pp. 4, 10; Herbert E. Alexander and Anthony Corrado, *Financing the 1992 Elections* (Armonk, N.Y.: M. E. Sharpe, 1995); Federal Election Commission, "Presidential Campaign Disbursements" (inception through August 31, 1996).

As a result of this landscape created in part by the party's nomination reforms, candidates need to raise and spend significant sums of money just to try to get their party's nomination. (For the aggregate prenomination spending for candidates from the two major parties for each election year since 1976, see Table 7.2.) Given the landscape that has developed, candidates need to look for any financial advantage that they can obtain, which leads to exploiting loopholes and calls into question the need for further reform.

These changes also have called into question the key tenets of what the original reforms were supposed to achieve. Although they attempted to open the process and make running more accessible, in essence they have closed the process to those who cannot afford to mount a viable campaign. Further, this has put a lot of emphasis on the known candidate and made those of lesser status fearful of running. Finally, the pressure to raise enough funds to be competitive has not only seen good candidates shy away or step out, but also has encouraged others to take advantage of the loopholes in the system. The very ends of keeping some control of the system were undermined by the fact that candidates in 2000 saw a real advantage in opting out of the public financing system in favor of raising private funds, an option, one might remember, that led to the initial reforms in the first account.

THE CLINTON LEGACY: CANDIDATES WORKING THE RULES SO THAT THE RULES WORK FOR THEM

Clearly, the problems that haunt current presidential campaign financing are not new, nor are they Bill Clinton's doing. These problems, or at least their precursors, have been prevalent since the current financing rules were established in the 1970s. Indeed, candidates have long tried to work in and outside the system to address the problems raised by increased costs; by increased competition, both for votes and money; and by a declining base of public funds and so on. Nevertheless, with all its well-documented faults, the system—to a degree at least— worked. Bill Clinton and the 1996 election, however, changed all that when, as one scholar put it, the fund-raising system crumbled.[22]

In 1992 and 1996, Ross Perot and Steve Forbes used their own fortunes in lieu of public funding as their campaigns' base resource.[23] Doing so allowed them to spend and raise money in the way they saw fit. While these decisions in and of themselves emphasize some of the problems of the current nomination system, they also placed greater pressure on other candidates to pursue alternative avenues for fund-raising and spending. In 1996, Clinton, already politically weakened by ineffectiveness during his first few years in office and the Republican gains in Congress during the 1994 midyear elections, responded to this pressure by making a fine art form out of stretching the loopholes that already existed to, and quite possibly beyond, their outer limits.

Much of the story of Clinton's fund-raising successes and excesses are now well known. Both chambers of Congress held hearings to investigate allegations of fund-raising abuses during the 1996 campaign. The Senate Governmental Affairs Committee, chaired by Senator Fred Thompson (R-Tenn.), produced an extensive 1,100-page report of its findings. Despite the partisan posturing in both the majority and minority sections, this report contains the most comprehensive discussion of the alleged campaign finance improprieties during the 1996 election, not only of the Clinton/Gore reelection campaign but also of the Democratic National Committee, the Republican National Committee, and a multitude of other actors.

Among the many allegations levied in the Senate report, two deserve particular attention. First, Clinton, as the nominal head of the Democratic Party, aggressively pursued soft money for the party with the implicit and allegedly explicit intention of using those funds to support his own campaign for reelection. Moreover, Clinton, through the White House staff, coordinated between the Democratic National Committee (DNC) and the Clinton/Gore 1996 campaign "the content, placement, and production of advertisements."[24] Federal law permits some coordination of hard money expenditures between a president's campaign and his party—that was not the issue.[25] Clinton's critics instead expressed their concern over the extent of his direction of the DNC and the focus on soft money. Senate Republicans called Clinton's control (through Deputy Chief of Staff Harold Ickes) over the DNC, which was required to receive prior approval from the White House for "all matters dealing with the allocation and expenditures of monies involving" the DNC, unprecedented.[26] They also quoted Clinton directly, who publicly stated to Democratic contributors that running "ads through the Democratic Party . . . meant that we could raise money in twenty and fifty and hundred thousand dollar lots, and we didn't have to do it all in thousand dollars."[27] Regardless of whether one considers these actions appropriate or not, they do reflect the Clinton campaign's focus on maximizing the funds that the Democratic Party raised to achieve the goal of reelecting Bill Clinton in 1996.

The second primary set of allegations that Senate Republicans levied against Clinton perhaps merits more attention. With his creative use of the perks of incumbency, Clinton brought phrases like "coffees," "Buddhist temples," and "sleepovers in the Lincoln Bedroom" to the forefront of the campaign finance lexicon. Whatever fictitious line in the past may have separated incumbent presidents as candidates from their role as chief executive, Clinton obliterated it. As the political scientist George Edwards has noted, Clinton ushered in the idea of the perpetual campaign in office.[28] In doing so, he used and, as many perceived it, abused the resources of his office for his benefit. As Senate Republicans correctly lamented, Clinton turned the "White House and the presidency itself [into] fund-raising tools."[29] In a campaign financing system that prompts each candidate to find innovative and sometimes questionable ways to raise funds, Clinton took advantage of the one resource he had that no one else did—the power and prestige of the bully pulpit.

During the 1995–1996 election cycle, Clinton used his office as a fund-raising tool by providing access to senior decision makers; allowing contributors to spend the night in the White House; holding coffees in the White House, including the Oval Office, that often lasted at least an hour; and providing flights on Air Force One, seats in the Kennedy Center's presidential box, and use of the White House recreational facilities. The presidential coffees particularly emphasize the financial rewards that Clinton reaped by using his office. Although not all the coffees were necessarily fund-raising events, they proved to be an effective means of generating revenue for the president's campaign. According to Senate Republicans, guests at the coffees contributed a total of $26.4 million during the 1996 election cycle, with one-third of that amount coming within one month of a donor's attendance at a coffee and with much of it directed to the DNC. Furthermore, White House documents purportedly tracked the "projected revenue" that each coffee would raise and how the resulting donations would be allocated between hard money and soft money accounts.

By using the presidency as a fund-raising tool, Clinton responded to the immediate pressure that he felt from other candidates who could raise substantial funds. In doing so, he may have ended up changing the parameters of what sitting presidents do in terms of seeking reelection. Clinton turned the need to raise money into what George Stephanopoulis, Clinton's former press secretary and confident, called an "obsession"; he turned campaigning from what traditionally had been an election-year-only activity into an ongoing concern of primary import.[30] Bill Clinton proved to be an effective and busy fund-raiser in 1996. He attended at least 237 fund-raisers during that year alone, more than twice the amount President George Bush attended in 1992 when seeking reelection.[31] He raised almost $120 million for himself, the Democratic Party, and other Democratic candidates.

But what were the costs of President Clinton's perpetual campaigning? As his hectic schedule became overcrowded with fund-raising events, other matters suffered. The increased use of presidential coffees often cut into his daily morning briefings with his chief of staff and national security adviser. For a period of time, Clinton called off weekly economic briefings; when the briefings were reinstated, they occurred only on a monthly basis. The need to coordinate and to follow up on the many fund-raising events held in the White House also placed great strain on his staff. He also lost several hours in the afternoon that he had previously set aside as "thinking time" as well as "down time" during which to relax, all to a schedule that required him to work eighteen to twenty hours a day. Indeed, he himself often complained to his staff of the hectic fund-raising schedule he maintained, but he kept pursuing campaign funds with a fervor that no other sitting president had exhibited previously.[32]

Clinton's supporters claim that this schedule did not affect his performance or his ability to deal with the important political issues of the day. The message that Clinton's role of fundraiser in chief sends, however, is that reelection is paramount. Viewed in one light, securing reelection may be a necessary component of a president's long-term strategy to achieve specific policy goals. A second-term president, freed from future electoral concerns and with the experience of a full term under his belt, may be in the best position to implement his policy agenda. Thus, a sitting president would need to spend a significant amount of time during the last years of his first term campaigning and fund-raising for himself and his party so as to be in a position to take advantage of having a second term.

Viewed more critically, however, the role of fundraiser in chief puts the individual who holds the title of president at any given time above the institution of the presidency and the nation as a whole. It tells the American public that the most important concern of being president is maintaining one's hold on the office. And the message that Clinton's activities sent to those considering running for president in the post-Clinton era is that they can and must do anything they can—use whatever advantage they can gain—so that they can have the privilege of holding the office as well.

Clinton's tactics in response to these electoral pressures had other ramifications as well, ones that extend beyond the office of the presidency. First, the need for the funding of presidential campaigns drains money and resources away from other candidates. It used to be that the president would raise funds not only for himself but also for the party, to help congressional candidates in particular. Although presidential candidates in the past, most notably Ronald Reagan in 1984, pursued funding through two routes—directly for themselves and indirectly through the party—Clinton's party fund-raising model was distinctly one-sided. Even when he nominally raised funds for the party, he did so largely on his own behalf. This model of focusing the national party structure on the election of its presidential candidate and losing some focus on getting other partisans elected to Congress places additional strain on the national campaign finance system.

Presidential candidates who raise funds for their party with the intention and ability of using such funds for their campaign compete for the same contribution dollars as candidates from their own party seeking lower offices. This results in disadvantaging the other candidates, such as those running for the House or Senate, particularly since presidential candidates raise their funds throughout the country, as opposed to focusing on a single state or district. This practice could have the result of potentially drawing money away from key locations and key races for Congress. Furthermore, the resulting strain on the congressional campaign system may lead some congressional officeseekers to search for other innovative and perhaps improper ways of financing their elections.

Clinton also helped highlight the disadvantages that those candidates who adhere more strictly to the campaign finance rules face. For example, Clinton's Republican opponent in 1996, Bob Dole, accepted public financing during the nomination process. Before securing the Republican nomination, he received approximately $29.5 million in individual contributions and $13.5 million in federal matching funds. Dole, however, needed to spend most of his funds to win the nomination, and federal election laws prevented him from spending more. From the end of the nomination process through the National Convention, Dole found himself at a severe disadvantage. He had to wait until after the Republican Convention, when his campaign would be infused with additional public funding, before he could undertake more aggressive campaigning.

Despite the traditional advantage that Republicans have in fund-raising, President Clinton was able to raise approximately the same amount in individual contributions ($28.2 million) and federal matching funds ($13.4 million) as Dole. Clinton's early fund-raising efforts helped deter a primary challenge.[33] Thus, in the months leading up to the national conventions, Clinton had substantial money left of his own as well as the public funding to run ads and attacks on Dole. He also drew on soft money expenditures by the Democratic National Committee to help fund these ads. Although the Republican Party ran its own set of ads paid with its soft money, Dole's reduced campaign resources limited his ability to defend himself in the wake of Clinton's barrage.

It is important to emphasize here that the difference in the amount of funds that each candidate had in the months before the conventions was not due to any unscrupulous behavior by Clinton, tactical errors by Dole, or even any shortcomings in the system. Dole simply did what he needed to do to secure the Republican nomination, but Clinton's focus on fund-raising did put him in a position to take advantage of this opportunity. Although the public financing system had been designed to place presidential candidates on equal footing, Clinton and Dole, each party's presumptive nominee, were in different positions as they entered the conventions—largely because Clinton's incumbency and financial advantages kept him from facing a primary challenge. In this regard, the 1996 election emphasized to future presidential candidates that along with receiving public funding came certain restrictions on spending, and those restrictions under certain circumstances could hinder a campaign more than federal matching funds might help it. Furthermore, Bill Clinton showed that by making key strategic decisions, the federal election laws designed to apply equally to all candidates could be worked to one's advantage.

Ultimately, Clinton's consistent focus on campaigning as a form of governing placed an ever-present, underlying emphasis on raising money. Although Clinton did not invent most of the loopholes, he did provide lessons on how to use them to the greatest effect. In pushing the boundaries surrounding acceptable behavior, he caused Republicans and Democrats in Congress and in the public to question his fund-raising practices. But little has been done to rectify these manipulations of the law. As a result, the lessons from the 1996 Clinton campaign raise serious questions for the future of the presidency as well as for those individuals who follow him. Moreover, his legacy has left open greater opportunities for exploiting the financing system rules, opportunities that came to fruition in the 2000 campaign.

LESSONS FOR 2000

The 2000 primary season saw new records of fund-raising and spending set (see Table 7.3 for a breakdown of the candidates' receipts through July 31, 2000). Taking a lesson from President Clinton's strategy, the candidates used 1999 to shore up their financial position well before the primary season opened. In fact, through January 31, 2000, the major party candidates collectively raised over $220 million and spent in excess of $180 million in hard dollars, and they had not even reached the New Hampshire primary. Even during the early stages of the 2000 campaign, many of the candidates seeking their party's presidential nomination seemed to have drawn upon lessons learned from the 1996 race.

First, candidates have recognized the disincentives for agreeing to play by the public financing rules. Millionaire Steve Forbes, who funded most of his run for the 1996 Republican nomination, elected to do so again in 2000 and ended up contributing over $42 million to his campaign. By doing so, Forbes was not constrained by the spending limits associated with receiving public financing. Given this situation, Republican George W. Bush, who early on was projected to be a favorite for the nomination, decided that Forbes's potential challenge was enough of an incentive for him to opt out of the public financing system. Although this choice meant Bush had to eschew federal matching funds, his spending was limited only by how much money he was able to raise and the timing of its receipt.

Bush undertook the most successful fund-raising effort in presidential campaign history, accumulating over $93 million in contributions from individuals

Table 7.3. Candidates' Receipts Through July 31, 2000 (in Dollars)

Candidate	Contributions from Individuals	Federal Matching Funds	Other Receipts	Total Receipts
Democrats				
Bill Bradley	29,270,589	12,462,045	409,931	42,142,565
Al Gore	33,871,206	15,317,872	13,667	49,202,745
Subtotal	63,141,795	27,779,917	423,598	91,345,310
Republicans				
Lamar Alexander	2,301,747	–	783,884	3,085,631
Gary Bauer[a]	7,553,317	4,632,803	(49,572)	12,136,548
George W. Bush	91,331,951	–	3,134,390	94,466,341
Elizabeth Dole	5,001,635	–	126,197	5,127,832
Steve Forbes	5,752,150	–	42,392,826	48,144,976
Orrin Hatch	2,124,707	–	428,016	2,552,723
Robert Kasich	1,702,668	–	1,488,415	3,191,083
Alan Keyes	7,663,253	3,325,340	11,159	10,999,752
John McCain	28,143,613	14,467,788	2,436,536	45,047,937
Dan Quayle	4,083,201	2,087,748	146,746	6,317,695
Bob Smith	1,522,128	–	92,070	1,614,198
Subtotal	157,180,370	24,513,679	50,990,667	232,684,716
Total (Major Parties)	220,322,165	52,293,596	51,414,265	324,030,026
Other				
Pat Buchanan	6,651,221	3,852,247	32,967	10,536,435
Ralph Nader	1,319,434	100,000	44,133	1,463,567
Others	5,291,555	1,498,507	143,774	6,933,836
Subtotal	13,262,210	5,450,754	220,874	18,933,838
Total	233,584,375	57,744,350	51,635,139	342,963,864

Source: Compiled from the Federal Election Commission website <http://www.fed.gov/finance/precm6.htm>
[a]Bauer's reported value for "Other Loans Minus Repayments" was ($63,249).

through the time of the Republican Convention (including approximately $7.5 million in addition to the more than $91 million listed in Table 7.3).[34] In particular, he used bundling—i.e., an intermediate agent collects contributions and delivers the whole lot to the candidate—to establish an effective and widespread network of contributors.[35] Usually the intermediate agent who bundles the contributions is a PAC, an interest group, or some other organization, and Bush raised considerable sums early on using this traditional form of bundling.[36] But Bush took bundling to another level by designating individual fund-raisers who brought in at least $100,000 in contributions from individuals and PACs as "Pioneers." At least 200 people earned Pioneer status, including a dozen current or former elected federal, state, or local officials; numerous attorneys; representatives from the oil, gas, and energy industries; and football Hall-of-Famer Roger Staubach. Although Bush took somewhat of a gamble in rejecting federal funding, the risk paid off for him. He saw how he could be hampered by the spending restrictions that receiving public financing would impose and used the Clinton example to pursue an even more aggressive fund-raising strategy. Like

Clinton, Bush took an all-consuming approach toward raising funds, and doing so provided him with the ability to overcome the challenges he faced in the primaries.

Other candidates also positioned themselves early in the campaign season to raise funds to demonstrate their viability. But the invisible primary indeed took its toll as Elizabeth Dole, for example, whom many pundits originally projected to be a serious contender for the Republican nomination, dropped out, primarily because of lack of funds.[37] Thus, voters were never given the opportunity to show their support (or lack thereof) for Dole other than, perhaps, in a public opinion poll. Instead, Dole's fate as a candidate was directed by where the contribution dollars went.

The 2000 campaign has raised questions regarding the integrity of the public campaign financing system for the presidential level. The incessant push to raise more dollars consumed the candidates, and the bar for what amount of funding was needed continued to rise as well. Al Gore (who raised $49.2 million in total funds through the time of the convention), Bill Bradley ($42.1 million), and John McCain ($45.1 million)—all of whom accepted public financing—each raised as much or more than Clinton and Dole in 1996.[38] These values compare with Steve Forbes's total funds but pale in comparison to George W. Bush. And by opting out of the campaign finance system, Forbes and Bush also had the advantage of not being bound by its spending restrictions.

Herein lies perhaps Bill Clinton's most significant legacy for presidential campaign financing. He so successfully worked the rules of the public funding system that he showed Democrats and Republicans alike how to succeed within the system. But he also showed candidates the necessity of exploiting any opportunity to gain an advantage over their opponents. One way to create an advantage over candidates who follow a set of rules designed to equalize certain financial disparities among them is simply not to play by those rules, that is, to opt out of the system. With Bush's success in doing so in 2000, future candidates will continue to look for unique and innovative ways to work the campaign finance rules to their benefit.

The fundraiser in chief function that President Clinton grafted onto the presidency's job description leaves open many questions for what this role means for the institution. For example, the president, who has ostensibly been the leader of his party, now has an exaggerated role in securing the party's economic viability. Furthermore, President Clinton demonstrated that this role can be exploited to raise funds not just for the party; the party, in turn, most likely will be expected to use this money to enhance the president's reelection possibilities. This relationship makes the president's role more self-serving and, in some instances, raises questions about possibly violating FECA's provisions prohibiting the parties from coordinating their soft money expenditures with their presidential candidates. The fundraiser in chief role, therefore, may put the president at odds with his party, which may become a competitor for necessary funds and thus could be perceived by some presidential candidates as a burden.

The fundraiser in chief function also raises concerns about the use of the office's incumbency advantages by the sitting president for his personal gain. This was one of the primary concerns that led to the early reforms discussed by the Progressives early in the twentieth century and to the eventual passage of the public financing provisions in the 1970s. The president has been given certain perks of the office—residence in the White House, use of Air Force One, and so on—at taxpayers' expense and so that he could serve the interests of his constituency, the American public. But Clinton's actions laid bare the fact that the White House and other accoutrements of the office could be exploited for reelection purposes and, as a result, he cheapened them in the eyes of the public. It will be hard for the American public to venerate something that is for sale at a premium nightly fare.

The introduction of this new job description calls into question how the president could still accomplish his everyday responsibilities when he must spend an extraordinary amount of time raising funds. As President Clinton demonstrated, it can be done, but the job does suffer. This result leads many observers to ask what this strain on the presidency does to policy development and the furtherance of institutional goals. Something has to give—and the risk is that it will not be the president's fund-raising schedule. Under these circumstances, any situation could become a potential crisis.

President Clinton's use of this new role leads one to ask if this constant fundraising has led to a new form of reelection imperative for the presidency. Although this reelection imperative has been noted for many other elected offices, it generally has not been as much of a concern for the presidency. Clinton's actions raise the issue as to whether first-term presidents in the future will go to such extremes to get reelected and thus transform what is expected, and one might argue desired, by the candidates facing this position. One might also question whether the Twenty-second Amendment, restricting the president to two terms, coupled with the need for campaign funds, has become a volatile cocktail that could lead to national disaster where a first-term president becomes consumed with securing a second term and waits until his fifth year in office, assuming he is able to secure a second term, before undertaking significant policy initiatives.

Further, this new role raises fundamental issues for the representational role of the presidency. The president is supposed to represent the whole nation and the American public, and the public finance system is supposed to facilitate that representation. But the presidential campaign finance system has started to look once again like the unregulated world before FECA, where the well-heeled and private money dominated the process. Yet FECA's formal rules remain in place, so that a candidate can take advantage of private money (at least to some extent) and still be subsidized by public funding. This system, however, where rules are bent, ignored, and possibly broken on a routine basis, is also rife with rhetoric and position taking on the need for campaign finance reform. Even though potential nominees in 2000 from both parties released positions on the need for campaign reform, they remained more than willing to exploit loopholes in the rules until others disarmed.

Thus one must ask the question: if large donors and special interests become essential to winning a presidential election, can the nation continue to assume the president is representative of all or of just a special moneyed few? Further, as the public financing system threatens to become increasingly irrelevant in choosing the nation's leader, the presidency will no longer be shielded from the campaign finance concerns that have plagued other areas of the government. Certainly, reforms that would address soft money and candidates' incentives to seek more avenues of private financing might be the impetus necessary to make the public financing option more attractive; if candidates could not rely on such alternatives, they would be more likely to use the public financing system as their primary campaign resource, as Congress envisioned when it originally passed FECA and its amendments. This approach, however, does not allay the reality that campaigning nationally has significantly increased in cost. As a result, the hopes and aspirations of reformers may be dashed in the name of raising the funds necessary for a candidate to be able to call the White House home.

POSTSCRIPT

As this book went to print, the Senate had passed the 2001 Bipartisan Campaign Reform Act (S. 27), popularly known as the McCain-Feingold campaign finance reform bill. This bill, if enacted, would represent the most sweeping legislative changes to the campaign finance system since the 1974 FECA amendments. Some of the bill's major components included a ban on unregulated soft money and an increase in the amount of regulated, hard dollar contributions that individuals can make to candidates and parties during an election cycle. Examining the full effects that this legislation may have on presidential campaign financing is beyond our scope here, but some initial thoughts on the subject are warranted.

The ban on soft money would eliminate one type of funding on which presidential candidates could rely to get out their message. Perhaps the scenario in which this ban would have its greatest effect is one similar to 1996: where an incumbent president does not face a primary challenge, thus allowing his party to throw its resources behind him, and where candidates in the other party are battling each other in the primaries. In 1996, Clinton conserved his campaign's money, raised through individual contributions and federal matching funds early on, while the Democratic Party ran anti-Republican ads financed by soft money expenditures. Although the Republican Party countered with some soft money ads financed after Dole became the party's presumptive nominee, the Democratic Party ads provided the Clinton campaign more flexibility in managing its funds, allowing the campaign to attack Dole at a time when his campaign resources were depleted from his primary battles. With McCain-Feingold's ban on soft money, such strategic management of campaign funds and the flexibility offered by soft money expenditures would be eliminated.

Potentially the most significant aspect of McCain-Feingold is the decision to increase the hard money caps on individual contributions. On the one hand, this would provide a boost to candidates who accept public funding and the constraints that the system places on a candidate. The increased caps should help these candidates raise more funds from individuals and, as a result, obtain more matching funding. Thus, for candidates who believe that their supporters will be willing to contribute more than $1,000 each (i.e., the existing cap), the changes that McCain-Feingold would bring offer a greater chance to be financially competitive with other candidates. On the other hand, the increased caps would apply, regardless of whether a candidate receives public funding or not. In 2000, one of the seemingly few constraints on George W. Bush's fund-raising ability was that individuals could contribute only $1,000 per election cycle. Imagine the additional funds that Bush could have raised if many of his contributors had given up to $2,000 (the McCain-Feingold limit). In other words, the increased caps also make it easier for candidates to work outside the public financing system.

The House, which has mustered support for a similar bill in both the 105th and 106th Congresses, continues to face a reluctant Republican majority and now a Democratic caucus with more to lose. The 2000 election cycle saw the Democrats raise more soft money than the Republicans, but the Republicans continue to maintain their hard money advantage. Taken together, these two facts provoke real questions about the fortitude the Democratic caucus will have in passing this bill in the House. Further, with the Senate no longer an impediment and the president now claiming he will sign a "real reform" bill, stakes are even higher. While the scenario set forth in this postscript is likely to happen if passage occurs, the 1996/2000 examples I have illuminated will continue, nevertheless, without any change. Either way, the fundraiser in chief is here to stay.

NOTES

1. Nelson W. Polsby and Aaron Wildavsky, *Presidential Elections: Strategies and Structures in American Politics*, 9th ed. (New York: Chatham House, 1996), pp. 68–69.

2. Stephen J. Wayne, *The Road to the White House, 1986* (New York: St. Martin's Press, 1996), pp. 40, 41.

3. Herbert Asher, *Presidential Elections and American Politics: Voters, Candidates, and Campaigns Since 1952,* 5th ed. (Pacific Grove, Calif.: Brooks/Cole, 1992), p. 221.

4. Polsby and Wildavsky, *Presidential Elections,* pp. 69, 70.

5. Herbert E. Alexander and Anthony Corrado, *Financing the 1992 Election* (New York: M. E. Sharpe, 1995), pp. 99–100.

6. Polsby and Wildavsky, *Presidential Elections,* pp. 70–71.

7. Tracy Westen, "Online Fundraising: Campaign Finance Solution or Gasoline on the Flames," in *The National Voter,* June/July 2000, p. 20. Westen notes, for example, that Senator John McCain, in his bid for the Republican presidential nomination in 2000, raised about one-fourth of his total campaign funds through the Internet, with about one-half of those online contributors having never given to a political campaign before (see p. 20).

8. Clyde Wilcox, "Follow the Money: Clinton, Campaign Finance, and Reform," in *Understanding the Presidency,* ed. James P. Pfiffner and Roger H. Davidson, 2d ed. (New York: Longman, 2000), p. 82.

9. Ibid., p. 81.

10. Much of the information presented in this section was compiled by Joseph E. Cantor, "The Presidential Election Campaign Fund and the Checkoff: Background and Current Issues," CRS Report no. 95-824 (Washington, D.C.: Congressional Research Service, 1997). For a historical discussion of the development of campaign finance laws generally, see Diana Dwyre and Victoria Farrar-Myers, *Legislative Labyrinth: Congress and Campaign Finance Reform* (Washington, D.C.: Congressional Quarterly Press, 2000).

11. In 1904 Congressman William Bourke Cockran and in 1907 President Theodore Roosevelt proposed public financing for presidential elections.

12. 424 U.S. 1 (1976). The Supreme Court upheld the voluntary components of the presidential public financing system but struck down certain mandatory limits on expenditures.

13. Numbers compiled from Cantor, "Presidential Election."

14. Between 1976 and 1996, three major candidates opted out of the system of public financing and spending limits: John Connally in 1980, Ross Perot in 1992, and Steve Forbes in 1996.

15. Anthony Corrado, *Creative Campaigning: PACs and the Presidential Selection Process* (Boulder, Colo.: Westview Press, 1992), p. 35.

16. Polsby and Wildavsky, *Presidential Elections,* p. 71.

17. Warren Weaver Jr., "By Law, This Will Be a Cheaper Campaign," *New York Times,* September 5, 1976, sec. 4, p. 1.

18. Warren Weaver Jr., "The Mixed Results of the Political Funding Law," *New York Times,* June 27, 1976, sec. 4, p. 2.

19. Ibid.

20. Wicker, "Improving the Next One," *New York Times,* November 2, 1976, B29; see also Weaver, "Mixed Result, sect. 4, p. 2, and Weaver, "By Law, sect. 4, p. 1.

21. Wicker, "Improving the Next One."

22. Wilcox, "Follow the Money," p. 83.

23. In 2000, Steve Forbes also relied on his own funds in seeking the Republican presidential nomination.

24. Senate Committee on Governmental Affairs, "Investigation of Illegal or Improper Activities in Connection with the 1996 Election Campaigns," 105th Cong., 2d sess., S. Rept. 105–167, sec. 5, p. 1 (Washington, D C.: U.S. Government Printing Office, 1998).

25. During the 1995–1996 presidential election cycle, political parties could spend approximately $12 million in coordinated hard money expenses. According to FEC records, the Democratic National Committee spent over $6.65 million in coordinated expenditures for Clinton/Gore, and the Republican National Committee paid $11.7 toward coordinated expenditures for the Dole/Kemp campaign.

26. From a memorandum from Harold Ickes, White House deputy chief of staff, to

Dan Fowler, DNC chair, April 17, 1986, quoted in S. Rep., Majority Views, no. 105–167, sec. 5, pp. 4–5. Senate Democrats countered that Ickes modeled his involvement with the DNC after systems established by Republican Ronald Reagan and continued by Republican George Bush (Minority Views, pp. 32–39).

27. The full excerpted quote in the Republican portion of the Senate Report reads: "We even gave up one or two of our fundraisers at the end of the year to try to get more money to the Democratic Party rather than my campaign this year, so I could spend all my money next year being president, running for president, and raising money for the Senate and House Committee and for the Democratic Party. And then we realized that we could run these ads through the Democratic Party, which meant that we could raise money in twenty and fifty and hundred thousand dollar lots, and we didn't have to do it all in thousand dollars. And run down—you know what I can spend which is limited by law. So that's what we've done. But I have to tell you I'm very grateful to you. The contributions you have made in this have made a huge difference" (Majority views, no. 105–167).

28. George C. Edwards III, "Campaigning Is Not Governing: Bill Clinton's Rhetorical Presidency," in *The Clinton Legacy,* ed. Colin Campbell and Bert Rockman (New York: Chatham House, 2000), p. 33.

29. S. Rep., Majority Views, no. 105–167, chap. 3, p. 1.

30. Quoted also in ibid., chap. 7, p. 1.

31. Glenn F. Bunting, "Clinton's Hard and Fast Ride on Donation Trail," *Los Angeles Times,* December 22, 1997, p. A1.

32. Dick Morris, Clinton's campaign strategist, told investigators from the House of Representatives, "A lot of times he would complain. . . . He would say, 'I haven't slept in three days; every time I turn around they want me to be at a fund-raiser. . . . I cannot think, I can't do anything; every minute of my time is spent at these fund-raisers'" (quoted in Bunting, "Clinton's Hard and Fast Ride."

33. As Bunting noted, "To scare off Democratic challengers, the Clinton-Gore campaign in 1995 arranged eight presidential fund-raising galas and quickly amassed $25 million" (ibid.).

34. The Center for Responsive Politics (CRP) reported that based on its analysis of FEC data released on August 2, 2000, Bush had raised total receipts of $93,260,829. As this book went to print, the FEC had not yet published this data (online at <http://www.opensecrets.org/2000elect/index/AllCands.htm>.

35. With bundling, both the individuals who make the contributions and the intermediate agent who collects and bundles them receive credit for the donations.

36. The Center for Responsive Politics reported in November 1999 that Bush had received bundles in excess of $50,000 from twenty-five different organizations, led by an $185,100 bundle from a prominent Houston-based law firm. By comparison, at that point Al Gore received eight bundled contributions exceeding $50,000 and Bill Bradley seven. See CRP's November 4, 1999, press release available online at <http://www.opensecrets.org/pressreleases/nov4_99_releast.htm>.

37. *New York Times,* October 24, 1999, p. A1.

38. The CRP reported that based on data released August 2, 2000, Gore's campaign raised a total of $52,568,089. See also Cantor, "Presidential Election."

8

The Impeachment of Bill Clinton

David Gray Adler and Nancy Kassop

The impeachment of President Bill Clinton and his subsequent acquittal on charges of perjury and obstruction of justice resurrect questions not only about the nature of impeachable offenses but also about the role of public opinion and political calculations in impeachment proceedings. It reminded all concerned, moreover, that impeachment is a complex, tumultuous, and unpredictable process, and it reaffirmed the wisdom of the delegates to the Constitutional Convention in placing the ultimate decision-making authority in the U.S. Senate and not in the House of Representatives. There was no doubt that President Clinton was guilty of serious wrongs; but the lying and cover-up of his reckless affair with a White House intern, which led to his impeachment, did not involve the abuse of power to political ends or the subversion of the Constitution, nor did it constitute the sort of "great and dangerous offenses" by "great offenders" or the crushing threat to the Republic that the Framers of the Constitution contemplated when they fashioned the impeachment power as an instrument for placing a "bridle on the executive."[1] Clinton no doubt deserved punishment, but in the form of sanctions imposed by the criminal and civil justice systems rather than by a court of impeachment.[2]

THE CONSTITUTIONAL CONVENTION

The convention was at pains to limit the presidency, mindful of the threat that executive power represented to the Republic.[3] Toward that end, as James Madison argued, presidential power should be "confined and defined," an approach employed by the Framers in their subsequent enumeration of executive powers and responsibilities.[4] But once presidential power was spelled out and the various checks and balances were in place, accompanied and reined in by the anticipated play of politics, grounded, as Madison wrote in *Federalist* no. 51, in the constitutional system's requirement of "ambition to counteract ambition," what else might serve to constrain the executive and protect the Republic from an errant president?[5]

The instrument of impeachment, familiar to the Framers as a mighty engine revved up by the House of Commons in the form of a "Grand Inquest" of the nation to safeguard what Edmund Burke had described as "the purity of the constitution," was urged as the ultimate restraint.[6] Benjamin Franklin warned his colleagues that impeachment was a necessary instrument; otherwise, the people would be forced to resort to assassination, a foreboding shared by others who feared violence as a grim alternative to executive repression and tyranny.[7]

The Framers' discussion, which certainly may be described as one that anticipates the use of the power, was focused on the president; the vice president and other "civil officers" were added in the last days of the convention. Those officers, as provided by Article 2, section 4, of the Constitution, might be removed from office "on Impeachment for, and conviction of, Treason, Bribery, or other high Crimes and Misdemeanors." The Constitution assigned to the House the sole power of impeachment, and it vested in the Senate the sole power to try all impeachments, with concurrence of two-thirds of the senators present required for conviction and removal. Treason, alone, is defined by the Constitution in Article 3, section 3, which provides, "Treason against the United States, shall consist only in levying war against them, or in adhering to their enemies, giving them aid and comfort." It seems clear that a corrupt use of power, as, for example, in the acceptance of a favor or money in exchange for the performance of an official action or inaction, represents the epitome of conduct judged impeachable as "bribery" under the Constitution. It is, of course, the category of "other high crimes and misdemeanors" that raises definitional problems in every impeachment controversy. Whatever uncertainty inheres in that phrase, which, as Raoul Berger has observed, was a term of art crafted by the English in the fourteenth century, it consists of crimes against the state, which the Framers intended to restrict to "great and dangerous offenses" by "great offenders."[8] Fortunately, our understanding has traveled well beyond such indefensible claims as that which asserts that an impeachable offense must be an indictable offense, or that it is illimitable, as urged in 1970 by then House Minority Leader Gerald Ford, who proposed the impeachment of Justice William O. Douglas and contended that an "impeachable offense" is whatever the House "considers [it] to be."[9] Uncertainty is not the equivalent of illimitability; and though the Framers, consummate craftsmen that they were, may not have applied their plane to the rough definitional edges of that category with quite the same precision that they applied to others, their cut remained focused on major offenses against the community. Indeed, the debates in the Philadelphia Convention, like those in the various state ratifying conventions, reflect an understanding that "high crimes and misdemeanors" involve subversion of the Constitution or serious abuses or usurpation of power. The initial drafts of the Constitution provided for impeachment for "mal-practice or neglect of duty," a formulation that was borrowed from state constitutional experience.[10] On July 20, 1787, in what was the first of two significant debates on the impeachment clause, the Framers adduced the necessity of impeachment as a means of restraining the president. William Davie believed the instrument provided an "essential security for the good behavior of the Executive."[11] Elbridge Gerry "urged the necessity of impeachment. A good Magistrate will not fear them. A bad one ought to be kept in fear of them. He hoped the maxim would never be adopted here that the chief Magistrate could do [no] wrong."[12] Without recourse to impeachment, Franklin reasoned, removal of the president would invite assassination, a concern echoed by Edmund Randolph, who also warned of a violent alternative, in the form of "tumults and insurrections."[13] As usual, Madison asserted strong and influential views:

> Mr. [Madison] thought it indispensable that some provision should be made for defending the community [against] the incapacity, negligence or perfidy of the chief Magistrate. The limitation of the period of his service, was not a sufficient security. He might lose his capacity after his appointment. He might pervert his administration into a scheme of peculation or oppression. He might betray his trust to foreign powers. The case of the Executive Magistracy was very distinguishable, from that of the Legislative or of any other public body, holding offices of limited duration. It could not be presumed that all or even a majority of the members of an Assembly would either lose their capacity for discharging, or be bribed to betray, their trust. Beside the restraints of their personal integrity and honor, the difficulty of acting in concert for purposes of corruption was a security to the public. And if one or a few members only should be seduced, the soundness of the remaining members, would maintain the integrity and fidelity of the body. In the case of the Executive magistracy which was to be administered by a single man, loss of capacity or corruption was more within the compass of probable events, and either of them might be fatal to the Republic.[14]

The final document was the result of several changes in the "high crimes and misdemeanors" category. In late July, the Committee of Detail changed the grounds of impeachment from "mal-practice or neglect of duty" to "Treason, Bribery or Corruption."[15] The Committee of Eleven reported to the convention on September 4 a draft that eliminated corruption; only treason and bribery remained.[16] On September 8, the delegates engaged in a second and final significant discussion of the impeachment clause. George Mason objected to the limitation of impeachable offenses to treason and bribery; those two categories, he said, would not cover "many great and dangerous offenses" such as "attempts to subvert the Constitution." Mason observed that the Constitution prohibited the use of bills of attainder as a tool to punish such offenses, and in urging an expansion of power he proposed the addition of "maladministration," a term used in the Virginia Constitution, among others. Madison objected that "so vague a term will be equivalent to a tenure during pleasure of the senate." Following Gouverneur Morris's observation that "an election every four years will prevent maladministration,"[17] Mason proposed "other high crimes and misdemeanors against the state," which the convention adopted by an eight-to-three vote.[18]

The Mason-Madison colloquy revealed the Virginians' search for an additional, but limited, category of impeachable offenses beyond treason and bribery. Madison's rejection of "maladministration," a term employed in his state constitution, is telling, given his well-known fears about the danger of executive power and his consequent proposal in Philadelphia to corral presidential power by confining, defining, and enumerating it so as to leave little doubt about its width, length, and breadth. And yet despite his concerns about the scope of executive power, he so valued the independence of the office that he wanted to ensure that the impeachment power would not permit such a vague, discretionary judgment so as to allow for the removal of the president merely at the will of Congress—for poor policy choices, personal distaste, or even inferior managerial skills. Let us put this in perspective: if twentieth-century Americans could trust Nixon to go to China, eighteenth-century Americans could trust Madison's judgment to constrain the impeachment power. The remedy for political, policy, and administrative failings was at the ballot box. Frequent elections supplied the means for policy changes, but impeachment, as Madison explained, was available for serious offenses for which the president's limited term did not provide a "sufficient security."[19]

In their aim to protect the president, as Morris explained, from "being dependent on the Legislature," a goal that he believed might be secured if impeachable offenses were "enumerated and defined," the Framers were aided by their firm grasp of the long history of the category of "high crimes and misdemeanors" and the role it played in English practice.[20] First used by Parliament in 1386, the category had its focus on great injuries to the state, which reflects the appellation "high," an offense akin to high treason or the betrayal of the Crown.[21] The evidence from the convention reveals that the Framers, like their English forebears, were concerned with an abuse of official power rather than with the personal misbehavior of the official. For the English, as Raoul Berger has observed, an illustrative, though not exhaustive, list of "high crimes and misdemeanors" would have included "misapplication of funds . . . , abuse of official power . . . , neglect of duty . . . , encroachment on or contempts of Parliament's prerogatives. . . . Then there are a group of charges which can be gathered under the rubric, 'corruption.'"[22] These offenses were recited by the Framers, who adopted the phrase "high crimes and misdemeanors" without debate, as an illustrative, though not exhaustive, list of offenses that would justify the impeachment and removal of the president. The essence of the offense for which impeachment might be brought, Hamilton explained in *Federalist* no. 65, is "the abuse or violation of some pub-

lic trust," the precise definition of which must be in the "awful discretion which a
court of impeachment must necessarily have, to doom to honor or to infamy the
most confidential and the most distinguished characters of the community."[23]
Madison shared this view; he observed that incapacity, negligence, or perfidy of
the president would justify his impeachment. Madison expounded at length: "He
might lose his capacity after his appointment. He might pervert his administration
into a scheme of peculation or oppression. He might betray his trust to foreign
powers."[24] Others in the convention weighed in the abuses of power that would
constitute impeachable offenses. Mason declared "corruption" to be impeachable,
a view echoed by Morris, who agreed that "corruption and some few other
offenses" ought to be impeachable. He added that the president "may be bribed
. . . to betray his trust" and noted that "Charles II was bribed by Louis XIV."[25]

The emphasis on the abuse of power and breach of trust was reiterated in the
state ratifying conventions. In South Carolina, General C. C. Pinckney stated that
impeachment would lie against those who betrayed their "public trust," an opinion shared by Edward Rutledge.[26] Presidential usurpation or violation of congressional foreign affairs powers were seen as impeachable offenses. In Virginia,
Madison remarked that "were the President to commit anything so atrocious as to
summon only a few states [that is, senators to consider a treaty], he would be
impeached for a 'misdemeanor.' "[27] In North Carolina, James Iredell, later a member of the Supreme Court, asserted that the president would face impeachment for
concealing "important intelligence" from the Senate in matters of foreign affairs,
or for giving "false information to the Senate," which would persuade it to ratify
a treaty favored by the president, neither of which was a trifling offense in the
eyes of Iredell, who told his colleagues that the "occasion for its exercise
[impeachment] will arise from acts of great injury to the community."[28]

The debates in both the Constitutional Convention and the state ratifying
conventions reflect a consensus that impeachable offenses are those that cause
great injury to the nation. Yet the subject itself defies precise delineation, if only
because Congress must determine on a case-by-case basis which acts represent
such a grave threat to the Republic that they warrant impeachment and removal
from office. Thus, while the Framers' discussion of the contours of the category
of "high crimes and misdemeanors" and some of the offenses that would trigger
impeachment affords valuable illumination and guidance, the fact is, as Hamilton observed in *Federalist* no. 65, impeachment "can never be tied down by . . .
strict rules, either in the delineation of the offence by the prosecutors, or in the
construction of it by the Judges."[29] Accordingly, the integrity of any impeachment inquiry will depend on the careful judgment of men and women of good
faith to determine the degree of danger to the nation represented in an official's
abuse of power. But it will not be easy, for the notion of impeachment, one part
legal and one part political, will, as Hamilton explained, "seldom fail to agitate
the passions of the whole community, and to divide it into parties more or less
friendly or inimical to the accused. In many cases it will connect itself with the

preexisting factions, and will enlist all their animosities, partialities, influence, and interest on one side or on the other; and in such cases there will always be the greatest danger that the decision will be regulated more by the comparative strength of the parties, than by the real demonstrations of innocence or guilt."[30] Thus the calamity of impeachment. But the system could not do without it, and no plan or approach can escape the potential for injustice.

CLINTON'S PATH TO IMPEACHMENT: THE PRESIDENT AND THE COURT

On December 19, 1998, President Clinton became the second president (and the first elected president) to be impeached by the House of Representatives on two counts of perjury and obstruction of justice. On February 12, 1999, the Senate acquitted him on both charges. Throughout the entire impeachment inquiry, every vote cast against President Clinton, from the House Judiciary Committee through the House of Representatives to the U.S. Senate, was cast by a Republican; no Democrat crossed party lines to vote against him. Hamilton's admonition of partisanship and party wrangling had been prophetic. More than three years have passed since the impeachment and Senate trial of President Clinton. There has been no shortage of analyses about the president's behavior and the effort to remove him that it spawned.[31] But the tangled elements, and the uncanny way in which calculations made to promote one goal tended to undermine another, constitute a variant of this story that has received little attention. The entire impeachment episode was replete with rich ironies, miscalculations, and errors of judgment. And yet it afforded the nation real insights into the impeachment process, and perhaps it yielded lessons for the future.

Miscalculations were made on both sides. All parties in this process faced choices at critical junctures, and all made decisions that advanced their interests in one forum at the expense of an equally important one in another. Second-guessing, a posteriori, is not the purpose here (although it is an inescapable feature); rather, the objective is to gain an understanding of why decision making during an impeachment process is such a zero-sum game, where an anticipated gain from one strategic choice is canceled out by the equivalent loss from another that was rejected in a different sphere. Recognizing that constitutional, legal, political, and institutional factors play equally crucial, competing, and often irreconcilable roles here, and examining some examples of how this worked in practice, adds a fuller context in which to comprehend the enigma of impeachment.

Everyone made mistakes. Unquestionably, President Clinton bore the sole responsibility for starting the spiral of unfortunate events, beginning with his inappropriate relationship with Monica Lewinsky and his subsequent efforts to withhold information and to mislead his advisers, prosecutors, the grand jury, and the public. The string of miscalculations began there, with the president's unrealistic and misguided belief that his initial relationship might remain hidden from public view, and it continued with his painfully transparent efforts to deny the existence of such behavior.

The implications of his conduct contained the potential to touch on all four factors that constitute the impeachment process: institutional, political, legal, and constitutional. Institutionally, his behavior diminished the dignity, integrity, and credibility of his presidency. Politically, he handed his opponents a "gift" too tempting to refuse: a salacious scandal that could capture the public's attention in a way that previous probes into Whitewater, the firings of staff in the White House Travel office, and the FBI files had not. Legally, judgments were needed about whether his behavior met the definitions of perjury or obstruction of justice. And constitutionally, questions arose as to whether impeachable offenses had been committed.

But what transformed this potential into reality was the 1997 Supreme Court's decision in *Clinton v. Jones*.[32] There, the Court needed to balance the president's concern for the interference that could arise with his official duties if he were subject to civil liability while in office against the claims of a litigant, Paula Jones, who wanted a judicial resolution of her long-dormant allegations of sexual harassment by the former governor Clinton. In *Clinton,* the Court rejected the president's arguments for temporary immunity from civil liability that were based on the uniqueness of the office, separation of powers, and the potential disruption that would be caused by the president's participation in a suit. The Court placed its faith, instead, in the broad discretion of federal district court judges to manage any civil litigation involving a president with sufficient sensitivity to a president's schedule and official duties. The Court assumed that, with the effective "case management" techniques at the district court level, there would be little danger that the president's participation in judicial proceedings would interfere with the performance of his official duties. Of course, the Court's assumption fell flat, but not so much because the premise itself was unsound. Rather, Clinton's own evasive and misleading testimony, for which he was held in contempt by Federal District Judge Susan Webber Wright, was primarily responsible for the fact that the Jones suit, and its consequences, came to dominate his presidency. Nevertheless, the warnings in Justice Stephen Breyer's concurring opinion provided a cautionary and prescient hint of what was to come: "I do not agree with what I believe to be an understatement of the 'danger.' And I believe that the ordinary case-management principles are unlikely to prove sufficient to deal with private civil lawsuits for damage unless supplemented with a constitutionally based requirement that district courts schedule proceedings so as to avoid significant interference with the President's ongoing discharge of his official responsibilities."[33]

The Court decided this case with a simple logic: the only way to guarantee the plaintiff's rights to a fair hearing was to require the president to submit to the judicial process without delay. It could not possibly have imagined that its ruling would pave the way for a full-dress impeachment proceeding of a president down the road, with far more intrusion in the functioning of the presidential office than ever could have been expected from a civil trial. But this decision removed any legal impediment to the president's deposition in the trial court in the Paula Jones case, where he was asked pointed questions about his relationship with Monica Lewinsky and where his answers would lay the predicate for the allegations of perjury that would form one part of Independent Counsel Kenneth Starr's investigation. It is reasonable to say that had President Clinton simply told the full truth in the deposition, the developments to come might have unfolded differently. Once he made the choice to respond to questions with misleading, evasive, and less-than-truthful answers, he bore the responsibility for that conduct. But it is equally reasonable to consider that had the Supreme Court decided more narrowly in *Clinton v. Jones,* or had it paid heed to Justice Breyer's admonition and higher standard for presidential liability, his deposition in the Jones case at the very least might have been postponed until after he left office, and the perjury charges stemming from that case would have never arisen in an impeachment context.[34] In short, the Court's resolution of the issue, in constitutional and legal terms, set the stage for an eventual outcome that would accomplish, in political and institutional terms, exactly the set of circumstances that the Court assumed it could avoid.

In retrospect, it is surely correct to suggest that, given the Court's decision, and given the potential for public embarrassment stemming from the president's relationship with Lewinsky, prudence and reason should have dictated a settlement of the Jones dispute at that juncture, which would have been in the president's best interests, despite any temporary political damage that he might have suffered. Clinton's refusal to settle led to the deposition that we now know inflicted an inestimable cost on him and his presidency, as measured by the personal, political, and institutional damage that resulted from his impeachment. A decision in one realm had disproportionately adverse consequences in the other three.

THE ATTORNEY GENERAL AND THE INDEPENDENT COUNSEL

With the reauthorization in 1994 of the independent counsel (IC) provision of the Ethics in Government Act of 1978, Robert Fiske, the independent counsel originally appointed in January 1994 by Attorney General Janet Reno to investigate Whitewater matters, was replaced by Kenneth Starr.[35] Fiske had been appointed during the period when the 1978 law had lapsed. Once the law had been reauthorized, to avoid any appearance of partisanship that might flow from a prosecutor handpicked by the attorney general, Reno began the process that resulted in the appointment of Starr by the Special Division, the three-judge panel constituted under that statute.

Four years later, on January 16, 1998, Attorney General Reno was in a position once again to apply the independent counsel statute. She needed to determine whether to recommend to the Special Division an investigation of allegations of perjury, obstruction of justice, and witness tampering in the Jones case that had been brought to her attention by associates in Starr's office after listening to tapes provided by Linda Tripp; and if so, whether to recommend the expansion of current independent counsel's jurisdiction to include these new charges or whether to appoint a separate counsel for these matters exclusively. Thus, the decision to add the Jones matter to Starr's jurisdiction was not automatic: Attorney General Reno could have recommended that another independent counsel should be named. Whether the outcome would have been different, had a separate counsel been appointed, cannot be known. But expanding Starr's jurisdiction to include this new investigation further fueled existing concerns about his lack of impartiality and his partisan and professional affiliations with Clinton's political opponents.

What were Reno's choices? Subsequent accounts have noted that the fast pace of events during the two days leading up to Clinton's impending deposition in the Jones case on January 17, 1998, played a role in her decision to recommend giving the expansion to Starr instead of asking the Special Division to appoint a new counsel, which would have caused a delay. Suspicions about Vernon Jordan's possible obstruction of justice in Whitewater coincided with his appearance in these new matters to provide Starr with the necessary nexus between the two cases. On Thursday, January 15, prosecutors from Starr's office met with Deputy Attorney General Eric Holder and presented him with information from tapes from Linda Tripp indicating that the president might have encouraged Lewinsky to submit a perjurious affidavit in the Jones case. Time was of the essence, since this information would certainly be relevant in the deposition questioning two days later and also because of a pending story in *Newsweek* about the tapes. Within twenty-four hours, Starr had received authorization from the Special Division, upon Reno's recommendation, to expand his investigation to include possible obstruction of justice in the Jones case.[36]

It appears that the restrictive timetable and political pressures for this appointment forced Attorney General Reno to take the path of least resistance. This crucial decision, made without complete information and against a relentless pace of events, shaped the journey toward impeachment.

THE INDEPENDENT COUNSEL AND THE HOUSE

Another conflict unfolded as a consequence of Independent Counsel Kenneth Starr's efforts to satisfy the legal requirement under the IC statute to "advise the House of Representatives of any substantial and credible information . . . that may constitute grounds for an impeachment."[37] That same section of the law also states that "nothing in this chapter . . . shall prevent Congress or either House from obtaining information in the course of an impeachment proceeding." Yet the effect of Starr's report to the House, magnified by his appearance during two days of testimony during the Judiciary Committee hearings and his political choice to become an advocate for impeachment, was to overwhelm and swallow up the constitutional requirement of Article 1 that "the House of Representatives shall have the sole Power of Impeachment." The House devolved its constitutional obligation to conduct an independent investigation to determine whether the information in Starr's report constituted grounds for impeachment when it chose to rely exclusively on his selective and untested presentation of evidence. Relatedly, its decision to hold the impeachment vote in a lame-duck session before adjourning sine die in December 1998 exposed its political insecurity and fear that a vote in the next session would have fewer Republican members, as a consequence of party losses in the 1998 elections, thus rendering the outcome in favor of impeachment far more uncertain in the new 106th Congress than in the waning hours of the 105th in December 1998.[38] Institutionally, as the governmental body solely entrusted with this power, the House relinquished this authority all too willingly and traded its solemn responsibility for tactical maneuvers.[39] Political and legal choices at this stage crowded out constitutional and institutional considerations.

A few other political choices that had an incalculable impact also were interjected at this stage. Most of these involved issues of management of evidence as well as access to evidence (both too much and too little), and all can be laid at the feet of the House Judiciary Committee. The White House lawyers Gregory Craig and David Kendall have aired three criticisms of the handling of evidence by the committee: that the president's lawyers were denied access to incendiary evidence (about possible "assaults" by the president) not included in the Starr Report that was stored in a House room for the exclusive viewing of committee members and staff (and later for all House members but not for the president's lawyers); that this extraneous evidence that was excluded from the Starr Report (and thus not part of the official record of evidence relating to the specific impeachment charges nor aired in House floor debate) was cited in David Schippers's report to the committee as being responsible for many votes in favor of impeachment; and that the release of the Starr Report in its raw form to the public (without advance release to the president's lawyers) and the more encompassing issue of conducting the entire investigation in public (as contrasted with the in camera investigation during the Nixon impeachment inquiry under Chairman Peter Rodino's leadership) raise the question of the impact and, also, issues of propriety that such unfiltered and total access had on the process as a whole.[40] Craig and Kendall recommended that future impeachment inquiries address these matters of access to evidence (i.e., whether the president's lawyers will have such access, as well as whether the public should have it, and, relatedly, the whole question of confidentiality during an investigation) at the outset and that there should be some instruction given to House members that they must vote solely on the record of evidence contained in the impeachment report and debated on the floor that related directly to the articles.

Other matters arose during the House proceedings that reflected political choices. House Democrats drafted a strong censure resolution, in the hope of substituting it for the articles of impeachment. The resolution stated that "the President made false statements concerning his reprehensible conduct with a subordinate" and that he "took steps to delay discovery of the truth," all but conceding that he had, indeed, committed perjury and obstruction of justice. The resolution was defeated in the committee by a twenty-two-to-fourteen vote, and parliamentary tactics to put it before the full House during the debate also failed, through the concerted efforts of the leadership. To be sure, doubts were aired about the constitutionality of substituting a censure resolution in the House for impeachment articles. But there is nothing in the Constitution, including the prohibition against bills of attainder, that precludes a resolution of censure, so long as the censure resolution does not include a fine or punishment but merely reflects the opinion of the House.[41] Still, the debacle over whether even to permit a vote on the resolution, and the resultant choice by the House leadership to deny that vote, marked a decision that did nothing to dispel the existent perception by the Democrats of the unfairness and partisanship that already characterized the process.

Thus, the issues that were handled during the independent counsel inquiry and House impeachment stages were critical and formative ones that served mostly to harden the partisan divide and mistrust that already colored the process. The end of that process left more questions than answers for the future, in such matters as the participation of a lame-duck Congress, the proper locus of an impeachment investigation, the role of White House lawyers, and the constitutionality of a censure substitution. If any conclusion can be drawn from the actions that framed this part of the impeachment process, it is the recognition of the necessity that, to be legitimate, only impeachment inquiries that are bipartisan in nature and that embody principles of fairness will satisfy that standard. An impeachment need not begin with bipartisan support, but one that ends without it and thus fails to acquire it along the way does not advance the purposes of the Framers or the objectives of government.

THE HOUSE MANAGERS AND THE WHITE HOUSE LAWYERS

At the Senate trial, both the House managers and the White House lawyers were confronted with conflicting legal and political considerations that caused each, at times, to make political decisions that may have undermined what would have been a more effective legal strategy and to make legal decisions that backfired politically. For example, the House managers' decision to select Sidney Blumenthal instead of Betty Currie as a witness—presumably because Blumenthal held more promise to be politically damaging to the president—may have sacrificed the legal advantages they might have gained from calling Betty Currie, whose testimony was far more central to the obstruction-of-justice charge and who might have strengthened their legal position. Similarly, the White House lawyers chose to act in a way that elevated political over legal considerations in deciding not to call witnesses, a move that sacrificed their client's legal right to pursuit of a greater political interest in ending the trial quickly.

Conversely, decisions about legal strategy that might not have been in their best political interests included the preference by the House managers for live witnesses or, at least, videotaped depositions—a step that ultimately proved irrelevant to the final vote and merely reinforced the hard-driving, partisan reputation they had already established for themselves in the public mind. For their part, the White House lawyers pinned their legal hopes on a strategy of hair-splitting legalisms that strained credulity and confirmed the public's impatience with Clinton's legendary, near-congenital inability to accept responsibility for his behavior. They dramatized their legal position of categorical denial of the charges by ending their four opening presentations and their closing argument with these stark, simple words: "William Jefferson Clinton is not guilty of the charges that have been brought against him. He did not commit perjury. He did not commit obstruction of justice. He must not be removed from office." Whatever legal advantage this garnered came at the price of further undercutting the president's political credibility, which had already been seriously eroded. In both sets, the White House lawyers and the House managers traded off one set of legal and political choices for another. Did either side gain much in the outcome? Probably not.

One incident in the Senate trial stood out for the simplicity and directness of its appeal. When the president's defense team took a chance on changing the dynamics in the trial by turning to former senator Dale Bumpers for the closing remarks at the end of the White House's presentation of its case, it reflected an understanding of the Senate as an institution—that an appeal to the senators by one of their own would, indeed, carry considerable weight. With the folksy, affable, and highly respected Senator Bumpers in the well, occasionally strolling about the chamber, the defense sought to appeal to a return to the Senate's sense of fraternity. The evocation of institutional membership served, if only temporarily, as a way to defuse some of the partisan tension. This may have been the only event within the entire impeachment episode in which all four elements—political, legal, constitutional, and institutional—coalesced in their purest form. Bumpers's approach was rambling, relaxed, and casual, the antithesis of the tight, orderly, and highly structured lawyerly appeals that had preceded him. Whether his manner changed any votes may never be known, but his presence was memorable for inducing the members, momentarily and collectively, to take a deep breath before completing the task ahead of them.

LESSONS LEARNED?

What are the lessons to be learned from this experience? What can we discern, in hindsight, that was not obvious in the eye of the storm? What are the consequences to the system of this impeachment episode? Has the presidency been weakened by the impeachment of Bill Clinton? Has the bar of impeachment been raised or lowered?

Some postmortems have warned that the impeachment bar will be lowered in the wake of the Clinton impeachment and that impeachment efforts will become more frequent and assume the posture of mere political weapons in the arsenal of confrontational politics. That fear seems exaggerated. There is just as much reason to imagine a reluctance to use the impeachment power anytime soon, since it has proven itself to be so uncontrollable, unpredictable, and, ultimately, unsuccessful, for those who wish to employ it. In purely rational terms, then, the question must be confronted: is it worth the risk to undertake the process?

The answer lies in the discretionary legal judgment and political calculations of those who think a president's actions warrant the deadliest constitutional scrutiny. In 1986, for example, Speaker of the House Jim Wright (D-Tex.), determined to block any impeachment inquiry against President Reagan arising from the Iran-Contra Affair, said, "I thought the last thing the country needed was . . . a frontal challenge to President Reagan's personal integrity." Speaker Wright observed that impeachment would have been "destructive," but it is quite likely that Democrats could find no political incentive in tackling a highly popular and elderly president nearing the end of his second term in office, despite evidence that Reagan's actions may have warranted an impeachment inquiry.[42] Similarly, the House Judiciary Committee in 1974 performed a calculation of sorts when it voted down an impeachment charge for tax evasion and another for illegal war making in Cambodia against Richard Nixon while agreeing to proceed with charges of obstruction of justice, abuse of power, and contempt of Congress.

How can the judgments in these two cases, which refrained from or restricted the use of impeachment, be reconciled with the decisions in the Clinton case, which proceeded to a full House vote and Senate trial? Are there lessons to be learned from comparing cases and in evaluating why they resulted in different choices with varied outcomes? Consideration of the four elements of impeachment provides some clarity.

In the Clinton case, political opponents of the president underestimated the force of the legal, constitutional, and institutional factors and calculated that the potential benefit to them of removing a president was worth the political risk to their party and to the system. Speaker Wright reached the opposite conclusion in the Reagan case, determining that the constitutional and institutional costs were not worth any possible political or legal benefits. With respect to the tax evasion and illegal war-making charges in the Nixon case, the House Judiciary Committee sifted the evidence to arrive at its result, as to the three charges that were advanced, their gravity and the degree of danger to the system that they posed argued for the conclusion that all four dimensions were equally satisfied here.

These approaches show that there was variation and nuance among the judgments, based on calculations of each of the four elements. From this examination emerges an analytic framework that may be useful for any future impeachment decisions. Efforts to unseat a president that are motivated by extreme partisan polarization, as in the Clinton case, are unlikely to succeed and instead may diminish the fortunes of the party pursuing the president. Only when enough members of a president's own party acknowledge the sufficiency of the evidence to make such an effort bipartisan will such a case make sense to pursue. And this is likely to occur only in these cases in which presidents have taken actions contrary to law and have usurped or disregarded the power of the other branches, as with Nixon and Reagan, those cases that implicate legal, constitutional, and institutional dimensions at the very least and, perhaps, political ones as well. In sum, this second model is of a higher order than the first and resembles the Framers' understanding of offenses of a public nature, with the necessary level of gravity and danger to the system that was, for them, a prerequisite to impeachment.

If this is true, then why did the Clinton impeachment effort actually proceed further into the process than the Nixon or Reagan cases? What accounts for the fact that the Nixon case was short-circuited, never to reach a vote on the floor of the House, and that the congressional investigating committee in the Iran-Contra scandal never formally recommended the bringing of impeachment charges against President Reagan?

Political judgment, or discretion, supplies the first crack at an answer. In the Nixon case, influential members of his own party reached the political judgment after the House committee voted that there were sufficient votes both to impeach and remove him, and they presented him with little option but to resign before becoming the first president to be removed from office through Senate conviction, causing irreparable harm to the party.

With Reagan, House leaders never had direct evidence that he knew of the diversion of funds to the Contras, and they determined that the backlash that would most likely ensue from launching an impeachment effort against a president with enormously high personal popularity would be politically unwise and could backfire to their detriment. Prudence, rational political judgments, as well as a healthy dose of self-preservation drove their decision, as Speaker Wright's comments illustrated. In other words, they were unwilling to go forward where the evidence was not at all clear or even present; and they acted, consequently, to protect their party's interests while still using Congress's investigative authority to maintain political pressure against the president's party and, ultimately, to weaken the president in his last two years in office.

The emerging factor here is the primacy of judgments by party leaders of the potential impact of the impeachment process on their party's short- and long-term interests. The question arises: did the House Republicans in 1998 learn from these two precedents? If they did, then their decision to pursue impeachment in 1998 can only be because either they believed that, in fact, there was sufficient evidence to succeed in impeaching and removing Clinton, or they were so motivated to move against him that they were willing to risk their party's reputation and interests, in the event that their efforts happened to fail.

Legally, the evidence to support the charges against President Clinton was stronger than that against Reagan in Iran-Contra, but that may be attributable to the suppression of evidence that may have directly implicated Reagan in that scandal. Clinton's behavior before the grand jury and his conduct with witnesses came either very close to or crossed the line of illegality. And, yes, perjury and witness tampering by a president are entirely incompatible with the president's constitutional duty to "faithfully execute the laws." The flip side of that argument, however, is that it was the extraordinarily embarrassing nature of the subject matter (illicit sex) that the president was under obligation to disclose, an issue that is prone to provoking less-than-candid answers whenever it is under inquiry.[43] If one separates the fact of his sexual behavior from his misleading statements about it, then the veracity of his statements can be judged on their own. But the obstacle comes from the fact that the two cannot be separated. One grows out of the other. And the sad lesson is, as one journalist observed in reference to many of the independent counsel investigations but the comment is equally relevant and aptly descriptive here, that this is another case in which "the cover-up became the crime even though there was no original crime to cover up."[44]

Constitutionally speaking, are we any closer to a consensus on what constitutes an "impeachable offense"? The best we can say is that a majority of the House believed that lying to a grand jury and tampering with evidence are such offenses while two-thirds of the Senate did not. Guidance from the 1974 staff report is instructive here and notes, "Not all presidential misconduct is sufficient to constitute grounds for impeachment. There is a further requirement — substantiality. In deciding whether this further requirement has been met, the facts must be considered as a whole in the context of the office, not in terms of separate or isolated events."[45] Did the charges here meet the test of substantiality? Reasonable people will disagree. But it may be worth noting the irony (and illogic) in the House votes that approved Article 1 perjury before the grand jury while defeating Article 2 perjury in the Paula Jones deposition when the grand jury testimony (and, thus, perjury) of Article 1 would never have occurred if there had been no deposition (and, thus, no perjury) in the Paula Jones case of Article 2.

Institutionally, the Clinton case provides a glimpse into the two different natures of the House and Senate in their roles in the impeachment process. The House stage of the process was fraught with partisan zeal on both sides of the aisle; it ended with more questions than when it began; and the outcome was clouded by the "lame-duckness" of the House vote, which included members who had been defeated just weeks earlier, in an election that was itself a referendum on impeachment, registering public disapproval for the Republican-led effort. The Senate procedures, in contrast, generated an atmosphere of greater fairness, warmth, and cordiality. Observers will long recall such details, right down to Senator Strom Thurmond's arm around the shoulder of Gregory Craig after his vigorous defense of the president at the trial and the centenarian's warm handshake and affectionate smile for Cheryl Mills after her striking presentation—although, as one reporter noted, "Strom always likes the ladies." And perhaps there was some detachment to be found in the eventual decision of ten Republicans to cross lines and vote against conviction on Article 1, and the defections of five on Article 2, a movement in sharp contrast to the closer party-line votes in the House on the two articles that were adopted.

Further, there is clearly much merit in the description of the Clinton impeachment as the "constitutionalization of politics," the conversion of political differences into constitutional battles, or, in other words, the utilization of constitutional means to address partisan conflicts. In the frame of American politics, it could hardly be otherwise. To those observers who believed that the Republicans were bent on ousting Clinton from office, this seems an apt description. To those who believed that Clinton's conduct in front of the grand jury and his efforts to impede the discovery process in the Paula Jones case did in fact constitute perjury and obstruction of justice, this may appear a harsh and unjustified rationalization. But it hardly seems an exaggeration to conclude that the political choices by House Republican leaders in 1998 to pursue impeachment to its very end reflected their conscious, single-minded determination to find any way to remove Clinton from office and that they were willing to sacrifice their party's standing, if necessary, to achieve that goal. Raw political strategy, converted into constitutional tactics, seemingly paved the way for their efforts, with far less regard for the consequences to their party than their comparable counterparts had in 1974 and 1987.

This business of impeachment is a tortuous, tumultuous process, filled with internal contradictions and unpredictable outcomes. It cast a hypnotic spell on most of the nation, forced to the sidelines consideration of most other matters, and seemed to impel an exclusive focus on an undeniably riveting, unfolding drama that defines who we are and what values we judge essential to governing. Further, it requires instinctive cost-benefit calculations at its inception and, continuously, at decisive steps along the way. One poor judgment or miscalculation can have a domino effect and can influence or circumscribe subsequent choices.

Viewing impeachment as a complex process with independent but interdependent variables is not a revolutionary approach. Richard Pious has written of the paradox of the "legal backlash" and "political frontlash" from the Clinton impeachment: Clinton's aggressive efforts to argue for broad presidential prerogatives in the courts resulted in net losses to the presidency as an institution, yet his political strategy yielded success in his triumph over impeachment and retention of office, at the cost of diminishing constitutional prerogatives and institutional prestige.[46] What needs to be acknowledged, and what these views urge, is a greater emphasis on recognizing the tangle of elements inevitably constituting impeachment decisions and driving the strategic choices that incur both costs and benefits to all players and indeed to the entire political system.

NOTES

1. Raoul Berger, *Impeachment: The Constitutional Problems* (Cambridge: Harvard University Press, 1973), p. 86; Hamilton, *Federalist* no. 65, in Alexander Hamilton, James Madison, and John Jay, *The Federalist*, ed. Edward M. Earle (New York: Modern Library, 1937), p. 485, referring to the fact that the English and the drafters of the state constitutions "seem to have regarded the practice of impeachments as a bridle in the hands of the legislative body upon the executive servants of the government. Is not this the true light in which it ought to be regarded?"

2. Ultimately, he was. Federal Judge Susan Webber Wright held the president in contempt and fined him. Clinton settled with Paula Jones in a civil suit for the sum of $850,000, which is suggestive of guilt. The Independent Counsel ultimately chose not to pursue criminal proceedings against Clinton under an arrangement where Clinton admitted that he gave false testimony in his deposition in the Paula Jones case and under a settlement with the Arkansas Bar Disciplinary Committee that included a five-year suspension of his law license and a $25,000 fine (see "Mr. Clinton's Deal," editorial, *Washington Post*, January 21, 2001, p. B6).

3. For a discussion of the Framers' fear of unilateral executive power see, generally, David Gray Adler, "Court, Constitution and Foreign Affairs," in *The Constitution and the Conduct of American Foreign Policy*, ed. David Gray Adler and Larry N. George (Lawrence: University Press of Kansas, 1996), pp. 19–56. The fear ran from the colonial period and was reflected in the post-Revolution state constitutions, which strictly limited the powers of the governors. As James Madison observed, state executives across the land were "little more than cyphers" (quoted in Max Farrand, ed., *The Records of the Federal Convention of 1787*, 4 vols. [New Haven: Yale University Press, 1911], 2:35). There was a deep fear of the potential for abuse of power in the hands of both hereditary and elected rulers. "The executive power," wrote a Delaware Whig, "is ever restless, ambitious, and ever grasping at increase of power" (quoted in Gordon Wood, *The Creation of the American Republic, 1776–1787* [Chapel Hill: University of North Carolina Press, 1969], p. 135).

4. At the convention, Madison addressed the issue of executive powers and observed that "a definition of their extent would assist the judgment in determining how far they might be safely entrusted to a single officer," and he added that executive power "shd. be confined and defined" (Farrand, ed., *Records*, 1 65–70). In the debate on impeachment, Gouvernour Morris thought that impeachable offenses "ought to be enumerated and defined" (ibid., 2: 65).

5. *Federalist* no. 51, p. 337.

6. Quoted in Raoul Berger, *Impeachment*, p. 299 n. 3.

7. See the discussion in Farrand, ed., *Records*, 2: 65.

8. Berger, *Impeachment,* p. 86.

9. Ibid., p. 56.

10. Farrand, ed., *Records,* 1: 78. This formulation was derived from the impeachment provision of the North Carolina Constitution.

11. Ibid., 2: 64.

12. Ibid., p. 66.

13. Ibid., p. 67.

14. Ibid., p. 65–66.

15. Ibid., 2: 145, 172, 185–186.

16. Ibid., p. 495.

17. Ibid., p. 550.

18. Ibid. The language was immediately changed to "against the United States" (p. 545).

19. Ibid., p. 65.

20. Ibid., pp. 69, 65. See Berger, *Impeachment,* pp. 54–55.

21. See Berger, *Impeachment,* p. 61; William Blackstone, *Commentaries on the Laws of England,* 15th ed., 4 vols. (Oxford: Oxford University Press, 1809), 4: 75.

22. See the discussion in Berger, *Impeachment,* pp. 70–73.

23. *Federalist* no. 65, p. 426.

24. Farrand, ed., *Records,* 2: 68.

25. Ibid., p. 69.

26. Jonathan Elliot, ed., *The Debates in the Several State Conventions on the Adoption of the Federal Constitution,* 5 vols. (1861; reprint, New York: Burt Franklin, 1974), 4: 281, 276.

27. Ibid., 3: 500.

28. Ibid., 4: 127, 113.

29. *Federalist* no. 65, pp. 425–426. Joseph Story stated, "Political offenses are of so various and complex a character, so utterly incapable of being defined, or classified, that the task of positive legislation would be impracticable, if it were not almost absurd to attempt it" (*Commentaries on the Constitution,* 5th ed., 3 vols. (Boston: Little, Brown, 1905), p. 581.

30. *Federalist* no. 65, p. 424.

31. See, e.g., Richard A. Posner, *An Affair of State* (Cambridge: Harvard University Press, 1999); Robert Spitzer, "Clinton's Impeachment Will Have Few Consequences for the Presidency," *PS: Political Science and Politics* 32 (1999): 541–545; Richard Pious, "The Constitutional and Popular Law of Presidential Impeachment," *Presidential Studies Quarterly* 28 (1998): 806–815; Pious, "The Paradox of Clinton Winning and the Presidency Losing," *Political Science Quarterly* 114 (1999–2000): 569–593; Jeffrey Toobin, *A Vast Conspiracy: The Real Story of a Sex Scandal that Nearly Brought Down a President* (New York: Random House, 1999); Symposium, "Scandal and Government: Current and Future Implications of the Clinton Presidency," *PS: Political Science and Politics* 32 (1999): 539–561.

32. *Clinton v. Jones,* 520 U.S. 681 (1997).

33. Ibid.

34. Richard Posner has commented that the Court "just did not understand the mischievous potential of the case" (*Affair of State,* p. 227). He noted that the Court, and the

president's lawyers, could have provided for a variable scope of temporary immunity, depending on the type of case. Here, unlike in other less sensational civil cases, the likelihood of intense public interest, due to the sexual nature of the charges, carried with it the "potential for humiliating the president and . . . disrupting the government" (ibid.). Moreover, Posner and Toobin have both suggested that the Court could (and should) have instructed the district court judge to determine the merit of the legal claim and weigh carefully the strength and validity of the sexual harassment charges in the Jones suit *before* ordering the president's deposition. As it happened, District Court Judge Wright dismissed the suit on April 1, 1998, for the precise reason that the claim of sexual harassment was not sufficient to constitute a legal injury (*Jones v. Clinton*, 990 Supp. 657 [E.D. Ark. 1998]; Posner, *Affair of State*, p. 65; Toobin, *A Vast Conspiracy*, pp. 206–213).

35. Public Law 103-270 (1994).

36. Posner, *Affair of State*, pp. 67–68; Toobin, *A Vast Conspiracy*, pp. 200–202; Bob Woodward, *Shadow: Five Presidents and the Legacy of Watergate* (New York: Simon and Schuster, 1999), p. 372.

37. 28 U.S.C. 595 (c).

38. Similarly, Gregory Craig, one of the White House lawyers who argued the case in the Senate, has noted that David Schippers, chief investigative counsel for the House Committee, has said that if Republicans had won the expected twenty to forty new seats in the House and four or five new seats in the Senate, as is often the case for the party out of power in midterm elections, the outcome might have been quite different (Gregory Craig and David Kendall, "Address: National Association of Criminal Defense Lawyers," Washington, D.C., aired on C-Span, August 28, 1999).

39. Some observers have gone so far as to claim that the House acted unconstitutionally by "delegating" its authority to conduct an impeachment investigation to an independent counsel (ibid.).

40. Craig described a published interview given to *Human Events Magazine* by David Schippers, where, in the days leading up to the House floor vote, Republican members were urged by their counterparts on the committee to view this additional evidence in the House evidence room. Craig quoted verbatim from Schippers's interview that "sixty-five individuals came over in the two- or three-day period before the impeachment vote in the House. We were really turning them over. Of these sixty-five, sixty-four went out and voted for impeachment, including a whole gaggle of them who, when they came in, told my staff that they were considering voting *against* impeachment. So that material that was in that room, I think, was the difference" (May 28, 1999, p. 2).

41. Article 1, section 9, paragraph 3 of the Constitution provides, "No Bill of Attainder or ex post facto law shall be passed." For an excellent discussion of the origins of the clause, see Francis D. Wormuth, "Legislative Disqualifications as Bills of Attainder," *Vanderbilt Law Review* 4 (1951): 603. See also Michael J. Gerhardt, "The Historical and Constitutional Significance of the Impeachment and Trial of President William Jefferson Clinton," *Hofstra Law Review* 28 (1999): 349, 376–377.

42. "In 1986, Another View of Impeachment," *National Journal*, December 19 and 26, 1998.

43. As Senator Bumpers commented in his remarks to the Senate, "When you hear somebody say 'this is not about sex,' it's about sex" (*Congressional Record*, 106th Cong., 2d sess., U.S. Senate, January 21, 1999, S 845).

44. David Grann, "Starr Wars: The Finale," *New Republic,* June 28, 1999, p. 22.

45. House, Committee of the Judiciary, Constitutional Grounds for Presidential Impeachment, 93d Cong., 2d sess., quoted in Michael J. Gerhardt, *The Federal Impeachment Process: A Constitutional and Historical Analysis* (Princeton: Princeton University Press, 1996), p. 27.

46. Pious, "Paradox of Clinton Winning," p. 592.

9

The Condition of the Presidency: Clinton in Context

David Gray Adler

The institutionalization and constitutional confinement of the executive represented the Framers' response to the royal prerogative which, as James I declared, inhered in the king by virtue of his royalty and not his office.[1] The American system of government was designed in part to overcome the personalization of executive power. In their replacement of personal rule with the rule of law, the Framers rejected the historical admiration of the executive and the claims of personal authority that at least since the Middle Ages, in one form or another, had conceived of executive rights as innate; they were derived not from the office but, one might say, from the "blood and bone of the man."[2] Executive power was personal, not juridical. For its part, the convention sought to transform personal rule into a matter of law and to subordinate the executive to constitutional commands and prescriptions. But the tremendous concentration of power in the modern presidency, some of which has been acquired through usurpation and some through congressional abdication, has left in its wake a long list of casualties, including the doctrines of separation of powers, checks and balances, and enumeration of powers. Given the diminution of the constitutional restraints imposed on the president, what Thomas Jefferson lamented as the conversion of the Constitution into "a thing of wax," it seems evident that in historical terms, the United States is marching steadily backward. This is the condition of the presidency: an overgrown office swollen with powers subject to few limitations.[3] No less a personage than the late Senator Sam Ervin questioned, in the course of hearings in 1973 on the unchecked executive practice of impoundment, "whether the Congress of the United States will remain a viable institution or whether the current trend toward the executive use of legislative power is to continue unabated until we have arrived at a presidential form of government." Senator Ervin justly criticized executive aggrandizement of legislative authority, but he also found Congress culpable for the rise of presidential dominance: "The executive branch has been able to seize power so brazenly only because the Congress has lacked the courage and foresight to maintain its constitutional position."[4]

It makes little difference whether we refer to this condition as the *Personal Presidency,* as Theodore Lowi has described it, or the *Imperial Presidency,* as Arthur Schlesinger Jr. has characterized it, or whether we consider it in light of the popular exaltation of the president as Superman, as Thomas E. Cronin has explained it; for the innovation of "Presidential Government" is triumphant in America.[5] The model for executive dominance found clear expression in the presidency of Richard Nixon, as manifested in the usurpation of warmaking authority and the aggrandizement of foreign affairs powers and in extended claims of impoundment authority, executive privilege, and secrecy. Professor Schlesinger has ably explained the problem: "The imperial Presidency, born in the 1940s and 1950s to save the outer world from perdition, thus began in the 1960s and 1970s to find nurture at home. Foreign policy had given the president the command of peace and war. Now the decay of the parties left him in command of the political scene, and the Keynesian revelation placed him in command of the economy. At this extraordinary historical moment, when foreign and domestic lines of force converged, much depended on whether the occupant of the White House was moved to ride the new tendencies of power or to resist them."[6]

Moreover, the coincidence of Nixon the man, and the presidency was pivotal: "With Nixon there came, whether by weird historical accident or by unconscious national response to historical pressure and possibility, a singular confluence of the job with the man. The Presidency, as enlarged by international delusions and domestic propulsion, found a President whose inner mix of vulnerability and ambition impelled him to push the historical logic to its extremity."[7]

In his expansion of executive claims and powers, Nixon had models. Harry Truman, for example, usurped the war power when he unilaterally plunged the nation into the Korean War and legislative authority when he invoked an "inherent" executive power to seize the steel mills.[8] And Nixon has had imitators. Each of his successors—Ford, Carter, Reagan, Bush, and Clinton—has asserted untrammeled executive authority to initiate war.[9] Like Nixon, they have aggrandized foreign affairs powers, including the authority to reinterpret and terminate treaties; negotiate executive agreements at the expense of congressional participation; and to order covert actions, military and otherwise. Presidents since Nixon have asserted broad claims of executive privilege and secrecy as well.[10]

The mushrooming growth in executive power also finds its roots in congressional abdication of its constitutional powers, which might strike a novitiate as counterintuitive, but an understanding of Congress yields the conclusion that most members are more concerned with "themselves and their reelection chances" than with the preservation of institutional authority.[11] Unmindful of the prohibitions imposed by the delegation doctrine, Congress has granted sweeping powers to the president.[12] Unmoved by concerns to harbor, preserve, and protect its exclusive authority over appropriations, Congress has facilitated executive control of the budgetary process and spending determinations.[13] Unconcerned about the maintenance of its lawmaking function, Congress has urged upon willing executives the concept of a line-item veto and, incredibly, the bizarre notion of an "inherent" line-item veto.[14] It hardly seems necessary to mention, moreover, that Congress has been unwilling to defend its broad powers over matters of war and foreign affairs; on the contrary, members seem relieved to unburden themselves of constitutional duties, responsibilities, and powers that they swore an oath to defend.[15]

Presidential government, built atop aggrandizement, usurpation, and abdication, has become firmly entrenched in the United States. This was the condition of the presidency that Bill Clinton inherited when he assumed office. It was imperial when he came to it and imperial when he left it. From a constitutional perspective, President Clinton made no effort to curtail executive aggrandizement of power or to stem the tide of legislative abdication, nor did he seek to restore congressional authority. Indeed, as we have demonstrated in this book, Clinton, like his predecessors, chose to ride the "tendencies of power" rather than "resist them."[16] He embraced, and in some respects extended, the doctrinal teachings, capacious claims, and unilateral actions that epitomize presidential government. Clinton followed a well-worn path of executive claims to a unilateral warmaking power, but in his defiance of constitutional metes and bounds he surpassed others' transgressions when he ordered in March 1999 an air and missile assault against Yugoslavia in the face of a direct congressional refusal to authorize the war. In his expansive exercise of executive privilege, moreover, Clinton rivaled President Nixon's abuse of the doctrine and exceeded by some distance the less controversial but still aggressive use of it by Ronald Reagan and George Bush. As Mark Rozell has indicated, Clinton's invocation of executive privilege on no less than six occasions before his substantive abuse of it in the Lewinsky scandal revealed a penchant for secrecy.[17] Several of President Clinton's eleventh-hour pardons, as well as those issued to FALN members, were as indefensible as any in our history, even if they did not carry the historical significance of Gerald Ford's pardon of Richard Nixon or George Bush's pardon of Caspar Weinberger. Clinton's broad claim of executive immunity represented a lawyer's plea and that of an anxious client, but it also represented the position of an executive light in his sensibilities toward the rule of law. Those same insensitivities were reflected, moreover, in his choice to dissemble during depositions and grand jury testimony in the Paula Jones proceedings, even if it was an act fully comprehensible in human and personal terms.[18]

At a minimum, the imperial or what we might call a plebiscitary presidency is suffused with swollen conceptions of executive power, it assumes that democracy is enhanced "if the capacity to govern is lodged in the White House," and it exhibits general indifference toward constitutional restraints so critical to the preservation of the enumeration of powers.[19] In its glory, it speaks of the investment of the sovereignty of the nation in the chief executive, and it exhibits contempt for the rule of law. Any doubts about the scope of this doctrine were laid to rest by Nixon himself in the third television interview with David Frost that was aired on May 19, 1977. In that interview, Nixon declared that the president, like the Stuart kings of England, could do no wrong. Not only was the president above the law, according to Nixon, but he could "authorize" staff members to violate the law as well.[20] The concept of a plebiscitary presidency, like its Latin root "plebiscite," is a "harsh term," as Professor Lowi has explained, "intended to evoke the powerful imagery of Roman emperors and French authoritarians who governed on the basis of popular adoration, with the masses giving their noisy consent to every course of action."[21] The "noisy consent" of American cit-izens is today "ascertained" through various means by the White House. Consent may be manufactured, as it surely was by President Nixon in his "silent major-ity" speech, designed to generate support for his conduct of the Vietnam War. Theodore Roosevelt may have equaled Nixon's arrogance, but at least he was more candid about his efforts to seek popular support: "People used to say of me that I . . . divined what the people were going to think. I did not 'divine.' I sim-ply made up my mind what they ought to think, and then did my best to get them to think it."[22] Moreover, White House efforts to build consent for its policies and actions may be rooted in its release of selective information, including reports and announcements tipped with deception. Then too, administrations routinely, perhaps excessively, conduct opinion polls not merely for the purpose of gaug-ing public reaction but occasionally to determine the course and direction of pol-icy pursuits. As Lyn Ragsdale has pointed out:

> Ronald Reagan modified speeches according to what internal White House polls and focus groups showed public opinion to support. George Bush received daily poll reports on American attitudes toward Iraq months before the start of the Gulf War. These polls helped administration officials to estab-lish the ultimate direction of American involvement in the war and to frame their justification for the war. In the aftermath of a Republican sweep of the House and Senate in the 1994 elections, Bill Clinton's specially prepared White House polls showed that the public felt the president should be more faithful to his centrist campaign promises. In the ensuing days, Clinton made announcements backing a middle-class tax cut, denouncing the size of the federal government, and calling for a line-item veto.[23]

There is certainly nothing inappropriate or improper in White House efforts to determine public opinion; indeed, such efforts are thoroughly Aristotelian and serve the cause of democracy. Nor is there any intrinsic harm in presidential efforts to promote their agendas, as Theodore Roosevelt explained, by "appeal-ing over the heads of the Senate and House leaders directly to the people, who were masters of both of us," an approach firmly rooted in American politics and aptly described by Sam Kernell and others as "going public."[24] The harm that occurs is a direct attribute of president-centered government. Whatever the public will support or even at a minimum, condone, becomes acceptable fare for a presidential agenda. The separation of powers is a principal casualty in the exercise of power under presidential government. Popular presidents adored by the public and presidents armed with popular issues who are seeking adoration, often sweep with indifference across constitutional boundaries and landmarks in pursuit of their goals and objectives. Presidents frequently have usurped the war-making power over the past fifty years, sometimes on the wings of popular support and high public approval ratings and sometimes in search of an improved status. The realm of foreign affairs may be fairly described as the last refuge of unpopular presidents. President Bush's unilateral invasion of Panama in December 1989 triggered a windfall of popularity and admiration. Though Bush had been unfairly labeled a "wimp" by detractors, the quick military attack brought widespread approval. His popularity soared to an 80 percent approval rating, and a senior Pentagon official characterized the strike as "a test of manhood"; indeed Bush had hit the "jackpot."[25] As the historian Alexander DeConde has justly stated, "Faced with this groundswell of acclaim for the president's machismo, few in Congress dared challenge his defiance of the War Powers Resolution or his failure to obtain legislative approval of the invasion beforehand as constitutionally mandated. Indeed, on February 7 [1990], the House of Representatives passed a resolution praising him for his decisive action."[26] President Bush's violation of constitutional law, as well as international law, was irrelevant to an American public that exhibits only selective concern for constitutional norms and that increasingly seems more interested in outcomes or ends than means or methods.[27] But Bush was buoyed by high approval ratings, which also served to deter congressional opposition to his action and any concern about its legality.

Arthur Schlesinger has captured the theory of the plebiscitary presidency in a passage worth quoting at length:

> What Nixon was moving toward was something different: it was not a parliamentary regime but a plebiscitary Presidency. His model lay not in Britain but in France—in the frame of Louis Napoleon and Charles de Gaulle. A plebiscitary presidency, unlike a parliamentary regime, would not require a new constitution; presidential acts, confirmed by a supreme court of his own appointment, could put a new gloss on the old one. And a plebiscitary presidency could be seen as the fulfillment of constitutional democracy. Michels explained in *Political Parties* the rationale of the "personal dictatorship conferred by the people in accordance with constitutional rules." By the plebiscitary logic, "once elected, the chosen of the people can no longer be opposed in any way. He personifies the majority and all resistance to his will is anti-democratic. . . . He is, moreover, infallible, for 'he who is elected by six million votes carries out the will of the people; he does not betray them.'"

How much more infallible if elected by 46 million votes! If opposition became irksome, it was the voters themselves, "we are assured, who demand from the chosen of the people that he should use severe repressive measures, should employ force, should concentrate all authority in his own hands." The chief executive would be, as Laboulaye said of Napoleon III, "democracy personified, the nation made man.[28]

Doubts about the vitality of Schlesinger's appraisal may be diminished by careful consideration, among other factors, of Nixon's portrayal of the president as above the law; routine acts of executive usurpation and aggrandizement of legislative powers by presidents since Nixon; the largely unstemmed flow of legislative authority from the legislature to the executive; and the Supreme Court's obeisance to the president in foreign affairs cases, including its opinion in *United States v. Curtiss-Wright Export Corporation* (1936) that the president embodies the "sovereignty" of the nation in its external relations.[29] In truth, in the context of American politics, the term "plebiscitary presidency" is an "exaggeration," as Professor Lowi has pointed out, "but by how much? Already we have a virtual cult of personality revolving around the White House."[30] The term may not be too wide of the mark, for the measure of its utility is to be found, in part, in the acquiescence of the public and Congress in presidential acts of usurpation and aggrandizement of powers assigned by the Constitution to Congress and in both extravagant claims of executive powers and presidential interest in assuming powers not vested in the office. No recent president has even remotely suggested the curtailment of executive power, and neither Congress nor the public has sought it. President Clinton's abuse of the pardon power, perhaps for motive of political gain and fund-raising interests, and his reliance on the doctrines of privilege and immunity in the Jones and Lewinsky matters are stark reminders that presidents will grasp for power and exercise it unilaterally to satisfy personal as well as political agendas. Clinton certainly is not the first president to abuse power; he is merely the most recent. The Framers regarded such temptations as a natural response to both opportunity and pressure. Madison echoed the sentiments of fellow delegates in Philadelphia when he observed that it is an "axiom that the executive is the department of power most distinguished by its propensity to war: hence it is the practice of all states, in proportion as they are free, to disarm this propensity of its influence."[31]

The tendency among executives to abuse their powers, particularly in an era that exalts the concept of a personal presidency at the expense of an institutional presidency, lays bare the paramountcy of a president's personal characteristics. Indeed, it is precisely in the realm of a personal presidency that a decidedly executive perspective, subject to the full measure of the president's talents, strengths, and temperament as well as his judgment, knowledge, and self-restraint, will be brought to the policy anvil. The historical portrait may not be pretty. Consider, for example, the arrogance and self-righteousness of Woodrow Wilson, the inclination toward dramatic posturing by Theodore Roosevelt, the inattentiveness of Ronald Reagan, and the imperfect personal judgment exercised by Bill Clinton. Then, too, there is the question of a president's ambition, political agenda, and personal distractions as well as a felt need to demonstrate one's machismo.

A considerable literature urges executive supremacy and extols the supposed virtues of presidential assertion, domination, and control; yet this body of work often ignores the dimensions of executive flaws, foibles, and frailties. The electoral process is not infallible; an elected president may lack the wisdom, temperament, and judgment, not to mention perception, expertise, and emotional intelligence to produce success in foreign and domestic affairs. Those qualities, which, to be sure, are attributes of the occupant and not of the office, cannot be conferred by election. Moreover, power and responsibility entail consequences. The duties and demands of the office are sure to produce stress, tension, and fatigue, which may lead to exhaustion, misperception, and impaired judgment. Theodore Sorenson's observation is illuminating: "I saw firsthand, during the long days and nights of the Cuban Missile Crisis, how brutally physical and mental fatigue can numb the good sense as well as the senses of normally articulate men."[32] Stress and strain may lead to an erosion of mental and physical health, which may distort perception and judgment. The tragic, final chapter of President Wilson's career is illustrative: isolation, obstinacy, mental deterioration, and distorted judgment impaired the pursuit of some of his objectives, including foreign policy goals. President Dwight Eisenhower suffered a stroke and a heart attack while in office. He worried about his ability to meet the duties of the office and arranged to be replaced by the vice president in the case of complete disability. President Reagan's gradual mental deterioration may have preceded the Iran-Contra Affair. Whether or not Richard Nixon's judgment and mental state were affected by prescriptions allegedly taken in response to depression, the fact that concerns about his mental state led Secretary of Defense James R. Schlesinger to take the extraordinary step of reminding all military units to ignore orders from "the White House" unless they were cleared by him or the secretary of state illustrates the grave potential of executive unilateralism. The central flaw of unilateralism remains: the most solemn and fateful decisions may be the result of the perceptions and misperceptions of a single person.

Essentially, presidential practice across two centuries confirms the wisdom of an institutionalized presidency, confined by the Constitution; the theory of executive unilateralism, as well as its traditional, underlying arguments, was exploded in the tragedy of the Vietnam War. The extollers' call for deference to the president is an argument that would reduce Congress to the role of spectator and exalt rule by presidential decree. It recalls the pervasive sentiment of the cold war, and a literature of advice, that urged blind trust of the executive on the ground that he alone possessed the information, facts, and expertise necessary to safeguard U.S. interests. Rarely has a sentiment been so troubling, dangerous, and antidemocratic. It led to the Vietnam War, the imperial presidency, and Iran-

Contra as well as to the entrenchment of presidential supremacy in foreign relations and war making, with its attendant military and policy failures, from Cuba
and Cambodia to Lebanon and Somalia. There is nothing, moreover, in the
broader historical record to suggest that the conduct of foreign relations by executive elites has produced wholesome results. Indeed, the wreckage of empires on
the shoals of executive foreign policies provides ample evidence that, as Lord
Bryce noted, the wisdom of "classes" is less than the "masses."

The contention that the wisdom of one is superior to that of many is philo-
sophically defective, historically untenable, and fundamentally undemocratic.
Since Aristotle, we have known that information alone is not a guarantee of political success; what matters are the values of the system and ultimately those of its
decision makers. Have Americans not learned from fifty years of implicit trust in
the president that despite its superior information the executive may be deficient
in perception, judgment, and vision? U.S. presidents failed to learn from the
French that Vietnam was a quagmire, a failure that confirms John Stuart Mill's
rhetorical derision of governmental infallibility. There is "nothing more fallible,"
wrote James Iredell, a delegate to the North Carolina Ratifying Convention and a
future Supreme Court justice, "than human judgement," a fundamental philosoph-
ical insight reflected in the Framers' embrace of the doctrine of separation of powers and checks and balances and in their rejection of presidential unilateralism.[33]

The Framers' design, which severed all ties to the royal prerogative and
which sought presidential confinement through institutional and constitutional
mechanisms, seems to have lost its currency. However, Robert Hirschfield's
acute analysis of the sources of presidential power, written four decades ago, has
lost none of its currency:

> Although theoretically the twin fountainheads of executive power are the
> "Constitution and the laws," in fact the sources of this prodigious authority
> are democracy and necessity.
>
> The Presidency, like all offices of government, is only a paper institution
> until the political process supplies the personality which brings it to life. . . .
> The real foundations of presidential power, therefore, are those forces which
> elevate the executive to a focal position in government, allowing him to
> interpret his authority broadly and to exercise it boldly.
>
> The most important of these forces lies in the democratic nature of the
> modern Presidency. Not only constitutionally but also politically and psy-
> chologically, the president is *the* leader of the nation.
>
> . . . The fact remains that its power flows from and is primarily dependent
> on its tribunate character.
>
> The other, and no less important, source of presidential power is necessity.
> Not only the psychological need for clearly identifiable and deeply trusted
> authority, but also the governmental necessity for centralized leadership and
> decisive action in times of crisis.

. . . The separation of powers, federalism, even the Bill of Rights and the rule of law, must sometimes be transcended under conditions of grave national emergency. Even under less pressing circumstances, the need for purposeful and efficient government is increasingly evident. But the legislative process—complex, deliberative, cumbersome, and designed to assure the compromise of manifold local interests—is ill-suited to meet these challenges. Only the President possessing (as Alexander Hamilton noted) both unity and energy, can meet the demand for leadership under critical conditions. . . .

. . . Under critical conditions there are no effective constitutional or governmental limits on executive power, for democracy and necessity allow the President to transcend the limitational principle and assert his full authority as trustee of the nation's destiny.[34]

Hirschfield's essay, an encomium to the executive, was reflective of a large academic literature of advice that offered little in the way of encouraging humility and self-abnegation. Rather, in the era of cold war tensions and fears, it counseled presidential domination and congressional and popular acquiescence. "Necessity" demanded it. Seldom has a literature of advice been so successful. Although the imperial presidency emerged from a complex of aggressive assertions of presidential authority, broad congressional delegations of power, friendly judicial decisions dating from the New Deal period. and scholarly promotions of a powerful executive, its most essential, most prominent, and most notorious characteristic was the presidential capture and control of powers that belong to Congress, including the usurpation of the war power. The cluster of foreign policy powers granted to Congress and, it may be usefully added, thus *denied* to the president, was nevertheless aggrandized by the executive. The treaty power and the critical role of the Senate in foreign policy were overwhelmed by presidential resort to executive agreements. Presidents increasingly claimed authority to withhold information from Congress on diplomatic, military, and national security grounds. Covert actions became the norm; secrecy was triumphant, and publicity and openness—critical values in a constitutional democracy—were in a state of eclipse.

The imperial presidency remains in full flight. It never was grounded, even if it did occasionally fly at a somewhat lower altitude. It remained aloft under Gerald Ford and Jimmy Carter, two presidents whose terms often are derided as disappointments or failures and whose actions, even on their best days in office, it seemed, led to their characterization as "caretaker" presidents. Yet both abused the war power—Ford in the *Mayaguez* incident and Carter in the aborted effort to rescue American hostages in Iran.[35] And Carter, it will be recalled, did not shrink from claiming unilateral authority to terminate treaties, a claim hardly consistent with the constitutional blueprint for foreign affairs.[36] In the hands of more aggressive executives—Reagan, Bush, and Clinton—the embrace of unilateralism and the cacaphony of capacious claims of presidential power were undeterred by constitutional restraints.

There is, moreover, no evidence that this trend will be curtailed. As this book went to press, the nation sustained on September 11, 2001, an insidious terrorist attack on the World Trade Center and the Pentagon that killed some 5,000 persons and caused tens of millions of dollars in damages. In an immediate response, the American government assumed a familiar posture, and it spoke with a voice that echoed the cold war literature. Congress abdicated its control of the war power when it passed within days of the attack the "Use of Force Resolution," essentially issuing to the president a blank check of military authority to name an enemy of the American people and to decide whom, when, and where to strike. It authorizes the president "to use all necessary and appropriate force against those nations, organizations or persons he determines planned, authorized, committed or aided the terrorist attacks that occurred on September 11 or harbored such organizations or persons, in order to prevent any future acts of international terrorism by such nations, organizations or persons."[37] The Constitution, as Madison observed, grants to Congress the authority to "commence, continue and conclude" military hostilities.[38] But the shopworn rhetoric of the need for "speed and dispatch" triumphed over constitutional principles. As a matter of law, the war power cannot be delegated.[39] Chief Justice John Marshall stated in 1825, in *Wayman v. Southard,* "It will not be contended that Congress can delegate to the courts, or to any tribunals, powers which are strictly and exclusively legislative."[40] The Constitution vests in Congress the sole and exclusive authority to move the nation from a state of peace to a state of war.[41] Chief Justice Charles Evans Hughes provided the classic explanation of the law of delegation a century later in *Schechter Poultry Corp. v. United States* (1935):

> The Congress is not permitted to abdicate or to transfer to others the essential legislative functions with which it is vested. We have repeatedly recognized the necessity of adopting legislation to complex conditions involving a host of details with which the national legislature cannot deal directly. We pointed out in the Panama Refining Case that the Constitution has never regarded as denying to Congress the necessary resources of flexibility and practicality, which will enable it to perform its function in laying down policies and establishing standards, while leaving to selected instrumentalities the making of subordinate rules within prescribed limits and the determination of facts to which the policy as declared by the Legislature is to apply. But we said that the constant recognition of the necessity and validity of such provisions, and the wide range of administrative authority which has been developed by means of them, cannot be allowed to observe the limitations of the authority to delegate, if our constitutional system is to be maintained.[42]

The law governing the delegation of power thus prevents Congress from passing legislation that would authorize the president to commence a war, for the simple reason that "it is impossible for Congress to enact governing standards for launching future wars."[43] Congress cannot anticipate the unpredictable twists and turns of warfare, which means it cannot lay down standards and policies that would give the president any meaningful directions. It has been justly observed that if Congress attempts to delegate the war power to the executive, "it is not determining policy for the future, it is casting dice."[44]

Congressional abdication of its war power has become a commonplace, but perhaps Americans would be justified in reacting with surprise to the abdication of its lawmaking authority. On October 8, 2001, President Bush announced that he had signed an executive order to create a Homeland Security Office, a cabinet-level position to which he immediately appointed Pennsylvania governor Tom Ridge.[45] As director of the office, Ridge was charged with the task of coordinating the antiterrorist activities of some fifty federal agencies, including those of the CIA and the FBI, as well as the efforts of state and local officials. Ridge would head a staff of nearly 100 persons and would be given "all the resources I need." He would report directly to President Bush and would be asked to certify whether funding levels for his office are "necessary and appropriate." At a press conference at which he announced the creation of the office and Ridge's appointment as its head, Bush explained that he had assigned to Ridge and the Office of Homeland Security "a mission to design a comprehensive, coordinated national strategy to fight terror here at home. We face a united and determined enemy. We must have a united and determined response." As head of Homeland Security, Ridge was vested with the authority and responsibility, Bush explained, to "take the strongest possible precautions against terrorism by bringing together the best information in intelligence" and to "respond effectively to terrorist actions if they come."[46] As part of his responsibilities, Ridge was named to the Homeland Security Council, a presidential policymaking committee chaired by the president, which would include the attorney general, the secretaries of defense, treasury, health and human services, and agriculture as well as the directors of the FBI and the Federal Emergency Management Authority (FEMA). U.S. Supreme Court Justice Clarence Thomas performed the swearing-in ceremony, at which Ridge pledged to "faithfully discharge the duties of the office."

The appointment clause of the Constitution, found in Article 2, section 2, provides that the president "shall nominate, and by and with the Advice and Consent of the Senate, shall appoint . . . all other Officers of the United States, whose Appointments are not herein otherwise provided for, and which shall be established by Law; but the Congress may by law vest the Appointment of such inferior Officers, as they think proper, in the President alone, in the Courts of Law, or in the Heads of Departments." In 1823, while riding circuit, Chief Justice Marshall held that the Constitution "directs that all offices of the United States shall be established by law."[47] The Framers, keenly aware that the king had used his authority to create offices for corrupt purposes, refused to grant that power to the president and accordingly placed it in Congress. No delegate proposed the placement of such authority in the presidency; indeed, the convention took for granted the principle that the creation of an office is a legislative act. Still, some efforts were undertaken to remove all doubt. On September 8, 1787, Elbridge Gerry moved "that no officer shall be appd but to offices created by the Constitution or by law." Madison stated, "This was rejected as unnecessary."[48]

Madison himself was concerned to remove any doubts about the fact that the legislative power encompassed the authority to create offices. His efforts were also seen as "unnecessary." On August 20, the convention considered a draft provision that eventually became known as the necessary and proper clause of the Constitution: "And to make all laws necessary and proper for carrying into executive the foregoing powers, and all other powers vested, by this Constitution, in the Government of the U.S. or any department or officer thereof." Seeking to remove all thoughts that the executive might create an office, Madison and Pinckney "moved to insert between 'laws' and 'necessary' 'and establish all offices' if appearing to them liable to cavil that the latter was not included in the former." Several Framers, however, urged that such an amendment "could not be necessary," and the Madison-Pinckney motion was rejected.[49]

President Bush's executive order to create the Office of Homeland Security thus constituted a rank usurpation of the legislative power. Congressional acquiescence in the act of usurpation supplies no constitutional warrant. It finds no support in the text of the Constitution, in its legislative history, or in judicial rulings.

The surge in Congress after the September 11 tragedy to concentrate even greater authority in the president was further fueled by legislative abdication of yet another of its fundamental powers—the spending power—when Congress approved on September 14 a massive $40 billion emergency-aid package, which included a grant to the president of $10 billion of nearly unbridled discretionary authority.[50] The spending bill provided an emergency appropriation of $40 billion to assist in recovery operations, repair damaged facilities, strengthen security, and fight terrorism. Under the legislation, Bush was granted authority to immediately spend $10 billion as he saw fit. Congressman David Obey of Wisconsin, the ranking Democrat on the House Appropriations Committee, said the measure "provides unprecedented grants of authority to the president, but it does retain reasonable congressional ability to make its own judgments about how this money ought to be spent."[51] Yet the congressional checks seem not to have applied to the initial allocation of $10 billion to the president; as a consequence, Congress has surrendered another of its great constitutional powers.[52]

In the aftermath of the impeachment of President Clinton, academics, journalists, and public officials, among others, engaged in a national dialogue on the future of the presidency: had Clinton's contretemps weakened the presidency? In light of the tremendous concentration of power vested in the presidency of George W. Bush as a response to the September 11 outrage, it is hard to believe that there was even a question about it. The fact is, as scholars have observed, the presidency is virtually indestructible. Presidential power was not diminished by Nixon's actions, nor was it sapped of its vitality by Clinton's deeds and misdeeds. On the contrary, presidential government was firmly entrenched when Clinton came to the presidency, and it remained firmly entrenched when he left it.

The Framers of the Constitution believed that certain political powers must be exercised only by Congress if republican government were to survive, among them, the lawmaking authority, the war power, and the spending power. For the Framers, history suggested that a strong executive might pose a continuous threat to a republic; American history has demonstrated it. The Framers could well have imagined an aggressive, even a commandeering president bent on aggrandizing legislative power. Accordingly, they improvised a system to confine the executive. But they could not have imagined a Congress unwilling to assert and defend its constitutional authority, seemingly indifferent to its institutional responsibilities, and one apparently uninterested in preserving its status and strength. Power, we are told, cannot resist a vacuum. Perhaps the rise of presidential government was irresistible, after all. Given the failings of Congress, a large body of literature extolling the virtues of a strong executive, and the emergence of a virtual cult of the presidency in America, perhaps the more interesting question to be addressed is, why did it take so long for the United States to succumb to presidential government?

That question resists a simple answer, and it must await another essay, but it is clear that the emergence of a plebiscitary or imperial presidency represents an assault on the rule of law, which, as Lord Dicey explained, requires, at a minimum that "absolute supremacy or predominance of regular law as opposed to the influence of arbitrary power, and excludes the existence of arbitrariness, or prerogative, or even of wide discretionary authority on the part of the government."[53] It is not possible, as Alexander Bickel has observed, for governmental officials to swear an oath to uphold the Constitution and at the same time to ignore its provisions or assert the authority to violate the Constitution and the laws of the land:

> There is a moral duty, and there ought to be, for those to whom it is applicable—most often officers of government—to obey the manifest Constitution, unless and until it is altered by the amendment process it itself provides for, a duty analogous to the duty to obey final judicial decrees. No president may decide to stay in office for a term of six years rather than four, or, since the Twenty-second Amendment, to run for a third term. There is an absolute duty to obey; to disobey is to deny the idea of constitutionalism, that special kind of law which establishes a set of pre-existing rules within which society works out all its other rules from time to time. To deny this idea is in the most fundamental sense to deny the idea of law itself.[54]

If, as we assume, the denial of arbitrary power—to Congress, the president, and the judiciary alike—was a preeminent goal of the Constitutional Convention, we are entitled to wonder whether the achievement of the goal is to be found in the resuscitation of constitutional mechanisms. We may seek such remedies for protection against presidential government, but they are likely to be unavailing. There seems little wrong with the constitutional blueprint; the principal problem, rather, is to be found in the unwillingness of the men and women in positions of power, those at the helm, duly to perform their duties and responsibilities. The remedy, it would appear, is to be found in a citizenry, from Main Street to Wall Street to Pennsylvania Avenue, that summons the will to nurture and nourish the virtues and values of constitutionalism. The historian Charles H. McIlwain has rightly observed, "The two fundamental correlative elements of constitutionalism for which all lovers of liberty must yet fight are the legal limits to arbitrary power and a complete responsibility of government to the governed."[55]

NOTES

1. See, generally, Francis D. Wormuth, *The Royal Prerogative, 1603–1649* (Ithaca, N.Y.: Cornell University Press, 1939); Wormuth, *The Origins of Modern Constitutionalism* (New York: Harper, 1949); Margaret A. Judson, *The Crisis of the Constitution: An Essay in Constitutional and Political Thought in England, 1603–1645* (New Brunswick, N.J.: Rutgers University Press, 1949); Donald W. Hanson, *From Kingdom to Commonwealth: The Development of Civic Consciousness in English Political Thought* (Cambridge: Harvard University Press, 1970).

2. Hanson, *Kingdom to Commonwealth*, p. 139.

3. In a letter to Spencer Roane, on September 6, 1819, Jefferson lamented that the Court had made the Constitution into "a thing of wax." He hoped that officials would be bound "from mischief by the chains of the Constitution" (quoted in Leonard Levy, ed., *The Supreme Court Under Earl Warren* [New York: Quadrangle Books, 1972], p. 7). In the Steel Seizure case, Justice Robert H. Jackson stated, "I cannot be brought to believe that this country will suffer if the Court refuses further to aggrandize the presidential office, already so potent and so relatively immune from judicial review, at the expense of Congress" (*Youngstown Sheet and Tube Co. v. Sawyer,* 343 U.S. 579, 638 [1952]).

4. Quoted in Louis Fisher, *Congressional Abdication on War and Spending* (College Station: Texas A&M University Press, 2000), p. 119.

5. See, generally, Theodore J. Lowi, *The Personal President: Power Invested, Promise Unfulfilled* (Ithaca, N.Y.: Cornell University Press, 1985); Arthur Schlesinger Jr., *The Imperial Presidency* (Boston: Houghton, Mifflin, 1973); Thomas E. Cronin, *The State of the Presidency* (Boston: Little, Brown, 1980); James MacGregor Burns, *Presidential Government* (Boston: Houghton, Mifflin, 1966).

6. Schlesinger, *Imperial Presidency,* p. 212.

7. Ibid., p. 216.

8. The Supreme Court rejected Truman's claim of "inherent" power in the Steel Seizure case, 343 U.S. 579 (1952).

9. See, generally, David Gray Adler, "The Constitution and Presidential Warmaking: The Enduring Debate," *Political Science Quarterly* 103 (1988): 1–36; Adler, "Clinton, the

Constitution, and the War Power," chap. 2 of this book; Louis Fisher, *Presidential War Power* (Lawrence, University Press of Kansas, 1995); David Gray Adler and Larry George, eds., *The Constitution and the Conduct of American Foreign Policy* (Lawrence: University Press of Kansas, 1996).

10. See, generally, Adler and George, eds., *Constitution and Foreign Policy;* Harold Koh, *The National Security Constitution* (New Haven: Yale University Press, 1990); Michael Glennon, *Constitutional Diplomacy* (Princeton: Princeton University Press, 1990); Schlesinger, *Imperial Presidency;* Fisher, *Presidential War Power.*

11. Fisher, *Congressional Abdication,* p. 163.

12. See, e.g., an analysis of the "War Powers Resolution of 1973," in Louis Fisher and David Gray Adler, "The War Powers Resolution: Time to Say Goodbye," *Political Science Quarterly* (1998): 1–20.

13. See, generally, Fisher, *Congressional Abdication,* pp. 115–161.

14. See ibid., pp. 137–152.

15. This has become a familiar theme in the literature. For a recent discussion, see Bert Rockman, "Reinventing for Whom? President and Congress in the Making of Foreign Policy," *Presidential Studies Quarterly* 30 (March 2000): 133–153.

16. See Schlesinger's apt description of presidential preference for abusing power rather than adhering to the Constitution and laws in *Imperial Presidency,* p. 212.

17. See Mark J. Rozell, "The Clinton Legacy: An Old or New Understanding of Executive Power," chapter 3 of this book.

18. See Michael A. Genovese and Kristine Almquist, "The Pardon Power Under Clinton: Tested but Intact," chapter 4, and Evan Gerstmann and Christopher Shortell, "Executive Immunity for the Post-Clinton Presidency," chapter 6, both in this book.

19. Lowi, *Personal President,* p. xi.

20. *New York Times,* May 19, 1977, p. 1.

21. Lowi, *Personal President,* p. xi.

22. See Lyn Ragsdale, "Disconnected Politics: Public Opinion and Presidents," in *Understanding Public Opinion,* ed. Barbara Norrander and Clyde Wilcox (Washington, D.C.: CQ Press, 1997), pp. 229–251.

23. Ibid., pp. 229–230.

24. Quoted in ibid., p. 228. See Samuel Kernell, *Going Public: New Strategies of Presidential Leadership,* 3d ed. (Washington, D.C.: Congressional Quarterly Press, 1997).

25. See the insightful discussion in Alexander DeConde, *Presidential Machismo: Executive Authority, Military Intervention, and Foreign Relations* (Boston: Northeastern University Press, 2000), pp. 246–250. DeConde's analysis lays bare presidential exploitation of foreign affairs and warmaking opportunities for fame and public approval ratings. For the impact on Bush of the allegations of "wimpishness," see Bob Woodward, *Shadow: Five Presidents and the Legacy of Watergate* (New York: Simon and Schuster, 1999), pp. 171–224; Bill Clinton too, was vulnerable to the charge of "wimpishness" (see pp. 449–517).

26. DeConde, *Presidential Machismo,* p. 249.

27. Few Americans, including governmental officials, possess a substantial knowledge of the Constitution, and, in terms of substance, many citizens seem not to mind their relative ignorance. The role of the Constitution will not ascend to a higher place until the constitutional tradition is integrated into the practice of politics. For a good discussion of

this theme, see Daniel Lessard Levin, *Representing Popular Sovereignty: The Constitution in American Political Culture* (Albany: State University of New York Press, 1999); for an insightful discussion of the "culture of the Constitution" in the United States, such as it is, see Michael Kammen, *Sovereignty and Liberty: Constitutional Discourse in American Culture* (Madison: University of Wisconsin Press, 1988), and his earlier, acclaimed work, *A Machine That Would Go of Itself* (New York: Knopf, 1986).

28. Schlesinger, *Imperial Presidency,* p. 254.

29. For a discussion of the Court's reflexive bow to the president in foreign affairs jurisprudence, see David Gray Adler, "Court, Constitution and Foreign Affairs," in Adler and George, eds., *The Constitution and Foreign Policy,* pp. 19–56. The *Curtiss-Wright* opinion was extravagant, to say the least (299 U.S. 304 [1936]).

30. Lowi, *Personal President,* p. xi.

31. "Letters of Helvidius," in James Madison, *The Writings of James Madison,* ed. Gaillard Hunt, 9 vols. (New York: Putnam, 1900–1910), 1: 138. Moreover, as Alexander Hamilton explained in *Federalist* no. 75, the Framers rejected the practice of granting to the president the unilateral authority to make treaties because the "history of human conduct does not warrant that exalted opinion of human virtue which would make it wise in a nation to commit interest of so delicate and momentous or kind, as those which concern its intercourse with the rest of the world, to the sole disposal of a magistrate created and circumstanced as would be a President of the United States" (Alexander Hamilton, James Madison, and John Jay, *The Federalist,* ed. Edward M. Earle [New York: Modern Library, 1937], p. 487). The Framers' discussion of impeachable offenses reflected their concerns about executive corruption and abuse of power. See, generally, Raoul Berger, *Impeachment: The Constitutional Problems* (Cambridge: Harvard University Press, 1973), pp. 53–102; see also, David Gray Adler and Nancy Kassop, "The Impeachment of Bill Clinton," chapter 8 of this book.

32. Theodore Sorenson, *Decision-making in the White House* (New York: Columbia University Press, 1963), p. 78.

33. Jonathan Elliot, ed., *The Debates in the Several State Conventions on the Adoption of the Federal Convention,* 2d ed., 4 vols. (Washington, D.C.: J. Elliot, 1836), 4: 14.

34. Robert Hirschfield, "The Power of the Contemporary Presidency," in *Parliamentary Affairs* 14 (1961): 353, 360, 362, 363 (emphasis in original).

35. For discussion, see Fisher, *Presidential War Power,* pp. 136–140.

36. President Carter's termination of the 1954 Mutual Defense Treaty triggered a lawsuit, *Goldwater v. Carter,* 344 U.S. 997 (1979), in which the Supreme Court invoked the political question doctrine and thus declined to reach the merits. There are good reasons to believe that the president lacks the unilateral authority to terminate treaties. For the argument that the termination power is shared by the president and the Senate, see Adler, "The Framers and the Termination of Treaties: A Matter of Symmetry," *Arizona State Law Journal* (1981): 891–923, and Adler, *The Constitution and the Termination of Treaties* (New York: Garland, 1986).

37. "Use of Force Resolution," S.J. Res 23, signed into law by President Bush on September 18, 2001. Public Law 107-40.

38. "Letter of Helvidius," in Madison, *Writings,* 6:148. In 1798, Madison wrote to Jefferson, "The Constitution supposes, what the History of all Govts. Demonstrates, that the Ex. Is the branch of power most interested in war, and most prone to it. It has accord-

ingly with studied care vested the question of war in the Legisl." (p. 312). Thus he rejected doctrines that "will deposit the peace of the Country in that Department which the Constitution distrusts as most ready without cause to renounce it" (ibid.).

39. See the penetrating analysis of Francis D. Wormuth, "The Vietnam War: The President versus the Constitution," in *The Vietnam War and International Law*, ed. Richard Falk, 2 vols. (Princeton: Princeton University Press, 1969), pp. 710, 780–799, and Wormuth and Edwin B. Firmage, *To Chain the Dog of War: The War Power of Congress in History and Law* (Dallas: Southern Methodist University Press, 1986), pp. 197–218.

40. *Wayman v. Southard*, 23 U.S. (10 Wheat.) 1, 42–43 (1825).

41. See, generally, Adler, "The Clinton Theory of the War Power," *Presidential Studies Quarterly* 30 (March 2000); Fisher, *Presidential War Power*, pp. 1–12; Adler, "The Constitution and Presidential Warmaking," pp. 1–17.

42. *Schechter Poultry Corp. v. United States*, 250 U.S. 495, 529–530 (1935).

43. Wormuth and Firmage, *To Chain the Dog of War*, p. 198.

44. Ibid., p. 199.

45. See "Text: President Bush, Tom Ridge," in *Washington Post*, October 8, 2001, p. A1, and Eric Pianin and Bradley Graham, "Ridge Is Sworn in as Anti-Terror Chief," ibid., p. A1.

46. Pianin and Graham, "Ridge Is Sworn," p. A1

47. *United States v. Maurice*, 26 F. Cas. 1211 (C.C.D. Va., 1823); see also *Op. Atty. Gen.* 10 (April 12, 1861): 11. I owe this citation and much, much more, to my mentor, the late Francis D. Wormuth, who provided it to me some twenty years ago in connection with another project.

48. Max Farrand, ed. *The Records of the Federal Convention of 1787*, 4 vols. (New Haven: Yale University Press, 1911), 2: 550.

49. Ibid., 2: 345. Madison's notes do not record whether his coauthor was Charles or Charles Cotesworth Pinckney, both delegates from South Carolina.

50. John Lancaster and Helen Dewar, "Congress Clears Use of Force, $40 Billion in Emergency Aid," *Washington Post*, September 15, 2001, p. A4.

51. Ibid.

52. Granting the president unfettered authority to expend funds threatens the constitutional power of Congress to determine budget priorities, and it violates the republican principle that the power of the purse should be exercised by Congress. See the excellent discussion of congressional abdication of its spending power in Fisher, *Congressional Abdication*, pp. 115–161.

53. A. V. Dicey, *Introduction to the Study of the Constitution*, 10th ed. (London: Macmillan, 1959), pp. 202–203.

54. Alexander Bickel, *The Morality of Consent* (New York: Harper and Row, 1975), p. 75. Once limits are prescribed, Chief Justice John Marshall explained, they may not "be passed at pleasure." It was because constitutions were bulwarks against oppression that, in his words, "written constitutions have been regarded with so much reverence" (*Marbury v. Madison*, 5 U.S. (1 Cranch), 137, 178 [1803]).

55. Charles H. McIlwain, *Constitutionalism: Ancient and Modern*, rev. ed. (Ithaca, N.Y.: Cornell University Press, 1947), p. 146.

Epilogue:
Constitutional Violence

Louis Fisher

These chapters send a powerful legal message. To an increasing extent, presidential conduct is uninformed and undirected by statutory and constitutional constraints. More than Edward Corwin ever realized, we have a "high-flying" executive.[1] Presidents seem more motivated in doing what is "right" (i.e., in their political self-interest) than what is authorized. White House aides, flush from the triumph of an electoral victory, often have scant patience for restrictions placed in statutes and the Constitution. When necessary they cut corners, or do worse. If their misdeeds are uncovered, by that time they are probably back in the private sector, with little concern about prosecution or penalty.

The Framers thought they broke free from monarchy and the philosophy that the "king can do no wrong." They believed that an elaborate system of checks and balances would bring abuses to light and keep wayward officials in line. Each branch, they assumed, would fight off encroachments and protect institutional prerogatives. Ambition would counter ambition, as James Madison told us. Yet this carefully calibrated political system has barely functioned in recent decades. Members of Congress not only fail to fight off encroachments (as with the war power), they dream up ways of voluntarily surrendering other powers (such as the item veto). The contemporary public seems unconcerned about constitutional violations. The president has just acted in a way that offends the Constitution? So what? The stock market is soaring and jobs are plentiful. Inflation and interest rates are down. Everything is coming up roses. Why worry?

Those who believe in constitutional limits, separation of powers, and the rule of law have great cause to worry. Democratic and Republican presidents show progressive disregard for legal boundaries. When offenders are caught red-handed, the lesson is not to avoid future illegalities; instead, officials figure out how to lessen the chance of being caught. If some people must be sacrificed, the penalty falls on midlevel officials and perhaps private citizens, not the officials (including the president) who generate the policies and decide to do what law forbids.

TRUMAN IN KOREA

President Truman's deployment of U.S. troops to Korea in June 1950 marked a watershed in presidential power. For the first time. a president had acted unilaterally in taking the nation into a major war, without bothering to come to Congress for authority. Second, by seeking "authority" from the UN Security Council, Truman established a damaging precedent (later used by Bush and Clinton) to bypass Congress and rely on an international body for approval.

Truman cited two resolutions of the UN Security Council to justify his action in Korea. However, the first did not call for military operations, and he acted before the second was passed.[2] Under Article 43 of the UN Charter, whenever there is any threat to the peace, breach of peace, or an act of aggression, all UN members shall make available to the Security Council—in accordance with "special agreements"—armed forces and other assistance. These agreements would spell out the numbers and types of forces, their degree of readiness and general location, and the nature of the facilities and assistance to be provided. Each nation would then ratify these agreements "in accordance with their respective constitutional processes."

While the Senate debated the UN Charter, President Truman wired a note from Potsdam to Senator Kenneth McKellar on July 27, 1945, making this pledge: "When any such agreement or agreements are negotiated it will be my purpose to ask the Congress for appropriate legislation to approve them."[3] Senators had more than Truman's word. The specific procedures needed to bring Article 43 into conformity with the "constitutional processes" of the U.S. Constitution were included in the UN Participation Act of 1945. Section 6 spells out the understanding in clear language. The agreements "shall be subject to the approval of the Congress by appropriate Act or joint resolution." Presidents would have to first come to Congress for authority before acting militarily in UN operations. The restrictions in Section 6 were later clarified by amendments adopted in 1949, allowing the president on his own initiative to provide military forces to the UN for "cooperative action." However, the 1949 amendments subject presidential discretion to stringent conditions. The armed forces can serve only as observers and guards, they may perform only in a noncombatant capacity, and they cannot exceed 1,000 in number. In providing these troops to the UN, the president must ensure that they not involve "the employment of armed forces contemplated by chapter VII of the United Nations Charter."[4]

With these statutory safeguards and understandings in place, how could Truman bypass Congress and act militarily in Korea under the UN umbrella? The short answer is that he ignored the procedure for special agreements. The United

States has never entered into a "special agreement" with the Security Council, nor has any other country. The very procedure established to protect congressional prerogatives became a nullity by executive action. Having been snookered, members of Congress never fought back. One legislator after another took the floor to praise Truman for his leadership and to express fealty to presidential authority. Only a handful of members raised constitutional objections.[5]

At a news conference on June 29, 1950, Truman announced, "We are not at war." He agreed with a reporter that it was more correct to call the conflict a "police action under the United Nations."[6] Of course it was a war, not a police action. Moreover, it was a U.S. war, not a UN operation. Measured by troops, money, casualties, and deaths, it remained an American war from start to finish. Federal courts, asked in life insurance cases whether the conflict in Korea amounted to war, had no trouble in reaching a conclusion: "We doubt very much if there is any question in the minds of the majority of the people of this country that the conflict now raging in Korea can be anything but war."[7] Another district judge remarked, "No unsophisticated mind would question whether there was a war in Korea in 1952."[8]

The federal judiciary finally checked Truman in 1952 when he advanced a broad theory of presidential power to justify seizing steel mills to prosecute the war in Korea. Newspapers from around the country published editorials that condemned his theory of inherent executive power. They attacked him for acting in a manner they regarded as arbitrary, dictatorial, dangerous, destructive, highhanded, and unauthorized by law.[9] In striking down the seizure, District Judge David A. Pine said that a nationwide strike "would be less injurious to the public than the injury which would flow from a timorous judicial recognition that there is some basis for this claim to unlimited and unrestrained Executive power, which would be implicit in a failure to grant this injunction." The Supreme Court affirmed his ruling.[10] I wonder if the general public and the courts today have the capacity to respond so forthrightly to presidential abuse of power.

Truman finally got his comeuppance, but not before setting a dangerous precedent that would be used later by Bush and Clinton. Presidents now go to the UN Security Council for a resolution expressing support for a military action, whether it is Bush in Iraq or Clinton in Haiti and Bosnia. Through this mechanism they bypass Congress and seek "authority" from an international institution. Similarly, President Clinton sought "authority" from NATO for military operations, even though NATO is a defensive pact and contains the same language as the UN Charter regarding "constitutional processes" (meaning joint action by Congress and the president for offensive military actions).[11]

WATERGATE

It is important to revisit Watergate. Executive officials who strayed from the legal arena paid a price—a stiff one. Future transgressors within the executive branch would not receive such penalties, or at least not those serving in top positions. The White House learned how to cope with intrusive and potentially damaging investigations.

In June 1972, five people were arrested for trying to burglarize the headquarters of the National Democratic Committee at the Watergate complex. Within a few days it became clear that others—connected to the Republican Committee to Re-Elect the President (CRP)—were involved. As a condition for his appointment to become attorney general, Elliot Richardson agreed to appoint Archibald Cox as special prosecutor to investigate the scandal. Scathing criticism has been leveled at Kenneth Starr's performance as independent counsel because of his association with Republican and conservative causes, but consider Cox's background. He had done substantial work for Senator John F. Kennedy, helped in his 1960 presidential race, and served as solicitor general in the Kennedy administration (working directly under Attorney General Robert Kennedy). At Cox's swearing-in ceremony as special prosecutor, at least ten members of the Kennedy family were present, including Senator Ted Kennedy and the widow of Robert Kennedy, Ethel Kennedy. Erwin Griswold, a former dean at Harvard Law School and solicitor general under President Nixon, said, "I thought it was a terrible mistake. But I kept my mouth shut.' Cox understood that "he still had plenty to learn about politics." Cox's biographer, Ken Gormley, has noted that political acumen "was never Cox's strong suit."[12]

Cox's insensitivity to political considerations is stunning. Given his previous identification with the Kennedys and the imperative of maintaining the appearance of neutrality and independence, it is almost inconceivable that he could have allowed his swearing-in ceremony to be debased in this manner. President Nixon did not need additional reasons to believe that Cox was "out to get him." As Nixon noted in his memoirs, "No White House in history could have survived the kind of operation Cox was planning. If he were determined to get me, as I was certain that he and his staff were, then given the terms of their charter it would only be a matter of time until they had bored like termites through the whole executive branch."[13]

Similar to complaints about Justice Department cover-ups during the Clinton years, the Watergate investigation ran into severe difficulties because of the techniques used by the three-man team led by Assistant U.S. Attorney Earl Silbert Jr. As Gormley notes, they seemed to ' steer away from the most puzzling questions: Who had authorized the burglary who had paid for it, and to whom did the defendants report?"[14] Seven men eventually pled guilty or were found guilty, but Judge John L. Sirica was not satisfied. He did not believe that any of the defendants had told the truth and suspected that the "whole case looked more and more like a big cover-up."[15] Yet he was stumped, unable to find a motive behind the burglary.

Now enters Lady Luck. Three days before sentencing, one of the defendants, James McCord, walked into Sirica's office with a letter, revealing that political pressure had been applied to the seven men to have them plead guilty and remain silent. McCord said that all of them had committed perjury during the trial and that their operation had help from others. He approached Sirica directly because he had no trust in the Justice Department: "I cannot feel confident in talking with an FBI agent, in testifying before a grand jury whose U.S. Attorneys work for the Department of Justice."[16]

Relations between the prosecutors and the head of the Criminal Division, Henry Petersen, were severely strained. Cox became aware that "the White House knew what the grand jury testimony was going to be on any day before the grand jury knew it." Evidently Petersen was serving as a conduit between the Justice Department and the White House. In a memo to Attorney General Richardson, Silbert said that "Petersen himself was a potential 'witness' to obstruction of justice and improper links between the FBI and the White House.'" Silbert concluded that Petersen "cannot, accordingly, remain in charge of the Watergate investigation, examining grand jury minutes of other witnesses and making prosecutive decisions." Silbert felt that Petersen had become "fearful" and "timid" in the company of high-level officials, especially in the White House and particularly with President Nixon. Even before Cox arrived, Silbert and the prosecutors were "increasingly 'concerned' about Petersen's close contact with the White House."[17]

White House Counsel John Dean had known Petersen for a number of years. In his twenties, Dean had served as associate deputy attorney general and worked with Petersen. After Dean moved to the White House, he stayed friendly with Petersen. Even after Watergate, Dean said, "It was very easy for me to talk to him, and get information from him." According to Dean, shortly after the Watergate break-in he told Attorney General Richard Kleindienst and Petersen that the White House could not take "a wide-open investigation" and that the Justice Department should limit its investigation to the Watergate incident without getting into other matters, such as campaign act violations and the break-in at Daniel Ellsberg's psychiatrist's office. Dean said that Peterson agreed to those ground rules.[18]

Actions by L. Patrick Gray III, the acting FBI director, further compromised the investigation. Dean had given him sensitive materials from the safe of Howard Hunt, one of the burglars. After some delay, Gray decided to destroy the documents, apparently burning them in his backyard.[19] An acting director of the FBI had destroyed potential evidence in a criminal case!

Cox initially urged Sam Ervin, chairman of the Senate Watergate Committee, not to hold televised hearings. He feared that the pretrial publicity would jeopardize his prosecution efforts and that the committee would grant immunity to key witnesses. Undeterred, Ervin proceeded. Cox later conceded that the hearings "certainly were a contribution to the public good as it turned out. None of them did interfere in any way with prosecution, and they may have produced some evidence . . . that might not otherwise have come out."[20] The hearings disclosed to the public a remarkable fact about White House operations. Alexander P. Butterfield, administrator of the Federal Aviation Administration, told committee staff about the existence of listening and recording devices in the Oval Office of the president.

After much legal maneuvering, some of these tapes wound up in the hands of Sirica. They revealed unmistakable evidence of a cover-up, such as Nixon's remark at a March 22, 1973 meeting: "And, uh, for that reason, I am perfectly willing to—I don't give a shit what happens. I want you to stonewall it, let them plead the Fifth Amendment, cover-up or anything else, if it'll save the plan."[21] Other tapes, released as a result of the Supreme Court's decision in *United States v. Nixon* (1974), demonstrated that Nixon had agreed that the CIA should put a halt to the FBI investigation.[22] With the release of these tapes, Nixon recognized that a House vote of impeachment "is, as a practical matter, virtually a foregone conclusion."[23] He announced his resignation on August 8, 1974, to be effective the next day.

What would have happened without the tapes, or if people outside the White House had not been allowed to listen to the tapes? Nixon would probably have survived. Cox had expressed interest in a White House proposal that the actual tapes would not be released to him. Instead, the president or the president's designate would prepare a transcript, omitting material that was outside Cox's jurisdiction. Nixon selected Senator John Stennis to play the role of this neutral arbiter. He would receive a "preliminary record" (prepared by the White House) of the nine tapes requested by Cox. It would consist of verbatim transcripts, except for portions "not pertinent" to the special prosecutor's investigation. Stennis could paraphrase language that might be "embarrassing" to Nixon and delete material related to "national defense" if it might "do real harm." This version, as edited by Stennis, would be given to Cox.

Members of Cox's staff found the proposal offensive. First, summaries of transcripts would most likely be useless in a court of law. Second, although Stennis had a reputation for "probity," his strong support for the military and presidential power would tilt toward nondisclosure. Third, his age and recent wounds in a gun attack raised questions whether he had the time and energy for such an exhaustive enterprise. Fourth, the person who would most likely prepare the transcript for Stennis was J. Fred Buzhardt, who had worked with Stennis in the past and had also worked for the Pentagon.[24] This proposal was eventually dropped.

The larger conspiracy of Watergate, reaching into the upper levels of the White House, was nearly suppressed. The prosecution conducted by the Justice Department imposed strict limits on the grand jury investigation. At a pretrial session, Sirica urged Silbert to trace the source of the money given to the burglars and to explore the motive and intent for entering the Democratic National Committee's headquarters. Silbert replied cautiously, giving little indication that he was willing to follow the story wherever it led. Sirica was disappointed by Silbert's opening statement, calling it "the most limited view of the case it was possible to take."

Silbert told the jury that McCord and G. Gordon Liddy "were off on an enterprise of their own."[25] (Defenders of the Reagan administration would later dismiss the Iran-Contra Affair as a "rogue operation.")

Through a fortuitous chain of events—McCord walking into Sirica's office, the availability of incriminating White House tapes, and the willingness of a number of administration officials to talk to prosecutors and reporters—we learned just about everything there is to know about Watergate. Carl Bernstein and Bob Woodward had access to a number of people who could round out the story: Hugh Sloan, treasurer for the CRP; the "Bookkeeper," who worked for Maurice Stans; "Deep Throat," who had extensive and accurate information about the CRP and the White House; an FBI agent; a Justice Department attorney; "Z," a woman knowledgeable about the CRP and the White House; Kathleen Chenow, secretary for the "Plumbers," the White House group that investigated leaks to the news media; friends and acquaintances of Howard Hunt, one of the men involved in the Watergate burglary; someone from the CRP; and a White House official.[26] Because of these sources, the outside world could penetrate and illuminate the corruption within the White House.

The result was political accountability, in spades. Nixon left office, and jail sentences were meted out to former attorney general John Mitchell and top officials in the administration, in the CRP, and to private citizens who had assisted the administration. In addition to the seven men who participated in the burglary, many individuals spent time in jail: Dwight Chapin, Charles Colson, John Dean, John Ehrlichman, Bob Haldeman, Herbert Kalmbach, Egil Krogh, Frederick LaRue, Jeb Magruder, Herbert Porter, and Donald Segretti. Others went to prison for related activities, such as illegal campaign contributions.

IRAN-CONTRA

Never again would investigation of a White House scandal reveal so clear a picture. In the years since Watergate, the executive branch has retained and possibly improved its capacity for cover-up. Efforts to understand the full dimension of the Iran-Contra Affair—reaching to the CIA, the Pentagon, and the White House—were regularly thwarted by the strategy of destroying or withholding information, denying classified documents, and issuing presidential pardons. We know a fair amount about the criminal activities of midlevel people. For the policymakers at the top, including President Reagan, Vice President Bush, Defense Secretary Caspar Weinberger, and CIA Director William Casey, the door largely closed and remains closed. There is hardly a shadow of political accountability.

As part of the investigation into the Iran-Contra Affair, Independent Counsel Lawrence Walsh looked into the activities of Joseph Fernandez, the CIA station chief in Costa Rica who helped Oliver North supply the Nicaraguan Contras in violation of the Boland amendment. On June 20, 1988, the grand jury in the

District of Columbia indicted Fernandez for false statements, obstruction of the investigations, and for conspiring with North and others to carry out the covert action. The conspiracy count was later dropped. When Attorney General Richard Thornburgh refused to release classified information needed for the trial, the case was dismissed and, with it, an opportunity to understand the full scope of the CIA's role in the Iran-Contra Affair.[27]

On June 16, 1992, a grand jury indicted Weinberger for five felonies, including one count of obstructing a congressional investigation, two counts of making false statements, and two charges of perjury. The obstruction charge was based on his concealment of diary notes and other memorandums that Congress had requested. President George Bush was likely to be called to Weinberger's trial to testify. Although Bush denied knowing that Secretary of State George Shultz and Weinberger opposed selling arms to Iran, the indictment revealed that Bush had attended a January 7, 1986, White House meeting "in which President Reagan had overridden Shultz and Weinberger and authorized the sale of missiles to Iran."[28]

The Weinberger indictment again raised questions of what Bush knew about the Iran-Contra Affair. That issue came into sharp focus on October 30, 1992, on the eve of the presidential election, when Walsh and his prosecutors supplemented Weinberger's indictment by releasing a quotation of his notes from the January 7, 1986, meeting. Attendees included President Reagan, Vice President Bush, Secretary of State Shultz, Secretary of Defense Weinberger, CIA Director Casey, Attorney General Edwin Meese, and National Security Adviser John Poindexter. Weinberger wrote that the "president decided to go with Israeli-Iranian offer to release our 5 hostages in return for sale of 4,000 TOWs to Iran by Israel. George Shultz and I opposed—Bill Casey, Ed Meese, and VP favored— as did Poindexter."[29] In the remaining days of the 1992 campaign, Bush had to fight off questions about how he could possibly claim he was "out of the loop."[30]

It looked as if Weinberger's trial would finally shine a beam into the participation of executive officials who operated at a level above Poindexter, North, and former national security adviser Robert McFarlane. However, on December 24, President Bush issued a pardon to six people involved in the Iran-Contra Affair. Heading the list was Weinberger. Fred Barnes of the *New Republic* commented on Bush's personal interest in granting the pardon: "It would avert a highly public trial at which Weinberger and . . . Shultz might give testimony contradicting Bush. . . . [Bush did not] want to be accused of a blatant cover-up."[31]

Bush's pardon also included three members of the CIA involved in the Iran-Contra Affair: Duane Clarridge, Alan Fiers, and Clair George. Clarridge had been indicted on seven felony counts. Fiers, facing indictment for felony, agreed to plead guilty to two misdemeanors and to cooperate with Walsh's investigation. George was charged with lying to three congressional panels and a federal judge. The first prosecution against George ended in a mistrial. The second trial found him guilty of two felony counts of lying to Congress. Clarridge's trial was scheduled for spring 1993.[32] The pardons wiped out the last chance to learn more details about the CIA's involvement in the Iran-Contra Affair.

In April 1975, during a speech to the American Chamber of Commerce in London, Cox reflected on his Watergate experience: "We have lost our innocence and have learned our capacity for evil. It takes honesty and courage to face those facts."[33] With Iran-Contra, evil retained its vitality but courage ran a distant second. Watergate did not cleanse the political system by teaching executive officials to avoid criminal activity. The lesson, instead, is to remove evidence. Conversations are less likely to be taped, and, if taped, to contain only exculpatory material. The paper trail is kept to a minimum. As few fingerprints as possible are left behind. If some executive employees must be punished, the brunt does not fall on those at the top, as it did with Watergate. It lands on those in the middle, like Poindexter, North, and McFarlane.

That result was facilitated in part by the nature of the congressional investigation. The Iran-Contra Committee did a good job of uncovering many of the criminal activities and elaborate deceptions. It also highlighted the administration's decision to finance the Contra rebels by seeking revenue from outside of Congress: from private citizens and foreign governments. However, the investigation was not conducted with such vigor that it might subject President Reagan to possible impeachment proceedings and implicate individuals within his cabinet.

After Bush had issued his pardon for the six Iran-Contra figures, Walsh said that it "demonstrates that powerful people with powerful allies can commit serious crimes in high office—deliberately abusing the public trust—without consequence." He suggested that Weinberger's notes evidence "a conspiracy among the highest-ranked Reagan administration officials to lie to Congress and the American public." Walsh offered this frank assessment: "What set Iran-Contra apart from previous political scandals was the fact that a cover-up engineered in the White House of one president and completed by his successor prevented the rule of law from being applied to the perpetrators of criminal activity of constitutional dimension."[34]

THE CLINTON ADMINISTRATION

A preview of how Clinton officials would wield executive power came in May 1993. In what could have been a routine operation without any political damage, presidential aides fired the seven employees of the White House Travel Office and implied that they had been involved in criminal activity. President Clinton had unquestioned constitutional authority to remove them. However, the manner of their dismissal was extraordinarily heavy-handed. They were booted out with the charge that they had followed poor management practices. Then Dee Dee Myers, Clinton's press secretary, let it be known that the FBI had been asked to examine Travel Office records, suggesting that the employees might have acted criminally.[35]

Aside from this casual charging of people with criminal conduct, other White House actions raised warning flags. Catherine Cornelius, who handled travel operations for Clinton's 1992 campaign, was slated to run the Travel Office. Other outsiders, also with financial interests, were involved. Harry Thomason, a Hollywood producer and close friend of Clinton, was co-owner of an airplane charter company and helped spur the White House inquiry that led to the dismissals. Penny Sample, brought in to handle press charters, was a close associate of Darnell Martens, co-owner with Thomason and Dan Richland of an airplane charter company. A White House review acknowledged that it was a mistake to let "people with personal interests in the outcome to be involved in evaluating the Travel Office" and that the White House had not been sufficiently sensitive "to the appearance of favoritism toward friends."[36]

Having worked in the White House for at least eight years and as many as thirty years, the employees could have been given several weeks' notice and gently eased out, perhaps with a nice letter of appreciation. Instead, they were abruptly fired, with a cloud hanging over their heads, and denied an opportunity to rebut charges of incompetence and possible illegality. The White House review conceded that the employees should have been treated "with more sensitivity" and with an opportunity "to hear the reasons for their termination, especially the allegations of wrongdoing, and should have been afforded an opportunity to respond." One wonders how the dismissals could have been handled this way, especially with the participation of attorneys who worked in the White House Counsel's office. Blackening and destroying reputations seemed far more important than recognizing and adhering to constitutional and procedural safeguards. Did any limits operate on White House power? That thought seemed far away.

Two of the Travel Office employees retired. The White House, embarrassed by its ineptitude, found federal jobs for the others. Billy Dale, who headed the Travel Office, was indicted on charges of embezzlement, but a federal jury took less than two hours to acquit him. Congress later appropriated funds to reimburse the Travel Office employees for the legal expenses they encountered related to their firings. Several lessons emerge. Even when the president operates on full constitutional authority through his removal power, a combination of political miscalculations, arrogance, and poor judgment can leave deep wounds and produce personal tragedies. White House lawyers ran roughshod over public servants.

Ever since President Harry Truman went to war against North Korea, without ever coming to Congress for authority, postwar presidents have seized more and more of the war power. These actions do violence to the Constitution, the UN Charter, the UN Participation Act, and such mutual security treaties as NATO. The concentration of the war power in the presidency reached its highest pitch under Clinton. Both Bush and Clinton used Security Council resolutions as "authority" to circumvent the constitutional power of Congress to initiate military action against other nations. Clinton also sought "authority" from NATO to conduct war against Yugoslavia.

At a news conference on March 23, 1993, a reporter asked Clinton about his difficulties with the Pentagon: "When you went to the USS *Theodore Roosevelt,* the sailors there were mocking you before your arrival, even though you are Commander in Chief. The services have been undercutting your proposal for permitting gays to be in the military. . . . Do you have a problem, perhaps because of your lack of military service or perhaps because of issues such as gays in the military, in being effective in your role as Commander in Chief, and what do you propose to do about it?"[37] Clinton denied that he had a problem being commander in chief. Within a few months, he would have what White House officials considered an opportunity to advertise his military "toughness."

On June 26, Clinton ordered air strikes against Iraq, explaining that the Kuwaiti government had uncovered what they suspected was a car-bombing plot to kill former president Bush during a visit to Kuwait. Sixteen suspects, including two Iraqi nationals, had been arrested. Although the trial of those suspects was still under way, Clinton relied on a CIA analysis that there was "compelling evidence" of an Iraqi plot to kill Bush. Clinton called the planned assassination of Bush "an attack against our country and against all Americans."[38] The twenty-three Tomahawk cruise missiles he launched against Baghdad did extensive damage to the Iraqi intelligence service's principal command-and-control facility, but three of the missiles destroyed homes in the surrounding neighborhood, killing eight people and wounding at least twelve others.

News analyses suggested that the White House appreciated that this use of military force would help build Clinton's image into that of a strong and decisive leader. White House aides told reporters that Clinton, after making an address from the Oval Office about the bombing, returned to the White House residence to watch a movie with his wife and slept "a solid eight hours."[39] The word was out: Clinton could make the tough military calls and not be bothered by them. Clinton justified the attack on Baghdad as a way "to send a message to those who engage in state-sponsored terrorism."[40] That argument is not credible. What Clinton did to Iraq he would not have done to other countries suspected of terrorist activity. Had he received evidence that Syria was behind a terrorist action, he would not have launched cruise missiles at intelligence facilities in Damascus.

Other military actions by Clinton followed, including a deepening involvement in Somalia and a threat to invade Haiti. Congress used its power of the purse to bring the U.S. military operation in Somalia to a halt. The planned invasion of Haiti was never carried out because of negotiations conducted by former president Jimmy Carter. Clinton's rationale for the invasion, however, merits scrutiny. On July 31, 1994, the UN Security Council adopted a resolution "inviting" all states—particularly those in the region of Haiti—to use "all necessary means" (i.e., military force) to remove the military leadership on that island. A number of lawmakers objected to the administration's seeking "authority" from the UN rather than from Congress. Senator Jesse Helms remarked that the administration "has gone, hat in hand, to the United Nations to ask the permission of the U.N. Security Council to invade Haiti. But the President . . . has not bothered to ask the approval of the United States Congress to go to war."[41]

In a nationwide televised address on September 15, Clinton told the American people that he was prepared to use military force to invade Haiti, referring to the Security Council resolution of July 31 and his willingness to lead a multinational force "to carry out the will of the United Nations."[42] He said nothing about carrying out the will of Congress or the American public. Acknowledging that the public and Congress were critical of the planned action, Clinton was determined to go ahead: "But regardless [of this opposition], this is what I believe is the right thing to do. I realize it is unpopular. I know it is unpopular. I know the timing is unpopular. I know the whole thing is unpopular. But I believe it is the right thing."[43] There seemed to be no interest on his part of doing the legal thing, the authorized thing, or the constitutional thing.

Clinton emphasized the need to honor commitments: "I'd like to mention just one other thing that is equally important, and that is the reliability of the United States and the United Nations once we say we're going to do something."[44] Notice the "we." The plural did not include Congress or the American public. It was a commitment made unilaterally by the president acting in concert with a Security Council resolution he helped pass.

In his first year in office, Clinton indicated that he would need authorization from Congress before ordering air strikes in Bosnia.[45] Before long, however, he began asking Congress only for "support" and then kept to that formula. Congress was no longer regarded as an institution that needed to authorize military activities. Throughout 1993, Clinton opposed any legislative language that "would make it unreasonably difficult for me or any President to operate militarily with other nations when it is in our interest to do so—and as we have done effectively for half a century through NATO."[46] Yet over that entire half-century, NATO had never once used military force. On the basis of nonexistent precedents, Clinton wanted the discretion to do what no president had ever done.

Air strikes in Bosnia began in February 1994 and continued into the next year. Decisions to use airpower were not based on statutory authority. They were taken in response to UN Security Council resolutions, operating through NATO's military command. Without constitutional amendment, Congress had been replaced by international and regional organizations. Curiously, Clinton would have to obtain approval from England, France, Italy, and other NATO allies but not from Congress. He dutifully reported to Congress about the air strikes, explaining that they were "conducted under the authority of U.N. Security Council resolutions and in full compliance with NATO procedures."[47] For Clinton, compliance with the Constitution did not have the same priority or urgency.

The next escalation came in 1995, with Clinton's decision to send about 25,000 ground forces into Bosnia. Members of Congress debated a number of legislative restrictions but in the end did nothing to limit Clinton. Addressing the nation on November 27, Clinton justified the deployment as a way of stopping "the killing of innocent civilians, especially children, and at the same time, to bring stability to Central Europe, a region of the world that is vital to our national interests. It is the right thing to do."[48] Once again Clinton was interested in doing the right thing, even if not the legal thing. For an attorney and former professor of constitutional law, he rarely showed an interest in legal or constitutional constraints.

Congressional prestige hit a low point on November 27, when Senate Majority Leader Bob Dole made it clear that legislative prerogatives were subordinate to presidential interests. It was Dole's view, based on three decades in the House and the Senate, that Clinton had "the authority and the power under the Constitution to do what he feels should be done regardless of what Congress does."[49] Imagine that. Regardless of what Congress did and what restrictions it enacted, Clinton could do whatever he wanted. There would be no checks and balances, no tussling for power, no search for constitutional authority. Once the president had announced his policy "to do what he feels," legislators would dutifully fall in line. Congress, as an independent and countervailing branch, did not exist. It was not interested in preserving its powers as a coequal branch.

The air strikes and ground operations in Bosnia set the stage for Clinton's war against Yugoslavia in 1999. Although Congress was to be given no role in authorizing the use of force against the Serbs, legislatures in other NATO countries took votes to authorize military action in Yugoslavia. The Italian Parliament had to vote approval for the NATO strikes. The German Supreme Court ruled that the Bundestag, which had been dissolved with the election that ousted Chancellor Helmut Kohl, had to be recalled to approve deployment of German aircraft and troops to Kosovo. The U.S. Congress, supposedly the strongest legislature in the world, was content to watch from the backseat. Congressman Ernest Istook (R-Okla.) remarked, "President Clinton asked many nations to agree to attack Yugoslavia, but he failed to get permission from one crucial country, America."[50]

Military operations from Truman to Clinton have brought us to the point where there appears to be no limit on what a president can do to commit the nation to war, deplete its treasury, and bring bloodshed to allies and enemies. The Framers thought they had put an end to that form of monarchy. It is back.

Clinton's impeachment showed how difficult it was for the country, and for members of Congress, to keep a focus on the principal charges: perjury and obstruction of justice. Was he guilty of those offenses? Did those actions, if true, rise to the level of "high crimes and misdemeanors"? Was Clinton fit to remain in office, or had he so damaged the political and legal system that he should be removed? Those questions—weighty and complicated—were repeatedly put on the back burner while Congress attended to distractions.

For example, was the whole matter simply about "sex"? At the Senate trial on January 21, 1999, Senator Dale Bumpers got a lot of laughs when he said, "When you hear somebody say, 'This is not about sex,' it's about sex." Actually, the impeachment was not primarily about sex. If Clinton had sex with other women and lied about it, those affairs—if uncovered—would have been an embarrassment but not grounds for impeachment. He was impeached because he chose to lie under oath, in front of a federal judge, and the purpose of that lie was not to cover up an embarrassing episode. It was to undermine Paula Jones's civil suit. She had to go through district court, appellate court, and finally to the Supreme Court to gain the legal right to sue Clinton while he was in office. Many people did not like her or the organizations that financed her case, but she had as much constitutional right to seek truth in court as any other litigant.

Clinton's lies in the Paula Jones deposition were followed by lies to the grand jury. The chief law enforcement officer in the country decided to commit perjury in front of a judge for the purpose of weakening someone's lawsuit. He did what he could to subvert justice. Having lied at the deposition, he kept on lying. Given his high office and low conduct, Congress could not ignore his actions.[51] As Judge Richard Posner notes: "Failure to prosecute would send a signal that the legal system smiles at obstructing justice."[52]

Extraneous issues constantly sidetracked the congressional inquiry. Some legislators denounced the impeachment as a coup d'etat, but it was nothing of the sort. A coup replaces the party in power with a rival group. Had Clinton been removed, Gore would have taken over. Another objection: Clinton's removal would nullify the votes of those who supported him in 1996. With that as a standard, no elected official could ever be impeached, including Nixon (who, like Clinton, was twice elected to the presidency). Again: Clinton was being impeached because Republicans hated him. No doubt some did, but the same could be said about the Democrats who hated Nixon in 1974. None of those issues had anything to do with the central questions: what did Clinton do, and should he be removed for those actions?

The seriousness of Clinton's conduct is reflected in the resolutions of censure drafted by Democrats in the House and the Senate. Toughly worded, they take Clinton to task for grave misconduct. House Democrats were prepared to censure Clinton because he "egregiously failed" in his obligation "to set high moral standards and conduct himself in a manner that fosters respect for the truth," made "false statements concerning his reprehensible conduct with a subordinate," and "wrongly took steps to delay discovery of the truth." House Democrats came as close as they could to admitting that Clinton committed perjury and obstructed justice. On December 11, 1998, in an effort to head off impeachment, Clinton said that should House members "determine that my errors of word and deed require their rebuke and censure, I am ready to accept that."[53] Senate Democrats, in their resolution, charged that Clinton had "deliberately misled and deceived the American people," gave "false or misleading testimony and impeded discovery of evidence in judicial proceedings," created "disrespect for the laws of the land," and "violated the trust of the American people."

Are we seriously to believe that this was all about sex, partisan coups, vote nullification, and Republican hate? Hardly. Other smokescreens and obfuscations helped divert attention from Clinton's actions. Monica Lewinsky was a "stalker." Kenneth Starr was "obsessed" by sex. Hillary Clinton claimed it was all a "vast right-wing conspiracy." The Supreme Court was "naive" in *Clinton v. Jones* to think that a sitting president could be a defendant without serious disruption to his official duties. No doubt the Paula Jones case was a nightmare for Clinton and beyond anything the justices expected, but the nightmare resulted largely from his brazen attempt to derail justice in and out of court. Judge Susan Webber Wright later held Clinton in contempt for repeatedly and willfully giving false statements and ordered him to compensate Jones's lawyers.

Throughout the impeachment process, many lawmakers seemed unable or unwilling to focus on Clinton's actions and to decide whether they merited removal. Instead, the discussion drifted off on the health of the economy, high levels of employment, low interest rates, low inflation, the booming stock market, and, most of all, the polls that indicated continued support for Clinton. Instead of looking inward to determine the standards that should guide impeachment and removal, lawmakers punted to public opinion. How would that have worked with Nixon? If the economy had been good and his polls strong, should he have remained in office? Conversely, if the stock market went south, would that have justified Clinton's removal? None of these economic indicators has any bearing on impeachment.

The Constitution gives to the House the sole power to impeach and to the Senate the sole power to remove. Members of Congress take an oath to "support and defend" the Constitution. The responsibility for impeachment and removal is given to them, not to the general public or to polls (or to independent counsels). Impeachment and removal require careful legislative deliberation and politically sensitive, seasoned judgment. Those legislative decisions cannot, or should not, be transferred to citizens and pollsters.

Watergate, Iran-Contra, and the Clinton scandals illustrate that even the ample resources available to an independent counsel are unlikely to penetrate the hardy defenses erected within the executive branch, especially when inquiries threaten top public officials. Cox, Walsh, and Starr conducted their investigations with vigor and diligence, but their efforts to reach a full understanding were stymied by a variety of executive roadblocks, including executive privilege and presidential pardons. To the extent that the picture unfolded at all, these probes (especially Watergate) depended on some fortunate breaks, including the willingness of some people to tell prosecutors and judges the truth. In Iran-Contra and the Clinton administration, no one involved in illegal or improper activities spoke out. The cover-ups stayed covered up. Political accountability disappeared.

The scandals from Watergate to Clinton demonstrate the capacity of executive officials for self-inflicted injuries. The loyalty of political officials to the president gives them little stake in the long-term operations of government and little interest in legal and constitutional prohibitions. They are quick to bridle at the frustrations and delays of orderly procedures. Shortcuts seem attractive. Officials try to circumvent laws with what they think are clever interpretations. Political appointees are so eager for results, and so ignorant about constitutional processes, that they seek immediate payoffs and leave to others the task of cleaning up the debris.

The cost to constitutional government is high, especially when other branches and the public fail to supply the necessary checks and to mete out the appropriate penalties. Until that happens, constitutional violence will continue. There is no reason to believe that the Justice Department can conduct credible investigations into illegal or improper activity at the White House. Independent counsels have the capacity and the independence to reveal the involvement of executive officials in criminal activity. Even if officials manage to escape in the end, the legal costs and public exposure may supply a prophylactic effect. But the kind of political accountability we had with Watergate is not likely to be repeated.

How did we reach our present comfort level with illegality and executive abuse of power? For decades, professors of history, law, and political science have indulged in idolatry and hagiography in their writings about the presidency. Readers are treated to a long list of imaginary virtues and strengths, with the highest accolade placed on action. At the same time, those disciplines downgraded the importance of Congress, legal constraints, collective judgment, and procedural safeguards. Unless we restore respect for checks and balances, legislative deliberation, and the rule of law, we can expect (and will deserve) continued constitutional violations by presidents and White House officials.

NOTES

1. Edward S. Corwin, "The President's Power," *New Republic,* January 29, 1951, p. 15.

2. For further details on Truman's action in Korea, see Louis Fisher, *Presidential War Power* (Lawrence: University Press of Kansas, 1995), pp. 84–90, and Louis Fisher, "The Korean War: On What Legal Basis Did Truman Act?" *American Journal of International Law* 89 (1995): 21.

3. *Cong. Rec.* 91 (1945): 8185.

4. 63 Stat. 735–36, sec. 5 (1949).

5. Louis Fisher, *Congressional Abdication on War and Spending* (College Station: Texas A&M University Press, 2000), pp. 42–44.

6. *Public Papers of the Presidents, 1950* (Washington, D.C.: U.S. Government Printing Office, 1950), p. 504.

7. *Weissman v. Metropolitan Life Ins. Co.,* 112 F. Supp. 420, 425 (S.D. Cal. 1953).

8. *Gagliormella v. Metropolitan Life Ins. Co.,* 122 F. Supp. 246, 249 (D. Mass. 1954). See also *Carius v. New York Life Insurance Co.,* 124 F. Supp. 388 (D. Ill. 1954).

9. 98 *Cong. Rec.* 98 (1952): 4029–4030, 4033–4034.

10. *Youngstown Sheet & Tube Co. v. Sawyer,* 103 F. Supp. 569, 577 (D.D.C. 1952), aff'd, *Youngstown Co. v. Sawyer,* 343 U.S. 579 (1952).

11. Louis Fisher, "Sidestepping Congress: Presidents Acting Under the UN and NATO," *Case Western Reserve Law Review* 47 (1997):1237.

12. Ken Gormley, *Archibald Cox: Conscience of a Nation* (Reading, Mass.: Addison Wesley, 1997), pp. 245–246, 250.

13. Richard M. Nixon, *The Memoirs of Richard Nixon* (New York: Simon and Schuster, 1978), p. 912.

14. Gormley, *Archibald Cox,* p. 253.

15, John J. Sirica, *To Set the Record Straight* (New York: W. W. Norton, 1979), p. 74.

16. Ibid., pp. 96–97.

17. Gormley, *Archibald Cox,* pp. 257–258.

18. Ibid., pp. 258–259. The same account appears in John W. Dean III, *Blind Ambition* (New York: Simon and Schuster, 1976), pp. 112–113.

19. Dean, *Blind Ambition,* pp. 169–171; John Ehrlichman, *Witness to Power: The Nixon Years* (New York: Simon and Schuster, 1982), p. 382; H. R. Haldeman, *The Ends of Power* (New York: Times Books, 1978), pp. 259–260; H. R. Haldeman, *The Haldeman Diaries: Inside the White House* (New York: G. P. Putnam's Sons, 1994), pp. 640, 645.

20. Gormley, *Archibald Cox,* pp. 270–273.

21. Sirica, *Set the Record,* p. 162.

22. H. Rept. 93-1305, 93d Cong., 2d sess., 1974, p. 53.

23. *Public Papers of the Presidents, 1974,* p. 622.

24. Gormley, *Archibald Cox,* pp. 311–312, 325–326, 329, 330, 332.

25. Sirica, *Set the Record,* pp. 56–57, 64, 84.

26. Carl Bernstein and Bob Woodward, *All the President's Men* (New York: Simon and Schuster, 1973); page references for Sloan (86, 174–175), the "Bookkeeper"(63–68, 74–76), "Deep Throat" (71–73, 130–135, 172–173, 195–196, 244–246, 270–271, 288, 306, 316–319, 333), FBI agent (175–177), Justice Department attorney (180, 255), "Z" (212–213), Chenow (215–217), friends and acquaintances of Hunt (251–254), someone from CRP (292), and a White House official (293).

27. Lawrence E. Walsh, *Firewall: The Iran-Contra Conspiracy and Cover-up* (New York: Norton, 1977), pp. 210–211, 218–219.

28. Ibid., pp. 415, 419.

29. Ibid., p. 448.

30. Ibid., pp. 459–464.

31. Ibid., pp. 487–489.

32. Ibid., pp. 313, 285–286, 423, 446, 447.

33. Gormley, *Archibald Cox,* p. 394.

34. Walsh, *Firewall,* pp. 493–494, 531.

35. This account of Travelgate is drawn from my book, *Constitutional Conflicts Between Congress and the President* (Lawrence: University Press of Kansas, 1997), pp. 77–83.

36. White House Travel Office Management Review, July 2, 1993, p. 3.

37. *Public Papers of the Presidents, 1993,* 1: 337.

38. Ibid., p. 938.

39. "Show of Strength Offers Benefits for Clinton," *Washington Post,* June 28, 1993, pp. A1, A14.

40. *Public Papers of the Presidents, 1993,* 1: 938–939.

41. *Cong. Rec.* 140 (1994): 19320.

42. *Public Papers of the Presidents,* 1994, 2: 1559.

43. Ibid., p. 1551.

44. Ibid., p. 1549.

45. *Public Papers of the Presidents, 1993,* 1: 594.

46. Ibid., 2: 1770.

47. Ibid., *1994,* 1: 355.

48. Ibid., *1995,* 2: 1784.

49. *Cong. Rec.* 141 (daily ed., November 27, 1995): S17529.

50. *Cong. Rec.* 145 (daily ed., April 28, 1999): H2419.

51. For a close analysis of Clinton's perjurious statements in his deposition in the Paula Jones case, in statements to the grand jury, and in his answers to questions put by the House Judiciary Committee, see Richard A. Posner, *An Affair of State: The Investigation, Impeachment, and Trial of President Clinton* (Cambridge: Harvard University Press, 1999), pp. 44–58, 84–86.

52. Ibid., p. 86.

53. *Public Papers of the Presidents, 1998,* 2: 2158.

Selected Bibliography

BOOKS

Adler, David Gray, and Larry N. George, eds. *The Constitution and the Conduct of American Foreign Policy.* Lawrence: University Press of Kansas, 1996.

Baker, Peter. *The Breach.* New York: Scribner, 2000.

Bennett, William J. *The Death of Outrage: Bill Clinton and the Assault on American Ideals.* New York: Free Press, 1998.

Berger, Raoul. *Executive Privilege: A Constitutional Myth.* Cambridge: Harvard University Press, 1974.

———. *Impeachment: The Constitutional Problems.* Cambridge: Harvard University Press, 1973.

Black, Charles L. Jr. *Impeachment: A Handbook.* New Haven: Yale University Press, 1974.

Corrado, Anthony. *Creative Campaigning: PACs and the Presidential Selection Process.* Boulder, Colo.: Westview Press, 1992.

Corwin, Edward S. *The President: Office and Powers, 1787–1984: A History and Analysis of Practice and Opinion.* 5th ed., rev. New York: New York University Press, 1984.

Cronin, Thomas E. *The State of the Presidency* Boston: Little, Brown, 1980.

———, ed. *Inventing the American Presidency.* Lawrence: University Press of Kansas, 1989.

Cronin, Thomas, and Michael A. Genovese. *The Paradoxes of the American Presidency.* New York: Oxford University Press, 1998.

Davis, Lanny J. *Truth to Tell: Notes from My White House Education.* New York: Free Press, 1999.

Dershowitz, Alan M. *Sexual McCarthyism: Clinton, Starr and the Emerging Constitutional Crisis.* New York: Basic Books, 1998.

Draper, Theodore. *A Very Thin Line: The Iran-Contra Affair.* New York: Hill and Wang, 1991.

Drew, Elizabeth. *The Corruption of American Politics: What Went Wrong and Why*. Sea-caucus, N.J.: Birch Lane Press, 1999.

Dwyre, Diana, and Victoria Farrar-Myers. *Legislative Labyrinth: Congress and Campaign Finance Reform*. Washington, D.C.: Congressional Quarterly Press, 2000.

Elliot, Jonathan, ed. *The Debates in the Several State Conventions on the Adoption of the Federal Constitution*. 5 vols. 1861. Reprint, New York: Burt Franklin, 1974.

Farrand, Max, ed. *The Records of the Federal Convention of 1787*. 4 vols. Reprint, New Haven: Yale University Press, 1996.

Fisher, Louis. *Constitutional Conflicts Between Congress and the President*. 4th ed., rev. Lawrence: University Press of Kansas, 1997.

———. *Presidential War Power*. Lawrence: University Press of Kansas, 1995.

Genovese, Michael A. *The Power of the American Presidency, 1789–2001*. New York: Oxford University Press, 2001.

Gerhardt, Michael J. *The Federal Impeachment Process: A Constitutional and Historical Analysis*. Princeton: Princeton University Press, 1996.

Ginsberg, Benjamin, and Martin Sheffer. *Politics by Other Means: Politicians, Prosecu-tors, and the Press, from Watergate to Whitewater*. New York: W. W. Norton, 1999.

Glennon, Michael J. *Constitutional Diplomacy*. Princeton: Princeton University Press, 1990.

Harriger, Katy J. *The Special Prosecutor in American Politics*. Lawrence: University Press of Kansas, 2000.

Henkin, Louis. *Constitutionalism, Democracy and Foreign Affairs*. New York: Columbia University Press, 1990.

———. *Foreign Affairs and the Constitution*. Mineola, N.Y.: Foundation Press, 1972.

Johnson, Loch K. *America's Secret Power*. New York: Oxford University Press, 1989.

Keynes, Edward. *Undeclared War: Twilight Zone of Constitutional Power*. University Park: Pennsylvania State University Press, 1982.

Levy, Leonard W. *Original Intent and the Framers' Constitution*. New York: Macmillan, 1988.

Lowi, Theodore J. *The Personal President*. Ithaca, N.Y.: Cornell University Press, 1985.

Pfiffner, James, and Roger H. Davidson. *Understanding the Presidency*. 2d ed. New York: Longman Press, 2000.

Pious, Richard M. *The American Presidency*. New York: Basic Books, 1979.

Polsby, Nelson W., and Aaron Wildavsky. *Presidential Elections: Strategies and Struc-tures in American Politics*. 9th ed. Chatham, N.Y.: Chatham House, 1996.

Posner, Richard A. *An Affair of State: The Investigation, Impeachment and Trial of Pres-ident Clinton*. Cambridge: Harvard University Press, 1999.

Robinson, Donald L. *"To the Best of My Ability."* New York: Norton, 1987.

———, ed. *Government for the Third American Century*. Boulder, Colo.: Westview Press, 1989.

Rossiter, Clinton. *Constitutional Dictatorship*. New York: Harcourt, Brace and World, 1948.

Rozell, Mark J. *Executive Privilege: The Dilemma of Secrecy and Democratic Account-ability*. Baltimore: Johns Hopkins University Press, 1994.

Schlesinger, Arthur M. Jr. *The Imperial Presidency*. Boston: Houghton Mifflin, 1973.

Spitzer, Robert J. *The President and Congress: Executive Hegemony at the Crossroads of American Government*. New York: McGraw-Hill, 1993.

———. *The Presidential Veto: Touchstone of the American Presidency*. Albany: State University of New York Press, 1988.

Story, Joseph. *Commentaries on the Constitution of the United States*. 3 vols. Reprint, Durham, N.C.: Carolina Academic Press, 1987.

Sutherland, George S. *Constitutional Power and World Affairs*. New York: Columbia University Press, 1919.

Toobin, Jeffrey. *A Vast Conspiracy*. New York: Random House, 1999.

Wayne, Stephen J. *The Road to the White House, 2000: The Politics of Presidential Elections*. Boston: Bedford/St. Martin's, 2000

Wormuth, Francis D., and Edwin B. Firmage. *To Chain the Dog of War: The War Power of Congress in History and Law*. Dallas: Southern Methodist University Press, 1986.

ARTICLES

Adler, David Gray. "The Clinton Theory of the War Power." *Presidential Studies Quarterly* 30 (March 2000): 155–169.

———. "The President's Pardon Power." In *Inventing the American Presidency*. Ed. Thomas E. Cronin, 209–235. Lawrence: University Press of Kansas, 1989.

———. "Virtues of the War Clause." *Presidential Studies Quarterly* 30 (December 2000): 777–783.

Alfange, Dean Jr. "The Quasi-War and Presidential Warmaking." In *The Constitution and the Conduct of American Foreign Policy*. Ed. David Gray Adler and Larry N. George, 274–291. Lawrence: University Press of Kansas. 1996.

———. "The Supreme Court and the Separation of Powers: A Welcome Return to Normalcy." *George Washington Law Review* 58 (1990): 668–761.

Amar, Akhil Reed. "The Unimperial Presidency." *New Republic,* March 8, 1999, 25–29.

Barrett, John Q. "All or Nothing, or Maybe, Cooperation: Attorney General Power, Conduct, and Judgment in Relation to the Work of an Independent Counsel." *Mercer Law Review* 49 (winter 1998): 519–551.

Beinart, Peter. "Private Matters." *New Republic,* February 15, 1999, 20–22.

Bestor, Arthur. "Respective Roles of Senate and President in the Making and Abrogation of Treaties—The Original Intent of the Framers of the Constitution Historically Examined." *Washington Law Review* 55 (1979): 1–136.

———. "Separation of Powers in the Domain of Foreign Affairs: The Intent of the Constitution Historically Examined." *Seton Hall Law Review* 5 (spring 1974): 527–666.

Blumenthal, Sidney. "The Friends of Paula Jones." *New Yorker,* June 20, 1999, 36–39.

Casper, Gerhard. "Constitutional Constraints on the Conduct of Foreign and Defense Policy: A Nonjudicial Model." *University of Chicago Law Review* 43 (spring 1976): 463–498.

Cook, Julian A. III. "Mend It or End It? What to Do with the Independent Counsel Statute." *Harvard Journal of Law and Public Policy* 22 (1998): 279–337.

Dash, Samuel. "Independent Counsel: No More, No Less a Federal Prosecutor." *Georgetown Law Journal* 86 (1998): 2077–2095.

Dworkin, Ronald. "The Wounded Constitution." *New York Review of Books,* March 18, 1999, 6–8.

Edwards, George C. III. "Campaigning Is Not Governing: Bill Clinton's Rhetorical Pres-idency." In *The Clinton Legacy.* Ed. Colin Campbell and Bert Rockman. New York: Chatham House, 1999.

Fisher, Louis. "Litigating the War Power with Campbell v. Clinton." *Presidential Studies Quarterly* 30 (September 2000): 564–574.

Harriger, Katy J. "Can the Independent Counsel Statute Be Saved?" *Law and Contempo-rary Problems* 62 (winter 1999): 131–144.

———. "The History of the Independent Counsel Provisions: How the Past Informs the Current Debate." *Mercer Law Review* 49 (1998): 489–517.

Kassop, Nancy. "The Clinton Impeachment: Untangling the Web of Conflicting Consid-erations." *Presidential Studies Quarterly* 30 (June 2000): 359–381.

Lewis, Anthony. "The Prosecutorial State: Criminalizing American Politics." *American Prospect,* January–February 1999, 26–31.

Lobel, Jules. "Covert War and Congressional Authority: Hidden War and Forgotten Power." *University of Pennsylvania Law Review* 134 (1986): 1035–1110.

Lofgren, Charles A. "War-Making Under the Constitution: The Original Understanding." *Yale Law Journal* 81 (1972): 672–702.

Mervin, David. "Demise of the War Clause." *Presidential Studies Quarterly* 30 (Decem-ber 2000): 770–776.

Miller, Randall. "Presidential Sanctuaries After the Clinton Sex Scandals." *Harvard Jour-nal of Law and Public Policy* 22 (1999): 647–734.

Sullivan, Terry. "Impeachment Practice in the Era of Lethal Conflict." *Congress and the Presidency* 25 (fall 1998): 117–128.

Wormuth, Francis D. "The Nixon Theory of the War Power: A Critique." *University of California Law Review* 60 (1972): 623–703.

———. "The Vietnam War: The President versus the Constitution." In *The Vietnam War and International Law.* Ed. Richard Falk. Princeton: Princeton University Press, 1969.

About the Contributors

DAVID GRAY ADLER is a professor of political science at Idaho State University and is the author of *The Constitution and the Termination of Treaties* and coeditor of *The Constitution and the Conduct of American Foreign Policy*. He has contributed numerous articles and essays on presidential power and the Constitution to various books and journals, including *Political Science Quarterly, Presidential Studies Quarterly,* the *Encyclopedia of the American Presidency,* and the *Encyclopedia of American Foreign Policy*.

KRISTINE ALMQUIST majored in political science and graduated from Loyola Marymount University in 2000.

THOMAS E. CRONIN teaches at and serves as president of Whitman College. He was a White House Fellow and a White House aide and has served as president of the Western Political Science Association. His many writings include *The State of the Presidency, U.S. v. Crime in the Streets, Direct Democracy: The Politics of Initiative, Referendum, and Recall,* and *Colorado Politics and Government,* and he is the coauthor of *The Paradoxes of the American Presidency.* Cronin is a past recipient of the American Political Science Association's Charles E. Merriam Award.

VICTORIA FARRAR-MYERS is an associate professor of political science at the University of Texas at Arlington. She is coauthor of *Legislative Labyrinth: Congress and Campaign Finance Reform,* and she has contributed articles to various journals and books, including *Congress and the Presidency, American Review of Politics,* and *White House Studies.* Farrar-Myers is a former Congressional Fellow.

LOUIS FISHER is senior specialist in Separation of Powers at the Congressional Research Service, Library of Congress. He has published more than two hundred articles in various journals and books in the areas of constitutional law, administrative law, and the Supreme Court. His books include *Constitutional Conflicts Between Congress and the President, Presidential War Power, Congressional Abdication on War and Spending,* and *The Politics of Shared Power, Constitutional Dialogues, and American Constitutional Law.* He has twice received the Louis Brownlow Book Award from the National Academy of Public Administration and was a coeditor of the *Encyclopedia of the American Presidency.*

MICHAEL A. GENOVESE is a professor of political science at Loyola Marymount University, where he holds the Loyola Chair of Leadership Studies and serves as director of the Institute of Leadership Studies. He is the author of eleven books, including *The Power of the American Presidency, 1789–2000, The Nixon Presidency: Power and Politics in Turbulent Times, The Presidency in an Age of Limits,* and *The Watergate Crisis,* and he coauthored *The Paradoxes of the American Presidency.*

EVAN GERSTMANN is an associate professor of political science at Loyola Marymount University. He is the author of several works in the field of constitutional law, including *The Constitutional Underclass: Gays, Lesbians, and the Failure of Class-Based Equal Protection.*

NANCY KASSOP is an associate professor of political science at the State University of New York at New Paltz, where she teaches and conducts research on the presidency and constitutional law. She has contributed numerous articles and essays to various journals and books, including *Presidential Studies Quarterly* and the *Encyclopedia of the Presidency.*

MARK J. ROZELL is associate professor of politics at the Catholic University of America in Washington, D.C. He is the author of several books, including *Executive Privilege: The Dilemma of Secrecy and Democratic Accountability.* He has contributed numerous articles and essays to various journals and books, including *Presidential Studies Quarterly, Minnesota Law Review, Bill of Rights Journal,* and the *Encyclopedia of the American Presidency.*

CHRISTOPHER SHORTELL is a graduate of Loyola Marymount University and a Ph.D. candidate in the Department of Political Science at the University of Southern California.

ROBERT J. SPITZER is Distinguished Service Professor of Political Science at the State University of New York at Cortland. He is the author of numerous studies on the presidency and American politics, including *The Presidential Veto, The President and Congress, The Politics of Gun Control, The Presidency and Public Policy,* and *The Right to Life Movement and Third Party Politics.* He has contributed many articles and essays to various journals and books, including *Political Science Quarterly, Presidential Studies Quarterly,* and the *Encyclopedia of the American Presidency.*

Index